ENCYCLOPEDIA OF THE

Animal World

Vol 1 Aardvark—Aquarium

Bay Books Sydney

Editorial Board

Authors

R. McN. A.	Professor R. McN. Alexander PhD *(University College of North Wales, Bangor)*
A. A.	A. Anderson *(University of Aberdeen)*
J. M. A.	J. M. Anderson BSc *(University of London, King's College)*
E. N. A.	E. N. Arnold *(British Museum Natural History, London)*
J. A.	J. Attridge PhD *(University of London, Birkbeck College)*
K. M. B.	K. M. Backhouse PhD *(University of London, Charing Cross Hospital Medical School)*
K. B.	K. Banister PhD *(British Museum Natural History, London)*
H. B.	H. Barnes PhD *(Marine Biological Station, Millport, Scotland)*
P. P. G. B.	P. P. G. Bateson PhD *(University of Cambridge)*
R. A. B.	R. A. Beaver DPhil *(University College of North Wales, Bangor)*
J. R. B.	J. R. Beck *(Monks Wood Experimental Station British Antarctic Survey, Abbots Ripton, Huntingdon)*
G. de B.	Sir Gavin de Beer FRS, FSA, MA, DSc (Oxon), Hon ScD (Cantab), Hon D de l'Univ (Bordeaux), Hon D-es-L (Lausanne), Membre Correspondent de l'Académie des Sciences de l'Institut de France) *(Bex, Switzerland)*
W. N. B.	W. N. Beeslev PhD *(University of Liverpool, School of Tropical Medicine)*
B. D. B.	D. B. Bell PhD *(University of Leicester)*
C. B.	C. Bertram PhD *(University of Cambridge, St. John's College)*
G. B.	G. Beven BSc, MD *(Esher, Surrey)*
J. G. B.	J. G. Blower *(University of Manchester)*
A. E. B.	A. E. Brafield PhD *(University of London, Queen Elizabeth College)*
C. D. B.	Mrs. C. D. Bramwell BSc *(University of Reading)*
R. S. B.	Professor R. S. Bray PhD, DSc *(Haile Sellassie University, Ethiopia)*
W. S. B.	W. S. Bristowe MA, ScD (Cantab) *(Battle, Sussex)*
E. B.	E. Broadhead DPhil *(University of Leeds)*
D. G. B.	D. G. Broadley PhD *(Umtali Museum, Rhodesia)*
G. J. B.	Professor G. J. Broekhuysen PhD *(University of Cape Town)*
L. D. B.	Professor L. D. Brongersma PhD *(University of Leiden, Netherlands)*
L. H. B.	L. H. Brown *(Karen, Kenya)*
H. K. B.	H. K. Buechner PhD *(The Smithsonian Institution, Washington D.C.)*
G. E. B.	G. E. Burghardt *(California Academy of Sciences, Steinhart Aquarium, San Francisco)*
M. B.	M. Burton, DSc *(Albury, Surrey)*
R. W. B.	R. W. Burton BA *(Albury, Surrey)*
D. B. C.	Professor D. B. Carlisle MA, DPhil, DSc *(Trent University, Peterborough, Ontario)*
J. D. C.	J. D. Carthy MA, PhD *(Field Studies Council, London)*
G. E. C.	G. Earl Chace *(Rapid City, South Dakota)*
R.F.C.	R. F. Chapman PhD *(Centre for Overseas Pest Research, London)*
A. C.	A. Cheke BA *(University of Oxford, Edward Grey Institute of Field Ornithology)*
W. E. leG. C.	Professor Sir Wilfrid E. Le Gros Clark FRS, MA, DSc, Hon DSc (Durham, Manchester), Hon MD (Melbourne, Oslo), Hon LLD (Malaya) *(University of Oxford)*
C. M. C.	C. M. Clifford PhD *(National Institute of Allergy and Infectious Diseases, Hamilton, Montana)*
A. J. C.	A. J. Cockbain PhD *(Rothamsted Experimental Station, Harpenden, Hertfordshire)*
H. G. C.	H. G. Cogger PhD *(The Australian Museum, Sydney)*
P. D. C.	P. D. Coker PhD *(University of London, King's College)*
P. J. C.	P. J. Conder *(Director, The Royal Society for the Protection of Birds, Sandy, Bedfordshire)*
N. J. C.	N. J. Conway *(Solihull, Warwickshire)*
G. B. C.	G. B. Corbet MA, PhD *(British Museum Natural History, London)*
P.S.C.	Professor P. S. Corbet PhD *(University of Waterloo, Ontario)*
L. C.	L. Cornwallis BA *(University of Oxford, Edward Grey Institute of Field Ornithology)*
W. A. M. C.	Miss W. A. M. Courtney PhD *(University of London, Westfield College)*
C. B. C.	C. B. Cox PhD *(University of London, King's College)*
F. E. G. C.	F. E. G. Cox PhD *(University of London, King's College)*
D. W. T. C.	D. W. T. Crompton PhD *(University of Cambridge)*
A. I. D.	Professor Anne Innis Dagg PhD *(University of Guelph, Ontario)*
R. P. D.	R. Phillips Dales PhD *(University of London, Bedford College)*
S. J. J. F. D.	S. J. J. F. Davies *(CSIRO, Division of Wildlife Research, Helena Valley, Western Australia)*
B. N. K. D.	B. N. K. Davis PhD *(Monks Wood Experimental Station, Abbots Ripton, Huntingdon)*
D. G. D.	D. G. Dawson BA *(University of Oxford, Edward Grey Institute of Field Ornithology)*
M. D.	M. Desfayes *(The Smithsonian Institution, Washington D.C.)*
M.E.D.	M. E. Dewar BSc London
J. S. D.	J. S. Dobbs *(Atlanta Zoological Park, Georgia)*
P. M. D.	P. M. Driver PhD *(Stonehouse, Gloucestershire)*
E. M. D.	Miss E. M. Dron BSc *(University of London, Westfield College)*
N. D.	Miss N. Duplaix BSc *(Université de Paris, Ecole de Médecine)*
K. F. D.	K. F. Dyer PhD *(Monash University, Clayton, Australia)*
R. D. E.	R. D. Eady *(Worcester Park, Surrey)*
R. E.	Mrs. R. Eastman *(Whitchurch, Hampshire)*
F. J. G. E.	Professor F. J. G. Ebling PhD *(University of Sheffield)*
B. E.	B. Edwards *(London)*
S. K. E.	S. K. Eltringham PhD *(Nuffield Unit of Tropical Animal Ecology, Uganda)*
R. H. E.	R. H. Emson PhD *(University of London, King's College)*
M. E. G. E.	M. E. G. Evans PhD *(University of Manchester)*
P. R. E.	P. R. Evans DPhil *(University of Durham*
R. C. F.	R. C. Fisher PhD *(University of London, University College)*

A. F.	A. Fisk PhD *(University of London, St Mary's Hospital Medical School)*
M. F.	M. Fogden *(Nuffield Unit of Tropical Animal Ecology, Uganda)*
E. B. F.	Professor E. B. Ford FRS, DSc *(University of Oxford)*
M. T. F.	Miss M. T. Franklin DSc *(Rothamsted Experimental Station, Harpenden, Hertfordshire)*
J. B. F.	J. B. Free PhD *(Rothamsted Experimental Station, Harpenden, Hertfordshire)*
V. F.	Miss V. Fretter DSc *(University of Reading)*
C. H. F.	C. H. Fry PhD *(University of Aberdeen)*
I. N. F.	I. N. Fuhn PhD *(Bucarest)*
P. D. G.	P. D. Gabbutt PhD *(University of Manchester)*
H. G.	Mrs H. Gauthier-Pilters PhD *(Saulieu, France)*
V. G.	Professor V. Geist PhD *(University of Calgary, Alberta)*
E. G.	Professor E. Gould PhD *(The Johns Hopkins University, Baltimore, Maryland)*
A. G.	Professor A. Graham *(University of Reading)*
A. G. C. G.	Miss A. G. C. Grandison BSc *(British Museum Natural History, London)*
Ja. G.	Professor J. Green PhD, DSc *(University of London, Westfield College)*
Jo. G.	J. Griffith PhD *(University of London, Westfield College)*
M. G.	M. Griffiths PhD *(CSIRO, Division of Wildlife Research, Canberra City, Australia)*
C. P. G.	C. P. Groves PhD *(University of Cambridge)*
L. B. H.	L. B. Halstead PhD, DSc *(University of Reading)*
M. P. H.	M. P. Harris PhD *(University of Oxford, Edward Grey Institute of Field Ornithology)*
W. V. H.	W. V. Harris OBE, DSc *(Commonwealth Institute of Entomology, London)*
C. J. O. H.	C. J. O. Harrison *(British Museum Natural History, London)*
B. H.	Mrs B. Harrisson *(Ithaca, New York)*
F. H.	F. Haverschmidt *(Ommen, Netherlands)*
S. E. H.	Miss S. E. Hawkins PhD *(University of London, King's College)*
I. N. H.	I. N. Healey PhD *(University of London, King's College)*
B. T. H.	B. T. Hepper *(Fisheries Experiment Station, Conway, Caernarvonshire)*
P. B. H.	P. B. Heppleston PhD *(College of Agriculture, Orkney)*
R. H.	R. Hewson *(Nature Conservancy, Banchory, Kincardineshire)*
N. E. H.	N. E. Hickin PhD *(Director, Rentokil Laboratories Limited, Sussex)*
C. W. H.	C. W. Holloway PhD *(Secretary, Survival Service Commission, Morges, Switzerland)*
D. T. H.	D. T. Holyoak *(London)*
J. H.	J. Horsley *(The Smithsonian Institution Washington D.C.)*
P. E. H.	P. E. Howse PhD *(University of Southampton)*
R. H.	R. Huddart BSc *(University of London, King's College)*
T. E. H.	T. E. Hughes PhD *(Rudgwick, Sussex)*
H. H.	H. Hunt *(G. V. Gress Zoological Park, Atlanta, Georgia)*
P. H.	P. Hutchinson PhD *(London)*
E. L. J.	E. L. Janecek *(John Shedd Aquarium, Chicago)*
J. B. J.	J. B. Jennings PhD *(University of Leeds)*
N. V. J.	N. V. Jones PhD *(University of Hull)*
P. J. J.	P. J. Jones BA *(University of Oxford, Edward Grey Institute of Field Ornithology)*
J. E. K.	Miss J. E. King BSc *(University of New South Wales, Australia)*
M. A. K.	Professor M. A. Kitching OBE, FRS, PhD, ScD *(University of East Anglia, Norwich)*
D. E. K.	Miss D. E. Kleiman PhD *(Rutgers University, New Jersey)*
K. K.	K. Klemmer PhD *(Forschungsinstitut Senckenberg, Frankfurt am Main, Germany)*
H. K.	H. Klingel PhD *(Technische Universität Carola-Wilhelmina, Braunschweig, Germany)*
R. M. L.	R. M. Laws PhD *(Cambridge)*
R. L.	R. Lawson PhD *(University of Salford, Lancashire)*
D. L. L.	D. L. Lee DSc *(Director, Houghton Poultry Research Station, Huntingdon)*
G. F. L.	G. F. Leedale PhD *(University of Leeds)*
A. P. M. L.	A. P. M. Lockwood PhD *(University of Southampton)*
P. L. L.	P. L. Long PhD *(Houghton Poultry Research Station, Huntingdon)*
F. A. L.	F. A. Lowe *(Bolton, Lancashire)*
K. M. L.	Miss K. M. Lyons PhD *(University of London, King's College)*
M. H. M.	M. H. MacRoberts PhD *(University of Oxford)*
S. M. M.	Miss S. M. Manton PhD *(British Museum Natural History, London)*
S. M.	S. Marchant *(Beaumoris, Victoria, Australia)*
R. D. M.	R. D. Martin PhD *(University of London, University College)*
P. F. M.	P. F. Mattingly DSc *(Caterham, Surrey)*
J. M.	J. Mauchline PhD *(Scottish Marine Biological Association, Oban, Argyll)*
J. M. M.	J. M. McMillan BSc *(University of London, King's College)*
J. H. M.	J. H. Mehrtens *(Columbia Zoological Park, South Carolina)*
H. M.	H. Milne PhD *(University of Aberdeen)*
R. D. M.	Professor R. D. Mitchell *(Ohio State University, Columbus, Ohio)*
P. D. M.	P. D. Moore PhD *(University of London, King's College)*
J. M. M.	J. M. Morgan *(London)*
P. A. M.	P. A. Morris PhD *(University of London, Royal Holloway College)*
J. M.	Professor J. Morton PhD *(University of Auckland, New Zealand)*
R. M.	R. Mykytowycz PhD *(CSIRO, Division of Wildlife Research, Canberra City, Australia)*
P. F. N.	P. F. Newell PhD *(University of London, Westfield College)*
R. C. N.	R. C. Newell PhD *(University of London, Queen Mary College)*
I. N.	I. Newton PhD *(Nature Conservancy, Edinburgh)*
M. N.	Miss M. Nixon PhD *(University of London, University College)*
F. B. O.	Professor F. B. O'Connor PhD *(University of London, University College)*
H. O.	H. Oldroyd MA *(British Museum Natural History, London)*
F. J. O.	Professor F. J. O'Rourke PhD, MB *(Kilmore Quay, Eire)*
A. L. P.	A. L. Panchen PhD *(University of Newcastle)*
M. J. P.	M. J. Parr PhD *(University of Salford, Lancashire)*
R. P.	R. Pawley *(Chicago Zoological Park)*
C. P.	C. Perrins DPhil *(University of Oxford, Edward Grey Institute of Field Ornithology)*
J. P.	J. Phillipson PhD *(University of Oxford)*
T. B. P.	T. B. Poole PhD *(University of Wales, Aberystwyth)*
I. P.	I. Prestt PhD *(Monks Wood Experimental Station, Abbots Ripton, Huntingdon)*
R. D. P.	Professor R. D. Purchon DSc *(University of London, Chelsea College of Science and Technology)*
D. P.	D. Pye PhD *(University of London, King's College)*
D. R. R.	D. R. Ragge PhD *(British Museum Natural History, London)*
U. R.	U. Rahm PhD *(Naturhistorisches Museum, Basel, Switzerland)*
T. B. R.	Professor T. B. Reynoldson DSc *(University College of North Wales, Bangor)*
R. B. R.	Père R. B. Richard *(Paris)*
J. R.	Professor Joan Robb MSc *(University of Auckland, New Zealand)*
N. J. R.	N. J. Robinson *(CSIRO, Division of Wildlife Research, Helena Valley, Western Australia)*
E. P. F. R.	E. P. F. Rose PhD *(University of London, Bedford College)*
A. R. S.	A. Russell-Smith BSc *(University of London, King's College)*
J. S. R.	J. S. Ryland PhD *(University College of Wales, Swansea)*
G. E. S.	G. E. Savage PhD *(University of London, Queen Mary College)*
D. R. S.	Professor D. R. Schenkel PhD *(University of Basel, Switzerland)*
D. A. S.	D. A. Scott BA *(University of Oxford, Edward Grey Institute of Field Ornithology)*
W. N. S.	Major W. N. Scott *(Universities' Federation for Animal Welfare, Potters Bar, Hertfordshire)*
G. D. S.	G. D. Sevastopoulo PhD *(University of Dublin)*
G. B. S.	Professor G. B. Sharman PhD *(Macquarie University, Eastwood, Australia)*
J. T. R. S.	J. T. R. Sharock PhD *(Cape Clear Bird Observatory, Bedford)*
K. S.	Professor K. Simkiss PhD *(University of London, Queen Mary College)*
K. E. L. S.	K. E. L. Simmons MSc PhD *(University of Leicester)*
C. S.	C. Simms *(Yorkshire Museum, York)*
M. A. S.	M. A. Sleigh PhD *(University of Bristol)*

.G.A.M.S.	F. G. A. M. Smit *(British Museum Natural History Zoological Museum, Tring, Hertfordshire)*
. C. S.	D. C. Smith DPhil *(University of Oxford)*
. J. P. S.	W. J. P. Smyly BSc *(Freshwater Biological Association, Westmorland)*
. K. S.	L. K. Sowls *(University of Arizona, Tucson)*
. S.	J. Sparks PhD *(Bristol)*
. P. S.	J. P. Spradberry PhD *(Sirex Biological Control Unit, Ascot, Berkshire)*
. S.	J. Stidworthy *(Zoological Society of London)*
. F. S.	A. F. Stimson *(British Museum Natural History, London)*
. M. S.	D. M. Stoddart PhD *(University of Oxford)*
. L. T.	Sir A. Landsborough Thomson CB, BSc, Hon LLD (Aberdeen) *(London)*
R. T.	R. Thorpe BSc *(Loughton, Essex)*
P. J. T.	P. J. Tilbrook BA *(Monks Wood Experimental Station, British Antarctic Survey, Abbots Ripton, Huntingdon)*
G. U.	G. Underwood DSc *(University of London, Sir John Cass College)*
K. V.	K. Vickerman PhD *(University of Glasgow)*
D. W.	D. Wakelin PhD *(University of London, Bedford College)*
J. A. W.	J. A. Wallwork PhD *(University of London, Westfield College)*
P. W.	P. Ward PhD *(Tropical Pests Research Institute, Arusha, Tanzania)*
E. E. W.	E. E. Watkin PhD *(University College of Wales, Aberystwyth)*
Ph. W.	P. Wayre *(The Ornamental Pheasant Trust, Norwich, Norfolk)*
J. E. W.	Professor J. E. Webb PhD, DSc *(University of London, Westfield College)*
R. W. W.	R. W. Webster BSc *(The Polytechnic, London)*
M. J. W.	M. J. Wells ScD *(University of Cambridge)*
H. W.	H. Wermuth PhD *(Staatliches Museum fur Naturkunde, Ludwigsburg, Germany)*
Y. L. W.	Y. L. Werner PhD *(Hebrew University of Jerusalem, Israel)*
G. K. W.	G. K. Whitehead *(Chorley, Lancashire)*
P. J. P. W.	P. J. P. Whitehead BA *(British Museum Natural History, London)*
N. V. W.	N. V. Williams PhD *(University of Salford)*
P. J. le B. W.	P. J. le B. Williams PhD *(University of Southampton)*
M. P. M. W.	Mrs M. P. McCrane Wolanek *(Old Bridge, New Jersey)*
D. W. Y.	D W. Yalden PhD *(University of Manchester)*
M. Y.	Sir Maurice Yonge CBE, FRS DSc *(Edinburgh)*

Preface

Readership

This encyclopedia seeks to present a concise but comprehensive guide to the animal kingdom for the interested non-specialist adult. It differs from other books on the subject in that it covers not only a large number of typical species of animals but also the concepts and principles of zoology. It should therefore also prove attractive to schools, colleges, and university audiences. Even the specialist may profitably turn to it for reading on the subjects outside his particular field of studies.

Contents

Its conciseness will facilitate usage and avoid overwhelming the reader. This has been further enhanced by an alphabetically arranged scheme which ensures easy reference. The number of entries is balanced to give full scope to the subject matter. This involves some 3,000 entries, most of them of sufficient length to be pleasantly readable yet fully informative. It also implies grouping together closely related animals and subjects. Thus, classes such as Mammals have their own entries as do orders of Mammals like Marsupials, Insectivores, Primates, Cetacea (Whales, Porpoises, Dolphins). These are further broken down into smaller entries on suborders like Anthropoidea (Monkeys and Apes), and even families like Lemurs. The more important species, for example, tiger, have their separate entries or they may be grouped together in their orders, like the Chiroptera or Bats. The same holds true for the general subjects.

Cross referencing has been kept to a minimum so that the reader will be able to find the information he needs without being referred from one page to another. For the same reason asterisks (*) have deliberately been kept to a minimum and are only used where it would not be obvious that the reader can look elsewhere for more information. An Index is provided containing the names of species which for various reasons do not form the key word of an entry, as well as scientific names and technical words; this will provide an alternative cross-referencing system. A Glossary explains the technical terms and assists the lay-reader to find what he may perhaps know under another more familiar name.

Illustrations

Special attention has been paid to illustrations which while attracting the reader will also amplify the text. There are a great number of them, taking up nearly 50% of the space, and they are deliberately varied to include both colour and black and white photographs, as well as artists' drawings from elaborate colour-work to simple diagrams and maps.

Proportion of Groups

Every effort has been made to deal with the various groups of animals and subjects in a zoologically balanced manner. Thus invertebrates, numerically so important, are extensively covered, for although less generally known to the lay-reader they include animals that are beautiful, bizarre, very large or extremely small, or are important because, for example, they carry or cause disease. Naturally, Mammals and Birds receive ample space for they contain some of the best known species. So, too, do Fishes, Reptiles and Amphibians. There is substantial treatment of such fascinating subjects as Animal Behaviour and Ecology, while for purposes of completeness and instruction adequate attention has been paid to Anatomy, Physiology, Reproduction and Zoogeography. A limited number of Biographies of some of the more important zoologists are included.

Writing

In order to achieve the highest standard, over 200 authors have been selected to write on topics in which they have specialized. In this way the latest and most reliable information becomes available. This has inevitably led to some sub-editing to achieve, as far as possible, a consistent presentation, but this sub-editing has been kept to a minimum.

Deliberately, most entries are so written that they will appeal more to the uninitiated. At the other extreme are subjects that cannot be dealt with except in more erudite terms. This means, however, that the completely uninformed reader may, if he so wishes, graduate with the help of the encyclopedia, from a purely dilettante interest to the zoologically well informed; metaphorically, from primary school to university.

The result is confidently expected to be the standard encyclopedia of zoology of the seventies and beyond.

Acknowledgements

All important entries are signed with the initials of the author. However, none of the entries on Fishes carries such acknowledgement as they are the cooperative effort of two authors, P. J. P. Whitehead and K. Banister. In the initial stages Joseph Lucas BSc has greatly contributed to the shape of the encyclopedia.

Introduction

'If we choose to let conjecture run wild, then animals – our fellow brethren in pain, disease, death, suffering and famine, our slaves in the most laborious works, our companions in our amusements – they may partake from our origin in one common ancestor, we may be all netted together.' So wrote Charles Darwin in his Notebook near the end of 1837.

Few today would disagree with these words. Yet, at the time, this conjecture must have appeared very wild, after 18 centuries of the Church's teaching that man was unique and a divine creation, whereas animals were only brutes. Darwin had returned from his journey round the world in the *Beagle* and was getting his observations, collections and ideas in order, when he came up with this idea which was to change the course of human thought. That it was the absolute truth, everything discovered since that date has confirmed. It means that all animals are related to each other and that man, also an animal, is related to them. More importantly, it means that everything learnt about animals has some bearing on man himself – not always to his liking or advantage. For example, man is the only species which claims to have an ethical code of behaviour – and he is also the only species in which individuals kill one another in large numbers. Indeed, in order to get out of this ghastly circumstance we might usefully study animals and their behaviour and see what has gone wrong in man.

Darwin incubated his ideas for another twenty years before publishing his epoch-making book on the *Origin of Species* in 1859. This, and many other historical features of the study of animals will be found in this encyclopedia, the object of which is to introduce the reader to what zoology, the study of animals, implies at the present day, for this science has made such great progress since Darwin's day that it has become split into a number of branches, each covering an enormous field.

The first branch is, quite naturally, comparative anatomy, or morphology, the science of form. It concerns itself with the shape of all animals, inside and out, and supplies information not only on the process of evolution whereby all animals are 'netted together', but also on innumerable puzzles in the structure of the human body. One of these is the presence of three tiny little bones in the middle ear, without which our hearing would be somewhat indiscriminating. These bones are the equivalent of three bones in the rear of the reptile's jaw. There they assist in the articulation of the jaw; in us they transmit delicate vibrations. An almost incredible transformation, but one we can trace by studying the position of these bones in related animals. And we can watch such transformation taking place in the developing embryo. Another is why the recurrent laryngeal nerve runs out from the back of the skull, goes down inside the neck to loop round the subclavian artery that runs into our arm before turning back up the neck and ending in the muscles of the larynx. This fails to make sense until we realize it is because our larynx is higher up in the throat than it is in some other animals. It is another of these puzzles that can only be explained by animal evolution.

The shape of any organ is inexplicable without the knowledge of how it works. This is the domain of physiology, which, with biochemistry, studies and explains, for example, how energy is obtained. We breath oxygen, which is carried about the body in the blood and used to burn the sugars and starches in various organs. These come from our food which is broken down by digestion and then built up again into the tissues. Physiology also explains how the kidneys, the lungs, and the skin get rid of the waste products of breakdown of these tissues; how the sense organs 'sense', how the nervous system conducts impulses in from the sense organs or out to muscles and glands; and how the brain co-ordinates or integrates the functions of the body.

Animals, except the very simplest, develop from a fertilized egg into the adult, passing through the stages of embryo and larva before growing up. This study, known as embryology, explains a number of conundrums. For instance, why the sensitive layer of the eye, the retina, in vertebrates including man, is inverted and turned away from the light entering the eye. In the embryo the eye grows out from the surface of the brain and becomes infolded to form a cup. As a result the light-sensitive cells are covered by a layer of nerve-fibres. Comparative embryology is, however, of the greatest value in the study of evolution, although there is another field in which it is important as a result of the introduction of experimental methods into its study. It is possible to operate on embryos at an early stage in their development, to change the order of their constituent parts. By taking some away and adding others, it has been possible to discover not only which part gives rise to which organ but to say that this or that organ develops because it has been induced to do so through the diffusion of chemical substances or the passage of nervous impulses. Cancerous growths may in some cases be regarded as a breakdown in this process of developmental mechanics.

Between one generation of animals and the next, there is a continuity brought about through the transmission of hereditary material, as a result of which offspring resemble or differ from their parents. The study of this is called the science of genetics, which has made such enormous progress in recent years that it is now possible to define the genes, the units of heredity, in chemical terms. So genetics is at the spearhead of what is called molecular biology.

The number of different kinds of animals now living – nearly a million and half are known and an even greater number remain to be discovered – is believed to represent less than 1% of the kinds which have lived on earth since life began. This means that the vast majority have become extinct. Their remains, if hard enough to undergo preservation, are the fossils, the study of which is known as paleontology. The geological record is necessarily incomplete, largely as a result of destructive changes in the earth's crust. Even fossils are not indestructible. Moreover, the remains of most animals are destroyed long before they can become fossilized. But sufficient fossils have already been discovered, and others are being constantly discovered, not only to show that evolution took place but also to give a general guide on how it proceeded. Many fossils show transitional forms between one group of animals and another or show how one species became transformed into another. This is particularly evident in the case of the evolution of man, the fossils showing man-like apes turning into ape-like men. Paleontology also makes use of radio-active materials in the rocks to assess their ages and to measure the speeds at which different lines or lineages of animals have evolved.

One very important branch of zoology is concerned with the correct naming and classifying of animals. This is known as systematics, or taxonomy, without which no zoologist or medical research worker anywhere in the world would know exactly what animal another worker was writing about. The scientific names are not only labels, they constitute a kind of international language. Only English-speaking scientists can be guaranteed to know what is meant by 'domestic dog', but scientists the world over know immediately what is meant by *Canis familiaris*.

After Darwin's 'bomb', showing that all animals were related to one another by ties of heredity and affinity, a curious and ironical result followed. Zoologists were so obsessed with the craving to know what the ancestral forms of animals, including those now living, were like, that they turned their backs on the very field studies which had enabled Darwin to make his discovery. They metaphorically rushed indoors, into their laboratories, to dissect, compare, and infer all sorts of conclusions, often useless, about the past history of animals. It was, indeed, some time before they remembered that animals are living things, and that the study of live animals is the domain of the naturalist. Yet the way to this had already been shown them by a country clergyman in England, Gilbert White of Selborne, whose patient study in the 18th century of the lives of birds, how to tell them apart by their shape and colour, their song, their nesting habits, the colours of their eggs, their food, and everything about their life and death in nature, led him to write a classic for all time, *The Natural History of Selborne*, a never-ending source of inspiration. Indeed, it inspired Darwin himself, and he did what he could on a world-wide scale to study the habits of the animals which he found in nature, and thereby initiated the science of ecology, which deals with where animals live and how they cope with the physical, chemical and biological factors in their environments, which together form the basis of the balance of nature. Attention is only now being paid to the effects, always unpredictable and often disastrous, of interfering with this balance by excessive use of chemical substances as pesticides, or by introducing to one region animals from another. Ironically man, himself an animal, has shamefully neglected his own ecology.

A special branch of ecology is represented by parasitology, the study of animals that have taken to living at the expense of others on which, or even in which, they live. It is only necessary to mention the malarial parasite, trypanosomes of sleeping sickness, amoebae of dystentery, worms of bilharziasis, threadworms of elephantiasis, liver-flukes and tape-worms, to realise how widespread this unpleasant phenomenon is, and also how dependent the science of medicine is on that of parasitology.

Finally, animal behaviour or ethology is another branch of zoology, to which Darwin made two contributions: in his principle of sexual selection and in his study of the expression of the emotions. It is now realised that ethology contains one of the keys to the question whether man will or will not detroy himself by his actions. The problem is tied up with the peculiar method by which man imparts knowledge (or superstition) and principles of conduct (ethical or brutal) to his offspring, during the very long period of childhood which is the cradle of what is called psycho-social evolution.

Like every other science, zoology has a history. But the fumblings of Aristotle the Greek, of Pliny the Roman, and of the few mediaeval or early Renaissance doctors who concerned themselves with describing animals, in bestiaries and other books, bear little relation to zoology as understood now. What they had to say is a subject for those who study the history of ideas, before such ideas became clarified by the words of Darwin and Mendel to mention only the giants. Zoology now enables animals to be not only studied, but appreciated, and often loved, with a sense of wonder and delight. For most readers, this is the most important part of the subject.

Sir Gavin de Beer

Geological Time and Prehistoric Life

The earth is almost 5,000 million years old, and for most of this time animals and plants have lived on its surface. Man has existed for about half a million years; translated into a different time scale – if the age of the earth is reckoned to be one year, then man has existed for a mere 50 minutes, and modern man, *Homo sapiens*, has been around for a considerably shorter time! Some knowledge of the history of the earth, and of extinct animals and plants, is essential to an understanding of the great diversity of life which we see around us today.

The Geological Succession. The earth around us at first appears to be extremely stable. Mountains, plains, rivers and seas seem to have changed very little since man first recorded his impressions of his geographical environment. But appearances can deceive, for in fact the earth's geography is continually changing. When this fact was first pointed out by early geologists such as Hutton in 1795, and Lyell in 1830, most people found it hard to accept because the life span of an individual, or even the whole of historical time, is minute compared with the age of the earth, and, because geological processes may be extremely slow, their effects may only become apparent after thousands or millions of years.

Among the most important geological processes are the breaking down of existing rocks and the formation of new ones – erosion and sedimentation. Both these processes are continuous. Rocks are broken down by the action of sun and rain, by glaciers on mountainsides, and by wave action on the seashore. In addition, chemical and biological agents are producing similar results in less spectacular ways. The products of erosion; fragments of rock, ranging in size from huge boulders to pebbles and sand grains, right down to clay particles less than $\frac{1}{2500}$ in (0.01 mm) in diameter, are carried by glaciers, wind and water. Eventually they come to rest; boulders and coarse gravels in stream beds; sands in rivers and lakes, or on dry land in desert regions; sands and muds around seashores, and the finest muds and silts in deep-sea water. Slowly, as these deposits accumulate, the layered rocks, known as sedimentary rocks, are formed. Each successive layer adds to the pressure acting on lower layers, and gradually the muds, sands and gravels, become compacted, while their particles become cemented together by minerals which percolate through them in solution, until mudstones, sandstones and conglomerates are formed. Other sedimentary rocks are formed, not from the products of erosion, but from the remains of animals. Thus limestones and chalks are often formed from the broken fragments of shells and the skeletons of marine animals.

The sedimentary rocks, then, form a sequence of layers or strata with older rocks lying below younger rocks. The total thickness of these strata may be thousands of feet, representing deposition during the past 3,500 million years. For convenience the geological history of the earth has been divided into four eras: Cenozoic, Mesozoic, Paleozoic and Precambrian, and the first three eras are subdivided into eleven periods: Quaternary and Tertiary through to Cambrian. Each of these periods is given a name based upon what is known as a type succession. A succession is a sequence of rock strata representing continuous deposition during one particular period of time. A type succession is the first one to be given a name. For example, one succession was first identified in Wales and was called the Cambrian, after Cambria, the old name for Wales. Once it was identified and named, this succession, wherever it is found in the world, is called Cambrian. Any newly discovered succession, anywhere in the world, can then be described by comparing it with the type succession. Another type succession is the Triassic (tri=three). This was found in Germany and is so called because there were three phases of deposition: Lower Triassic in lakes and rivers, Middle Triassic in the sea, and Upper Triassic again in lakes and rivers.

The Fossil Record. How does knowledge of the sedimentary history of the earth help our understanding of life? Imagine a scene of some 200 million years ago in an area now occupied by Utah USA. The landscape is flat, the Rocky Mountains are not due to be formed for another 100 million years, and the semitropical vegetation consists of tree

The effects of erosion and sedimentation. During the course of geological time, rocks forming mountains and hills are broken down by various agents such as sun, rain and ice action. The products of erosion are carried away by wind, ice and water, and are deposited in rivers and on the sea bed. As geographical features are erased, layers of sedimentary rocks are gradually accumulated.

ferns and ginkgos. A herd of dinosaurs, pursued perhaps by predators, is forced to ford a flooded river, and some of the weaker members are drowned and carried away in the current. Animal carcasses in such circumstances rot away, or are found by scavengers and devoured. On this occasion however, the dinosaur bodies are caught on a sand-bar onto which the flood water is depositing sediment at an unusually rapid rate. Before decomposition can take place, the dinosaurs are buried in sand. This sand was to become just one stratum within the thousands of feet of sands deposited during the following ten million years. Today they form the Morrison formation of the American Jurassic, and erosion has revealed within these rocks the skeletons of those hapless dinosaurs.

As in the example given above, organisms have been entombed in sedimentary rocks ever since the first known fossil, an alga, was preserved some 3,000 million years ago. Thus the rocks contain a record of the evolutionary history of past and present life, the fossil record. The fossil record of some animals is very complete, and the history of some groups, for example the Horses (Equidae), is known in great detail. Another example is that of *Micraster*, a Sea urchin, which consists of a series of fossils exhibiting almost imperceptible change during the Cretaceous. A more typical example is that of the Procolophonidae. These were small reptiles, probably living in the undergrowth and feeding on plants and insects. Their remains have been found in Permian and Lower Triassic rocks of South Africa and Europe, in Middle Triassic rocks of Europe, and in Upper Triassic rocks of America. In a study of these animals, Dr. E. H. Colbert, of the American Museum of Natural History, New York, arranged their skulls in order of their age, and it became apparent that certain changes had taken place. The eye became larger, spines developed on the head, the number of teeth decreased, the jaws became shorter and stouter and the jaw muscles became larger. From these observations, two main types of conclusion could be drawn. Firstly, changes in the tooth and jaw structure indicated that the procolophonids were becoming more dependent on plant food, paralleling rodents living today. Secondly, the gradual change in their structure suggested that the fossils were related, and a family tree could be constructed representing the way in which evolution in these animals had taken place.

In a similar way, paleontologists piece together the story of other prehistoric animals and their findings can be similarly expressed in evolutionary charts which are used to illustrate the evolution of the major groups in this encyclopedia. Obviously more is known about some than about others, because the fossil record is never complete. Fossils are more readily formed in the deposits of the sea bed, hence our knowledge of the history of marine animals is better than that of land dwellers. Only the hard parts of animals are usually preserved, and the fossil record of soft bodied phyla such as the worms (Annelida) is virtually non-existent. In spite of these gaps, however, the fossil record furnishes the zoologist with a most eloquent proof of the fact of organic evolution.

Peter Hutchinson

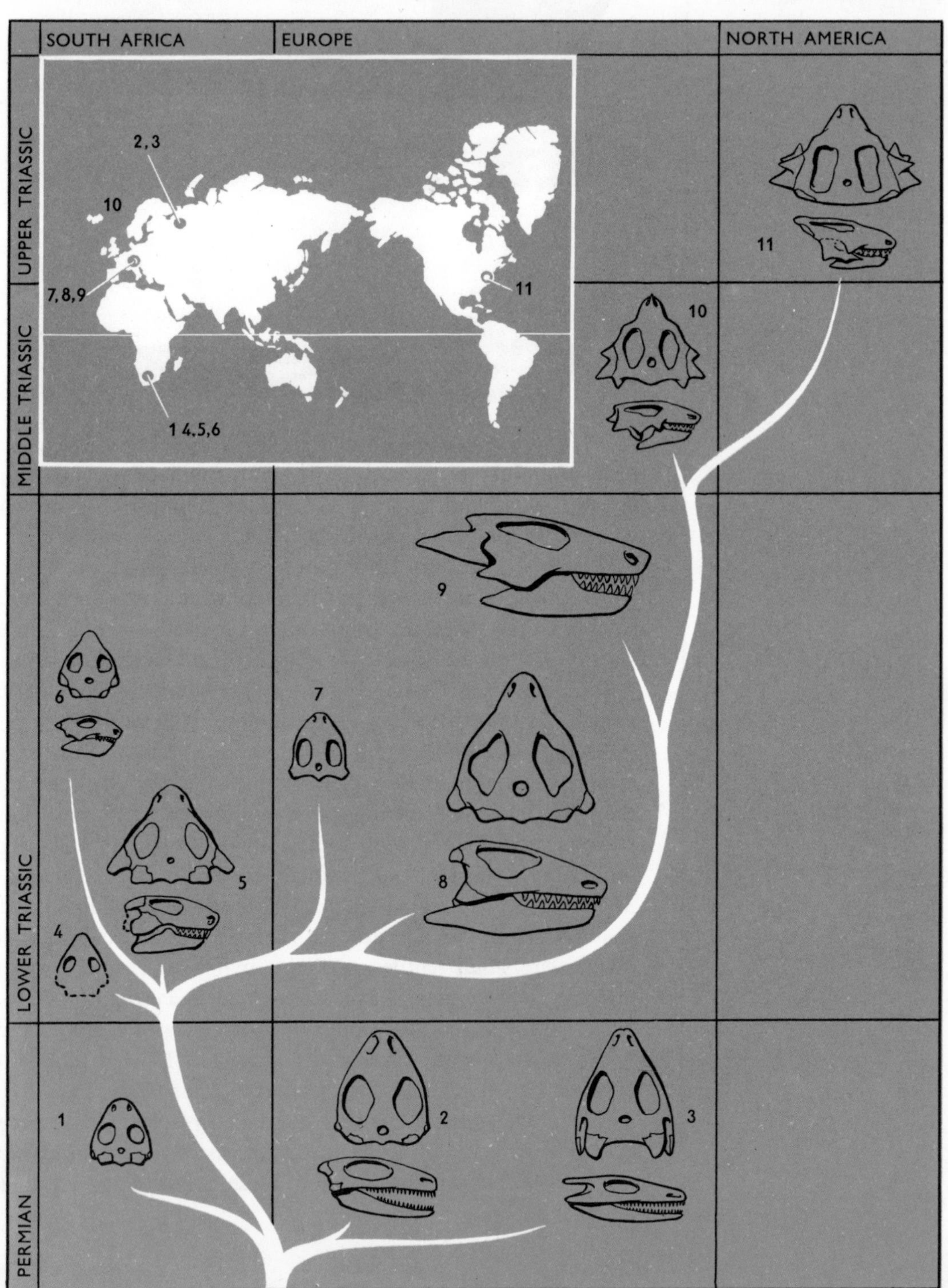

The construction of a family tree. Skulls of small reptiles called procolophonids, viewed from the side and top. The age of the rocks in which each type was found is indicated by the horizontal divisions, and the continent in which they were found by the vertical divisions. The skulls have been arranged to form a family tree. The line linking each type represent directions in which evolution is thought to have taken place, in other words, they represent theoretical lines of descent.

How animal remains become incorporated into the geological record. A dinosaur is drowned in a flooded river, and its body comes to rest on the river bed where it is rapidly covered with sand and mud. These sediments form the layers of rocks called sedimentary rocks. In this example the rock strata were tilted before erosion took place and fossilised remains of the dinosaur were revealed on the surface of a scarp face in Utah USA.

Overleaf: the geological time scale and the fossil record. On the left are the eras and periods into which the geological history of the earth is divided. The evolutionary chart shows the length of the fossil record of the major groups of animals and plants. 1 Protozoans 2 Algae 3 Xenusion 4 Sponges 5 Cnidarians 6 Brachiopods 7 Gastropods 8 Trilobites 9 Echinoderms 10 Ferns 11 Jawless fish 12 Lamellibranchs 13 Arthrodires 14 Rhipidistians 15 Crossopterygians 16 Dipnoans 17 Nautiloids 18 Arthropods 19 Primitive Ichthyostega 20 Cartilaginous fish 21 Actinopterygians 22 Lepidodendron 23 Reptiles 24 Mammal-like reptiles 25 Ammonites 26 Lizards and snakes 27 Turtles 28 Ichthyosaurs 29 Plesiosaurs 30 Cynognathus 31 Cycads 32 Conifers 33 Crocodiles 34 Pterosaurs 35 Archaeopteryx 36 Mammals 37 Amphibians 38 Dinosaurs 39 Birds 40 Insectivores 41 Angiosperms 42 Carnivores 43 Apes 44 Elephants 45 Marsupials 46 Whales 47 Bats 48 Man 49 Monkeys 50 Perissodactyls 51 Artiodactyls.

PERIODS
ERAS
EPOCHS
Age in millions of years
QUATERNARY
Recent
Pleistocene 4
CENOZOIC
Pliocene 11
Miocene 25
Oligocene 40
TERTIARY
Eocene 60
Paleocene 70
CRETACEOUS 135
MESOZOIC
JURASSIC 180
TRIASSIC 225
PERMIAN 270
CARBONIFEROUS
Pennsylvanian
350
Mississippian
DEVONIAN 400
PALEOZOIC
SILURIAN 440
ORDOVICIAN 500
600
PRECAMBRIAN 3500
1
2
3
4
5
6
7
8
9
11
12
13
14
15
16
17
18
19
20
21
22
23
24
25
26
27
28
29
30
31
33
34
35
36
37
38
39
40
41
42
43
44
45
46
47
48
49
50
51

AARDVARK *Orycteropus afer,* large African burrowing mammal with no close living relatives, at first placed in the order Edentata (the toothless ones) along with the armadillos and sloths because of its lack of front teeth. Now placed by itself in the order Tubulidentata (the tube-toothed) so called because of the fine tubes radiating through each tooth. The teeth themselves are singular in having no roots or enamel. A few fossil aardvarks have been found in North America, Asia, Europe and Africa but they give no help in tracing the aardvark's ancestry or its connection with other animals. Being nocturnal and secretive its habits are difficult to study, although it is in fact found throughout Africa, south of the Sahara, in most types of country except dense forest.

The aardvark (the Afrikaans name for 'earth-pig'), has a sturdy body, 6 ft (180 cm) long including a 2 ft (60 cm) tail and stands 2 ft (60 cm) high at the shoulder. The tough grey skin looks almost naked but is in fact very sparsely covered with hair. The head is long and narrow with a snout bearing a round pig-like muzzle and small mouth. The ears are large, resembling those of a donkey. The limbs are very powerful with four strong claws on the front feet and five on the hind feet.

Aardvarks excavate burrows, 3–4 yd (3m) long with their powerful limbs and sharp claws, working with incredible speed. When digging the aardvark rests on its hind legs and tail, pushing the earth back under its body with its forefeet and throwing it out with the hindlegs. Usually only one aardvark occupies a burrow, but each animal has several burrows sometimes several miles apart. In midsummer the female gives birth in her burrow to a single young, occasionally twins. After two weeks the young aardvark is strong enough to come out from the burrow and go foraging with its mother. At six months it is able to dig its own burrow and fend for itself.

As well as using the burrows for sleeping and breeding, an aardvark will retreat into an existing burrow or rapidly dig a new one if threatened by an enemy. It has many natural enemies; Hunting dogs, snakes, lions, leopards, cheetahs, Honey badgers or ratels. If unable to reach its burrow in time it will turn and fight back vigorously, striking at the enemy with its tail or feet and sometimes rolling on its back to kick with all four feet together. Flight and its rapid digging ability are its best defence for, having acute senses, like the moles and shrews even a moderate blow on the head in a fight may be fatal.

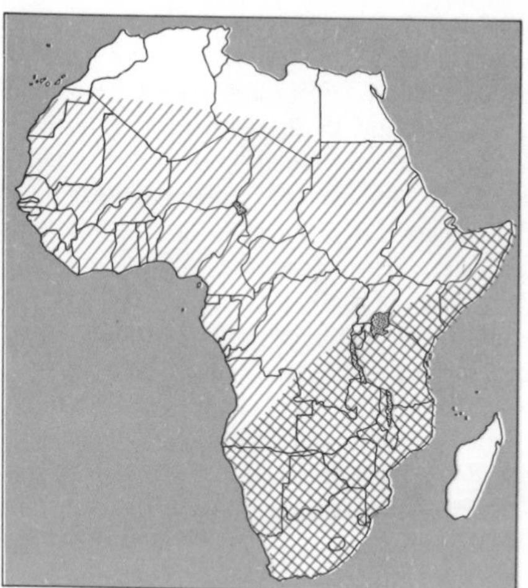

Distribution of the aardvark (blue) and the aardwolf (red).

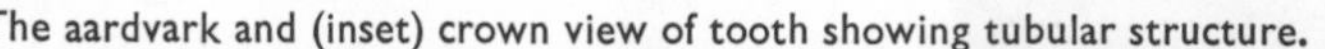

The aardvark and (inset) crown view of tooth showing tubular structure.

The aardvark feeds mainly on termites. It can rip a small hole in the rock-hard walls of the nests with its powerful claws, insert its muzzle and then pick out the swarming termites with its 18 in (45 cm) long, slender, sticky tongue. Its nose is protected from the termites by a fringe of stiff bristles and by its ability to close its nostrils. The aardvark also feeds on termites in rotten wood or while they are on the march but it is unable to eat true ants as its stomach is not adapted for dealing with hard-bodied insects. It will sometimes eat other soft-bodied insects and some fruit. Unlike other burrowing animals it will sometimes travel long distances in search of food. FAMILY: Orycteropidae, ORDER: Tubulidentata, CLASS: Mammalia.

N.J.C.

AARDWOLF *Proteles cristatus,* African relative of the hyaenas, in a separate family, the Protelidae. The aardwolf (the Afrikaans name for 'earth-wolf') is somewhat larger than a fox, weighing 50–60 lb (22–27 kg) with a yellow-grey coat with black stripes and black legs below the knee. The muzzle is black and hairless, the tail bushy and black-tipped. The hair along the neck and back is long and may be erected when the animal is frightened. It is found throughout southern and eastern Africa as far north as Somalia, in sandy plains or bushy country. It is not common anywhere throughout its range and is rarely seen, being solitary and nocturnal, spending the day in rock crevices or burrows which it digs out of the soil.

It differs in form from true hyaenas in having five instead of four toes on the front feet, larger ears and a narrower muzzle with weaker jaws and teeth. The main difference, however, is in its different feeding habits. The true hyaenas, with their powerful neck and jaw muscles and strong teeth, are hunters and carrion eaters. The aardwolf's teeth, except for the fairly large canines, are small and weak and there are few cheekteeth. It feeds, therefore, almost entirely on termites although, lacking strong claws to tear open the termite nests, it has to be satisfied with taking the insects from the surface or digging them out of soft soil. It sweeps up the termites in hundreds with amazing speed with its long sticky tongue.

When insects are short it may take mice, small ground-nesting birds and their eggs and it has been reported as killing lambs and chickens. This is unlikely except in cases of acute hunger as its teeth are inadequate for chewing such food.

Very little is known of the aardwolf's breeding habits. After a gestation of 90–110 days, a single litter of two to four blind young ones is born each year in November or December in the southern part of its range. FAMILY: Protelidae, ORDER: Carnivora, CLASS: Mammalia. N.J.C.

ABALONE *Haliotis,* the American name for the large Pacific ormer or earshell, a gastropod mollusc. The single flat shell is very beautiful with iridescent colours on the inside and also on the outside when the surface is cleaned of encrustations. There are usually a number of perforations on the side of the shell through which the water emerges after passing the abalone's gills. Abalones are found along the California coasts, the largest being the Red abalone *H. rufescens,* with a shell up to 10 in (25·4 cm) across. The Green abalone *H. fulgens* is thin-shelled and smaller up to 6 in (15 cm) and the Black abalone *H. cracherodii* 5 in (13 cm) across, unlike the other two that cling to rocks, lives among rocks in the surf and consequently has a clean and shining shell.

The flesh from the large muscular foot attached to the shell is regarded as a delicacy and eaten in many American cities along the Pacific coast and the shell is used for decorative work. Because of this the animal was in danger of extinction until minimum size limits for fishing were imposed and exports banned. Most of the abalones that are now eaten in the United States are imported from Mexico. FAMILY: Fissurellidae, ORDER: Diotocardia, CLASS: Gastropoda, PHYLUM: Mollusca.

ABYSSAL FAUNA, animals inhabiting the depths of the oceans, where there are low temperatures, permanent darkness, and enormous pressures. The lower limit of the abyss is, of course, the ocean floor, generally at a depth of about 13,000 ft (4,000 m), though deep troughs extending down to about 33,000 ft (10,000 m) occur. There is no firm upper limit to the abyss, though all waters below a depth of about 3,300 ft (1,000 m) may be called abyssal.

The abyss presents a remarkable habitat, which varies little with season and region. Even in tropical regions the temperature at a depth of 3,300 ft (1,000 m) is only about 40°F (5°C), and declines with increasing depth to about 33–35°F (1–2°C) at the ocean floor. The only light present is that made by the animals themselves. Pressure increases in the sea by one atmosphere for each 33 ft (10 m), so at a depth of 33,000 ft (10,000 m) the pressure is about 1,000 atmospheres, or approximately 6 tons per sq in (6 tons per 6·5 sq cm). At low temperatures viscosity increases: the water at the ocean floor, if at 32°F (0°C), will be twice as viscous as surface water at 77°F (25°C).

The fauna is specialized in various ways to be able to live in this environment. Movements of animals from the abyss into surface waters, and in the reverse direction, are rare. The animals are equilibrated to the outside pressure, so there is no danger of implosion and no need to guard against it. With moderate changes in depth there will be little change in volume for the body fluids are, like the water outside, practically incompressible. Only those fish with gas-filled swimbladders face dangers from the pressure, and most deep-sea fishes have lost the swimbladder, or use it as a fat store. Many members of the abyssal fauna have photophores, in which light is produced by the enzyme luciferase catalysing the oxidation of a substance known as luciferin. There are several functions of the resultant bioluminescence. The light from some photophores apparently lures potential prey to the predator's vicinity; that from others may discourage potential predators. The pattern of the photophores over the body surface may aid species recognition and sex recognition.

In or on the thick ooze of the deep-sea floor live such animals as sponges, anemones, Bivalve molluscs, crabs, brittlestars, Sea urchins and Sea cucumbers—a quantity and variety of animals larger than might be imagined. Above them swim squid, deep-sea prawns, and a surprising variety of fishes. Animals have been recovered from even the deepest troughs.

An abyssal food chain generally starts with the bacteria of the abyss rather than with members of the populations living at lesser depths. The bacteria digest and assimilate waste material which has drifted dowr. directly take up dissolved organic substances from the water, and also obtain energy by oxidizing inorganic substances. The bacteria in the ooze form food for the sand-swallowers (e.g. Sea cucumbers), these provide food for such bottom-crawlers as the crabs, and the crabs may in turn be taken by fishes swimming near the bottom. In ways such as these a self-maintained fauna lives in the remarkable conditions of the abyss. See also benthos, bioluminescence. A.E.B.

The aardwolf, although related to hyaenas, lacks their powerful teeth and jaws.

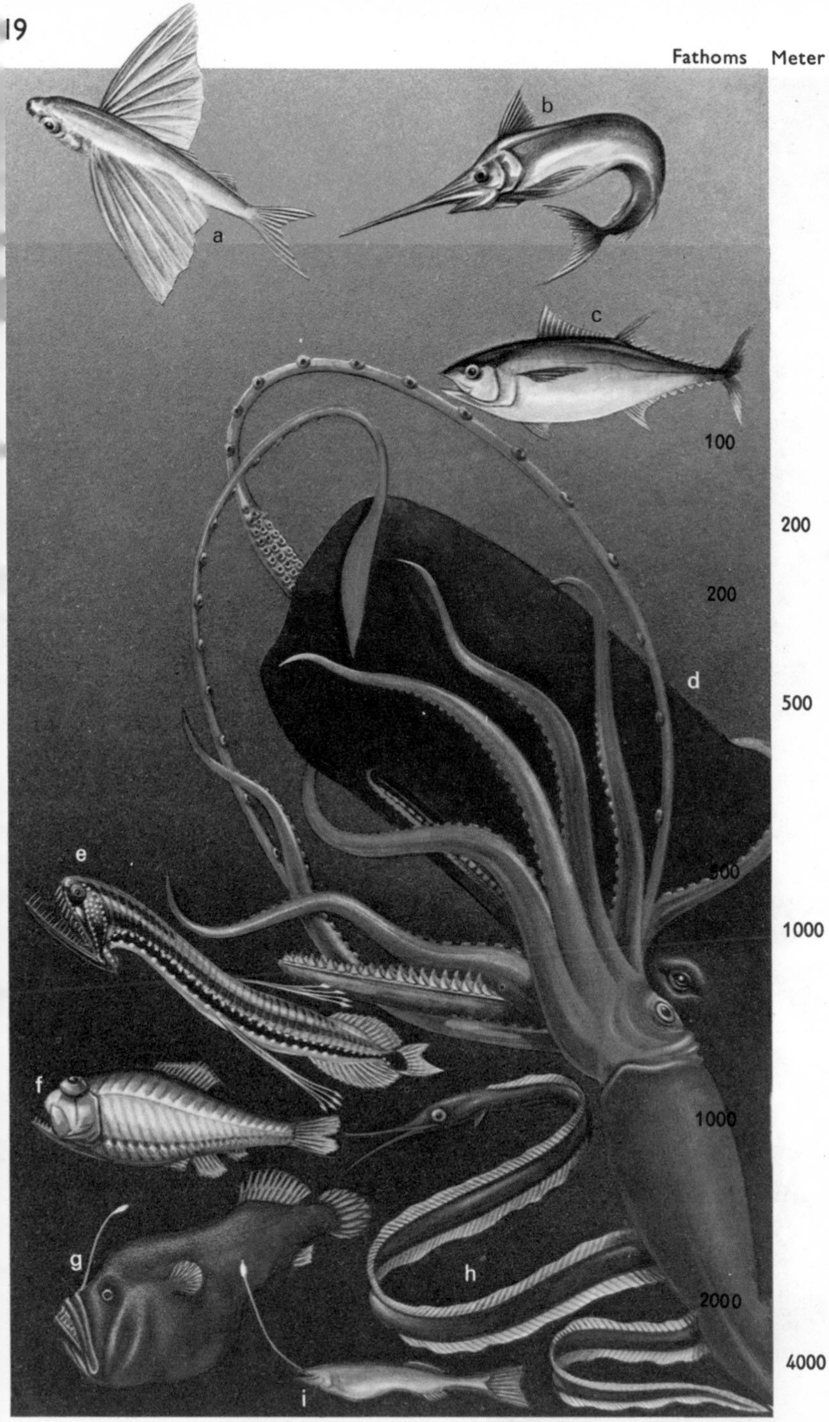

Types of animals found in the ocean at changing depths:
a. flyingfish *Exocoetus*,
b. swordfish *Xiphias*,
c. tunny *Thunnus*,
d. Sperm whale *Physeter* and Giant Squid *Architeuthis*,
e. Deep-sea fish *Photostomias*,
f. hatchetfish *Argyropelecus*,
g. anglerfish *Melanocetus*,
h. Snipe eel *Nemichthys*,
i. anglerfish *Gigantictis*.

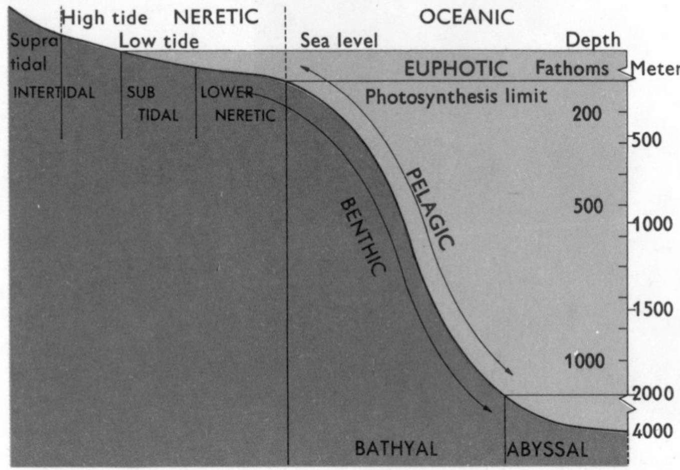

ABYSSAL FAUNA, in 1843 Edward Forbes an English lecturer, put forward the idea that there was no life in the sea below depths of 1,800 ft (550 m). He called this region the Azoic or Lifeless Zone. Many scientists accepted Forbes' arguments although Sir James Ross had collected starfish and other animals from 6,000 ft (1,800 m) some 25 years earlier. The discussions that ensued stimulated several attempts to test his theory and the foundation of deep-sea oceanography was assured when *HMS Challenger,* largely from efforts to test Forbes' theory, spent 3½ years cruising round the world while the scientists on board collected a wealth of specimens, many from several thousand feet deep.

ACANTHODIANS, fossil shark-like fishes that first made an appearance in the Silurian. One of the best known genera is *Climatius* of the Lower Devonian. Some authorities consider the acanthodians to have been ancestral to the shark-like fishes (Chondrichthyes) but others believe them to be early members of the bony fishes (Pisces or Osteichthyes). The acanthodians survived until the Lower Permian. See article Fossil fishes. SUBCLASS: Acanthodii, CLASS: Pisces.

ACARA, the common name given to certain freshwater fishes of the genus *Aequidens* (family Cichlidae). They are found in Brazil and Venezuela and certain species are now imported into Europe and North America as aquarium fishes. The best known are the Blue acara *Aequidens pulcher* and the Black acara *A. portalegrensis*. In the wild they grow to 8 in (22 cm) in length, but are very much smaller when kept in aquaria. The young tend to be rather pugnacious but older fishes will settle down well in a community tank. FAMILY: Cichlidae, ORDER: Perciformes, CLASS: Pisces.

ACARINE, or Isle of Wight disease, the name given to a disease of honeybees caused by an infestation of the parasitic mite, *Acarapis woodi*. The main seat of infection is the respiratory system of the bee, in particular the large tracheae of the thorax which connect with the exterior by breathing pores, or spiracles, located on the sides of the body. The initial infection, to which adult bees less than six days old are particularly susceptible, occurs when an adult female mite enters the trachea through a spiracle and lays eggs from which breeding populations become established. The mites may become so numerous that they block the trachea, which becomes blackened and shrivelled in appearance. They feed on the blood of the bee by pushing their stylet-like mouthparts through the wall of the trachea into the

Blue acara, a popular aquarium fish with blue-green spangled scales.

blood-filled body cavity. A heavily infected bee has a reduced flight capability, and tends to remain in the vicinity of the hive, fluttering its wings and crawling weakly with a distended abdomen. In England and Wales during the period 1958–67 approximately one in every ten colonies examined showed the presence of this disease. The survival of the colony is threatened when more than 40% of the bees are infected and this occurs more often during winter and early spring than in summer. The disease is treated by the use of fumigants, details of which are available from bee appliance dealers. J.A.W.

ACCENTORS, sparrow-like birds with short rounded wings, and fine pointed bills. They are generally brown or reddish-brown spotted or streaked above, and brown or grey below, usually with a reddish band on the breast or reddish streaks on the flanks. The twelve species are sufficiently alike to be included in the single genus *Prunella*. In most species, the nest is an untidy cup of grass, mosses and leaves, lined with wool or feathers, and placed low down or on the ground, in a small conifer, stunted shrub or crevice amongst boulders. The eggs are unmarked and vary in colour from pale blue to blue-green, the usual clutch size being between three and five. All species feed mainly on the ground, hopping about stiffly with a mouse-like action. Insects comprise a large part of the diet in spring and summer; in winter the food consists chiefly of small seeds and berries. Accentors are quiet, unobtrusive little birds, often extremely tame and confiding. They are usually rather solitary, but some species show a tendency to form flocks in winter. The song is short and simple, generally soft, and delivered at a hurried pace, from a rock or low bush.

Although showing certain affinities to the thrushes, chats and warblers (Muscicapidae), all species possess a true crop and muscular gizzard, characteristics of the finches (Fringillidae). Apart from isolated populations in southern Arabia, and perhaps also in Formosa, the group is exclusively confined to the Palearctic region and is characteristic of alpine meadows, juniper scrub and the coniferous-forest zones of the mountain ranges of Europe and central Asia, particularly the Himalayas. Two species, the Alpine accentor *Prunella collaris,* and the Himalayan accentor *P. himalayana,* commonly breed at elevations of over 15,000 ft (4,570 m), and few accentors occur below 5,000 ft (1,520 m) even in winter.

The dunnock or hedge-sparrow *P. modularis* of Europe is peculiar in that in some parts of its range it has descended from the coniferous-forest zone, and has become a characteristic bird of parks, gardens and hedgerows down to sea level. The Japanese accentor *P. rubida,* a bird very similar in

The dunnock, also called hedge-sparrow, (above) feeding nestlings, (left) close-up, showing slender bill typical of insectivorous birds.

appearance to the dunnock, breeds in the zone of dwarf birches and pines in mountainous regions in Japan and winters in the undergrowth of dense forests at lower altitudes. More typical is the Alpine accentor, which occurs in alpine meadows in mountainous regions from Spain and Morocco across Europe and Asia to Japan. This bird is commonly found around climbing huts and ski lifts in the Alps throughout the year. The Siberian accentor *P. montanella* breeds along the northern limits of the great coniferous forests of northern Asia from the Urals to Amurland, and is the only species which undertakes an extensive annual migration, its winter quarters being in northern China and Korea. Stragglers of this species have been recorded in Europe and in Alaska. The other species are either sedentary, or undertake short altitudinal migrations, descending in winter to lower snow-free areas, usually within their total breeding range. FAMILY: Prunellidae, ORDER: Passeriformes, CLASS: Aves. D.A.S.

ACCLIMATIZATION, is the process whereby animals adjust to changed or changing conditions in the environment to ensure the maintenance of normal body functioning. It is well known, for example, that humans living at high altitudes become adapted to the low levels of oxygen in the atmosphere by an increase in the amount of haemoglobin in their blood. Again, the chemical composition of the blood of certain crustaceans alters in response to changes in the salt content of their environment.

Many animals can become acclimatized and this ability is often shown by the way in which changes in the environmental temperature can be tolerated. An animal can normally tolerate a particular range of environmental temperature, its tolerance zone, but within this is a narrower zone, the preferred or optimum zone, in which the animal flourishes best and in which it would live if it had the choice. If exposed to temperatures outside the tolerance range for a given period of time, the animal will die and the temperature at which death occurs is known as the lethal temperature. Tolerance zones, optima and lethal temperatures are not fixed characteristics of an animal or species; they vary not only from animal to animal, but also from time to time in the same animal. Many cold-blooded animals are able to adjust, or acclimatize, to higher temperatures during the summer and lower temperatures during the winter, than they would be able to tolerate at other times of the year. This acclimatization is then a seasonal phenomenon and is stimulated by the animal being subjected to a particular set of temperature conditions. For example, the optimum environmental temperature for the Brook trout may be 54°F (12°C) in summer, but during the winter, when the fish is exposed to lower environmental temperatures for a period of several months, the optimum drops to 46°F (8°C). Similarly, an insect kept in temperature conditions at the lower end of its tolerance range for a period of several hours will become acclimatized. The temperatures at which it suffers heat death or cold death will then be lower than those for an insect of the same species maintained in conditions at the upper end of the tolerance range. These adaptations are of obvious benefit in increasing the chances of survival in habitats where there are large seasonal variations in temperature. In cold-blooded animals, the body temperature varies with the environmental temperature, and if these animals were not able to acclimatize, the metabolic rate would rise or fall as the body temperature increased or decreased. This would mean that such vital activities as growth, respiration and excretion would be seriously disturbed. In an acclimatized animal, an adjustment has been made so that the metabolic rate remains constant, even though the body temperature may have changed. The process of acclimatization in warm-blooded animals is rather different, however, for the body temperature usually remains more or less constant, despite variations in the environmental temperature, and any adjustments are designed to maintain this constancy. Many mammals sweat or pant when they are hot and shiver when they are cold, and these activities are directed towards keeping the body temperature steady within rather narrow limits. However, over a period of time, some mammals, at least, can acclimatize to endure cold or heat, and energy that would normally be expended in sweating, panting or shivering is therefore conserved.

The mechanisms which allow animals to acclimatize are not known in many cases and, indeed, they may vary from group to group. In cold-blooded animals, however, there are strong indications that the metabolic adjustments necessary for the development of heat or cold tolerance are made through adaptations of various enzyme systems. J.A.W.

ACORN WORMS, sluggish worm-like marine animals with the body in three clearly distinguishable parts: an anterior proboscis, shaped like a very elongate acorn, leading by a narrow neck to a 'collar', commonly wider than the third and main part, the 'trunk', which tapers gradually towards its rear end. The most obvious feature associating Acorn worms with the true *chordates is the paired gill slits or pores which open from the pharynx, the front part of the gut, through the body wall of the trunk just behind the base of the collar. These are numerous and their number increases with age. Externally, these gill slits appear as small pores, but internally they have the elongate U-shaped slit with a tongue bar in the middle reminiscent of the gills of the primitive chordate, the *lancelet (*Branchiostoma* or *Amphioxus*).

Most Acorn worms are 4 in (10 cm) in length, but *Balanoglossus gigas,* of Brazil, may be more than 3 ft (1 m) long. All are burrowers and *B. gigas* makes a burrow several metres in length. Acorn worms live in soft sand or muddy sand between tidemarks or just below low tide level. For the most part they feed on sand, digesting the minute organisms living on or between the sand grains. They make a U-shaped burrow, eating the surface sand or mud which is richest in nutrients. Like lugworms they form coiled castings on the surface.

The mouth lies between the proboscis and the collar. Feeding is by a combination of sand swallowing and *suspension feeding, the proportions varying from species to species. In suspension feeding particles in the water adhere to the mucus on the proboscis and are conveyed to the mouth, just as sand grains are. The food particles are directed across and down the proboscis to the mouth in a mucous string. *Cilia on the surface of the proboscis carry them into a preoral ciliary gutter-like organ and thence to the mouth. Particles too large or distasteful to be ingested travel along another ciliary tract onto the collar where they collect and are later rejected. The particles enter the mouth helped in by the ciliary current generated by the pharynx which acts as a gill, the water passing out through the gill pores. Probably these gill slits were evolved originally for feeding, but in Acorn worms they seem no longer to play this part but serve only for respiration.

Acorn worms have colourless blood circulated to the front of the body by a large dorsal vessel which opens into sinuses in the collar and proboscis at the base of which there is a complicated arrangement of vesicle and sinus forming what is known as the 'glomerulus', thought, at one time, to have an excretory function, though this now seems doubtful. Blood is directed back along the ventral vessel which supplies branches to the walls of the gills slits.

Acorn worms are localized in distribution but sometimes very numerous. The sexes are separate and when the breeding season approaches the gonads, producing the eggs or sperm, may often be detected by the series of bulges along each side of the trunk behind the gill-slit region. The edges of the trunk may even be extended into genital ridges or 'wings', in some species. The *gametes are shed through special pores from each gonad and fertilization of the numerous eggs takes place in the sea. In *Balanoglossus* each fertilized egg develops into a free-swimming larva, known as a tornaria, very like those of starfish and Sea urchins (echinoderms). The larva is at first a transparent globe with an apical tuft of long cilia, a band of cilia—the telotroch—towards the posterior end encircling the anus, and another characteristic curving band of cilia between the two which lengthens as the larva grows. The upper part of the larva becomes the acorn-shaped proboscis, the collar develops from the area between the mouth and the telotroch, and the part behind the telotroch becomes the trunk region as the larva settles on to a suitable sandy bottom to assume an adult mode of life. In some other genera development is more direct and the free larval life is shortened: in

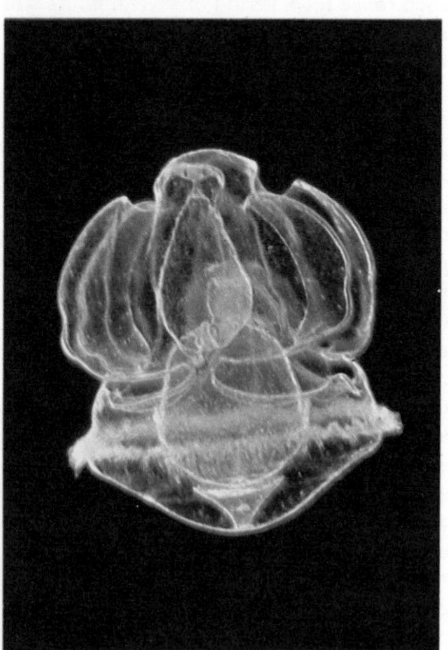

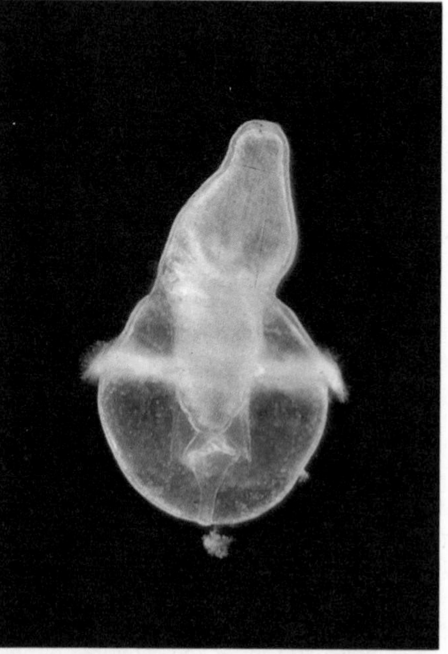

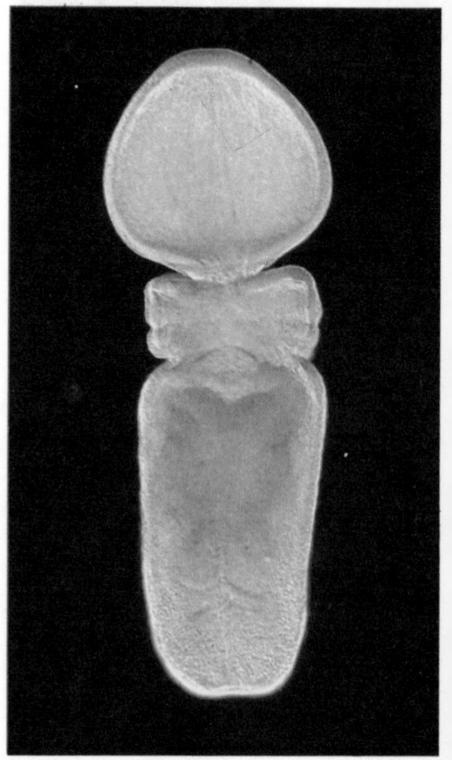

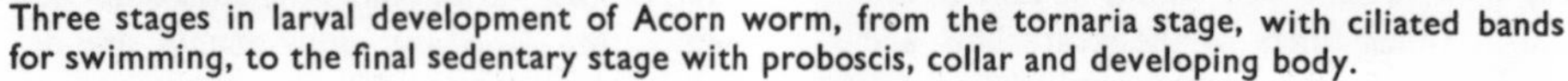

Three stages in larval development of Acorn worm, from the tornaria stage, with ciliated bands for swimming, to the final sedentary stage with proboscis, collar and developing body.

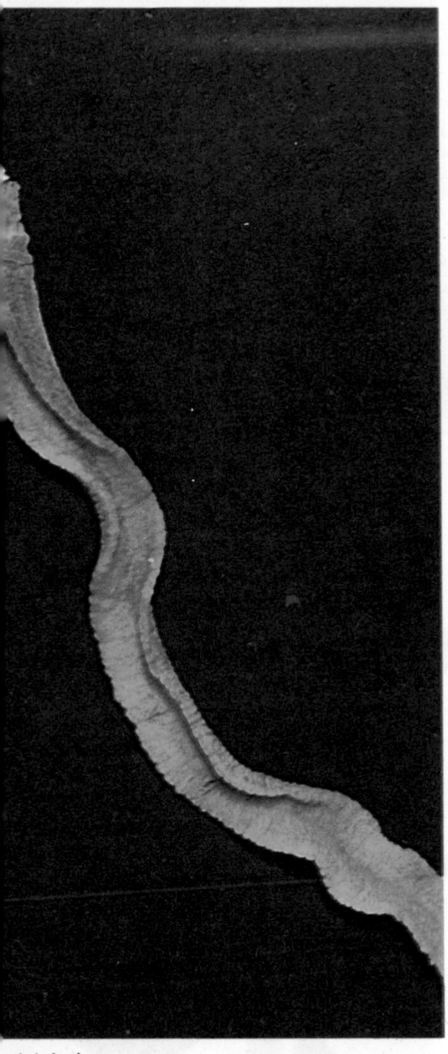

Adult Acorn worm.

the common *Saccoglossus kowalevskii* of northwest Europe, for example, the egg hatches into a larva which almost at once assumes an adult way of life. In *Saccoglossus horsti* spawning takes place when the tide is down. First the eggs are laid in coiled masses in mucus, and then the sperm are shed into the shallow puddles left by the receding tide. The males are stimulated to shed their sperm by the presence of the egg masses. Later the egg masses break up and the young larvae are swept away by the tide.

Acorn worms comprise one of the two classes of 'hemichordates' or half-chordates. As this name implies they show only some of the characters of chordates. They have gill slits like chordates, but no notochord, an essential characteristic of the chordates which is a skeletal rod that precedes the formation of the spinal column in vertebrates. The structure in Acorn worms once thought to be a notochord, which was called the 'stomochord' because of its connection with the mouth, is now thought to be merely a diverticulum of the gut and to be in no sense a true notochord. The larvae of *Balanoglossus* indicate a relationship with undoubted invertebrates and so does the way the body cavity or coelom develops. The coelom arises from the gut and is subdivided into three chambers, anterior, median and posterior, the first (anterior) becoming the proboscis cavity, the median and posterior arising as right and left parts and separated by the gut. In echinoderms the coelom develops in a similar manner, although each part later becomes adapted for rather different purposes. Other details of the anatomy also link the Acorn worms with the echinoderms.

The nervous system remains within the epidermis and is in many ways less differentiated even than that of echinoderms, but is organized in places into defined tracts, especially in the collar region where it is rolled into a 'neurocord'. This is like a chordate nerve cord in being hollow, but it is simply a concentration of nerve elements in a strip of epidermis which has been invaginated. It does however have giant nerve cells and is functionally adapted as a through conducting system and is said to play an important part in making the Acorn worm move backwards as an 'escape' movement. CLASS: Enteropneusta, SUBPHYLUM: Hemichordata, PHYLUM: Chordata. R.P.D.

ACTINOPTERYGIANS or ray-finned fishes, a broad grouping (subclass) within the class Pisces or bony fishes. See fishes and Fossil fishes. SUBCLASS: Actinopterygii, CLASS: Pisces.

ACUSHIS, which are assigned to the genus *Myoprocta,* are a group of about five species of South American rodents belonging to the same family, Dasyproctidae, as the better known agoutis. They are long-legged, agile rodents, differing from agoutis in their smaller size (about 14 inches or 35 cm) and longer tails (about 2 inches or 5 cm). They live on the ground in wet forests throughout the northern half of South America. One of the better known species is the Green acushi *Myoprocta pratti,* which is often seen in zoos. FAMILY: Dasyproctidae, ORDER: Rodentia, CLASS: Mammalia.

Four Acorn worms: 1. *Saccoglossus pusillus,* 2. *Balanoglossus numeensis,* 3. *Balanoglossus clavigerus,* 4. *Glandiceps* sp.

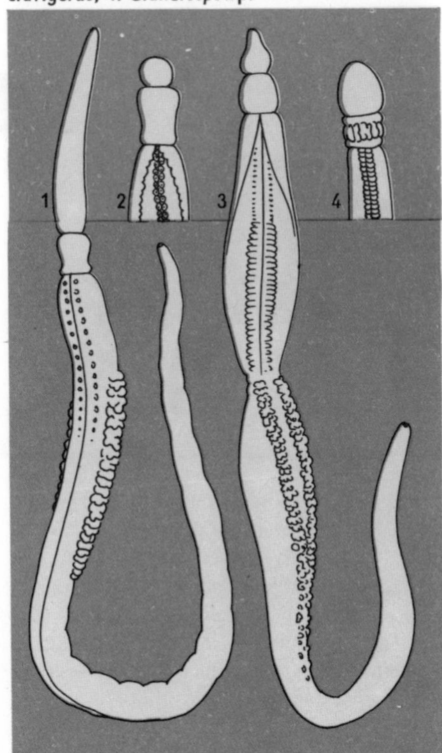

ADAPTIVE RADIATION. The concept of adaptive radiation is not easy to understand. Imagine an animal with four legs of about the same length. To move about quickly, to search for food or escape from enemies, it can either grow all four legs long, to give speed in running, or it can grow long hindlegs to bound along. It is then known as a cursorial or running animal. There are other lines it or its descendants can follow, however. It may burrow in the ground, so becoming fossorial, from the Latin *fossor,* meaning a digger. It may take to the trees and become arboreal or tree-dwelling. It may take to the air and become aerial, or flying, or it may take to water and become aquatic.

In fact, it has happened many times that the descendants of one species or type of animal have taken these radiating paths of development, some to remain terrestrial, others to become fossorial, arboreal, aerial or aquatic. They have become adapted, each to its own mode of life, by changes in structure, by growing long claws (fossorial), sharp claws for climbing (arboreal), wings (aerial) or flippers (aquatic).

Technically it is a term given to the evolutionary activity in certain animals which gave rise in comparatively short geological time to great diversification of species, genera etc. It can be ascribed to one or more of the following factors: geographical isolation (e.g. marsupials radiating in Australasia), physiological improvement in efficiency (e.g. placental mammals all over the accessible world eclipsing and making extinct previously dominant groups, such as reptiles and marsupials) and, most important of all, achievement of a break-through into a new kind of environment in which the ecological niches are numerous and vacant (e.g. power of flight in insects and in birds, throwing open the possibilities and opportunities of life in the air). Throughout the fossil record, in geological time, there has been a succession of adaptive radiations, of plants as well as of animals, belonging to groups each with more efficient powers of adaptation than the preceding group. The colonization of land and of fresh waters, after life in the sea, provided innumerable ecological niches which had never been occupied before.

From a common ancestor like *Euparkeria*, a primitive reptile of the Mesozoic period, evolved swimming, flying and terrestrial reptiles that were bipedal or quadrupedal. They also differed in their diet, some being fish eaters, other herbivores or carnivores.

Adaptive radiation is the modern equivalent of the 'Principle of Divergence' put forward by Darwin in answer to his question 'How does the lesser difference between varieties become augmented into the greater difference between species?' The solution is 'the more diversified the descendants from any one species become in structure, constitution and habits, by so much will they be better enabled to seize on many and widely diversified places in the polity of nature'. In other words, divergence is related to the existence of a multiplicity of ecological niches to which organisms, provided that they are capable of inheritable variation through crossing (see genetics), may become progressively adapted.

The opposite of adaptive radiation is the 'persistent types' which other groups of organisms show in lineages which have undergone scarcely any evolution at all during very long periods of time, and show very little diversification, their genera, families and orders having very few species, and sometimes only one. Examples of persistent types are the lampshell *Lingula,* almost unchanged since Ordovician times (500 million years ago), the coelacanth *Latimeria* since Devonian times (400 million years), the Horseshoe crab *Limulus* since Jurassic times (180 million years). It may be noticed that all these animals are marine and that life in the sea is characterized by a constancy of conditions with few new ecological niches.

It was because of the plentiful adaptive radiation which successive groups of animals had undergone that the Carboniferous and Permian periods have been called the Age of Amphibia, from the Permian to the Cretaceous, the Age of Reptiles, and the Tertiary Era, the Age of Mammals. The Jurassic period was also that of the adaptive radiation of insects and flowering plants. They were ecologically connected because the insects served to promote cross-pollination and hence inheritable variation in the plants, while the latter provided the insects with habitats and food. This is reflected in the great number of surviving species belonging to these complementary classes of organisms: 850,000 insects, 250,000 flowering plants. G.de B.

ADDAX *Addax nasomaculatus,* a medium-sized desert-living antelope, a member of the tribe Hippotragini (family Bovidae), the group that contains Sable and Roan antelope, and oryx.

The addax is 42 in (107 cm) high, with spiral horns up to 36 in (90 cm) long; in males the horns may form $2\frac{1}{2}$–3 spiral turns; in females, only $1\frac{1}{2}$–2. Addax normally weigh 265–330 lb (120–150 kg) but a big male in good condition will weigh as much as 440 lb (200 kg). Next to some of the gazelles, the addax is the most strongly desert-adapted of all antelopes, even more so than the oryx. It has big, splayed hoofs; in summer it is white with a grey-brown tinge; in winter, grey-brown. Calves are red. Like the oryx, it has a remarkable ability to tolerate high temperature without significant water-loss.

The addax is found only to the west of the Nile, but in the whole of the desert region between the Nile and the Atlantic Ocean. Formerly its range extended to the Mediterranean coast in Libya and Egypt, and the Atlas range in the Mahgreb, and south into northern Nigeria and northern Cameroun. Nowadays it no longer occurs in Algeria, Tunisia or Egypt; there is only a remnant in the extreme south of Libya; and it is nowhere found south of 15°N. In Mauretania and Mali it is still found in the El Djouf sand area; in Chad it is common in the district 70 miles (112 km) to the north of Fort Lamy, north to Tibesti, and east to Ennedi; in the Sudan it is found in northern Kordofan and the Dongola region. In the summer rainy season (July to September) it goes south to the southern Sahara and the Sudan savannah; in the winter rains (November to March), it returns north. Only 5,000 addax remain in the wild; fortunately it breeds well in zoos. Almost nothing is known of the addax's breeding except that one young is born at a time, in winter or early spring.

Addax, sandy coloured antelope of the Sahara.

Normally, addax are found in areas with large sand dunes and hard desert ground. They live in family groups of 5–15, of one male with several females and calves; other males live solitarily or associate with herds of Addra gazelle, *Gazella dama.* During the cold weather, they dig small holes in the sand with their hoofs, for shelter against the wind.

During the war, Allied soldiers, not allowed to tell their families where they were fighting, wrote to them of a large white spiral-horned antelope. From this, their families could discover they were in North Africa. FAMILY: Bovidae, ORDER: Artiodactyla, CLASS: Mammalia. C.P.G.

Map showing former (cross-hatched) and present (dark areas) distribution.

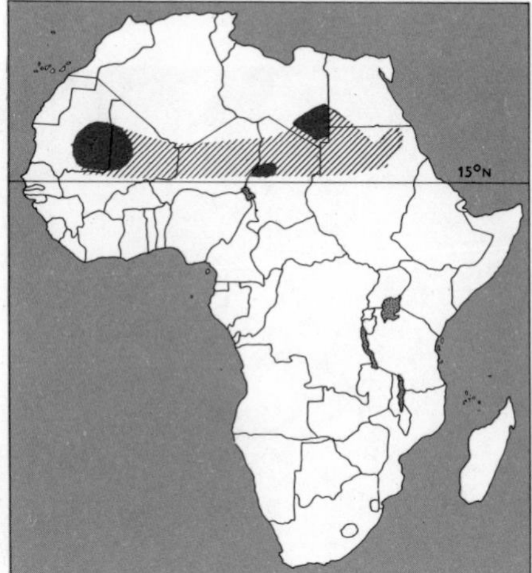

ADDER *Vipera berus,* or Northern viper, is a representative of the large family of venomous snakes known as the Viperidae. Adders are variable in colour and pattern but are most commonly cream, yellowish or reddish-brown with black or brown markings. They nearly always have a dark zigzag pattern down the middle of the back. These markings and the short, rather thick body, together with the copper coloured iris and vertical pupil make this snake easy to recognize, at close quarters. The adder occurs farther north than any other snake in Europe and Asia. It occurs within the Arctic Circle in Scandinavia and ranges well into southern Europe, where it tends to inhabit cooler mountainous areas. Dry, open moorlands and heaths, sunny hillsides and open woodland are its preferred habitats. Adders mate in April and May, and the young are born (usually free of the egg membrane) in August and September. They hibernate for much of the winter but may emerge early to bask in sunshine on warm days in February and March. In keeping with their northern distribution, they cannot tolerate very hot sun and retreat into shade during the hottest part of summer days. They hunt lizards and small mammals mainly in the evening and at night. Adder venom, like that of most of the Viperidae, is dangerously toxic to humans, especially small children. FAMILY: Viperidae, ORDER: Squamata, CLASS: Reptilia.

ADDERS, the viviparous habits of the adder gave our ancestors some strange ideas. According to the 12th century *Book of Beasts* translated by T. H. White the young adders or vipers did not wait to be born in the usual way but bit through their mother's body, so killing her. A later legend, recounted in Holinshed's *Chronicle* published in 1577, was that in times of danger the mother adder swallowed her young. Although the Anglo-Saxons were aware that the adder gave birth to live young, calling it *vipre* from the Latin *vivus* (alive) and *parere* (to bring forth), the explanation for the story is probably due to the speed at which the young adders dash to cover and to people finding unborn young in adders they had killed.

ADIPOSE FIN, a small fleshy fin on the back of some of the more primitive fishes, such as salmon and trout, near the tail, that is to say behind the normal dorsal fin. It is often little more than a small lobe whose function

Adder or viper, of Europe, with young. These, born alive, stay with the mother for a while, which has given rise to a hard-dying legend.

appears to be the control of the small eddies that are formed by any solid body when it moves through water. In some of the catfishes the adipose fin is large and may be preceded by a sharp spine, as in the African genus *Clarotes*. Many of the more advanced fishes have a second dorsal fin in place of an adipose fin but this is a very different structure since it is a membrane supported by finrays which are in turn supported internally by a series of small bones, the pterygiophores.

ADORNMENT, a word with two distinct meanings. It may mean the tufts of feathers or fur, frills, wattles or other outgrowths of skin, usually conspicuously coloured and used for conveying visual signals in courtship or aggressive display. Sometimes adornments function in breaking up the outline of an animal's body, so serving as camouflage. Examples are the flaps of skin on bottom-living fishes or those that live among seaweed, which simulate pieces of weed.

Adornment, in the sense of decorating the body with articles or materials not produced by the body, is an almost entirely human trait. Baby apes and a few young monkeys have, in captivity, been seen to place pieces of fabric or hollow vessels on their heads, in a spirit of fun, or have draped their shoulders with fabrics or with straw. Other than these we must go to the lower animals, such as some Foraminifera, which select broken sponge spicules and encase their bodies in coverings of geometric design, which may equally be protective rather than adornment.

AESCULAPIAN SNAKE *Elaphe longissima,* a large, slender, non-venomous snake, $4\frac{1}{2}$–$6\frac{1}{2}$ ft (1·5–2·0 m) long, with a small head and a long tapering tail. Its colour is brown, rarely black (melanic) and most of its scales are striped with white. There is a pair of yellow patches on each side of the neck. The belly is light yellow and there is a distinct dark stripe from the eye to the corner of the mouth. Young individuals have dark brown blotches on the back. The scales of the mid-body are in 23 (seldom 21) rows and there are 212–248 ventral plates. There are three geographical races or subspecies known as *longissima, romana* and *persica* respectively. The Aesculapian snake ranges across Europe but is not found in the British Isles, the Iberian Peninsula, Scandinavia and countries north of the 50° parallel. It is also found in Turkey, Armenia, the Caucasus and on the southern shores of the Caspian Sea. Its habitat is forest with clearings and rocky slopes with shrub or bush vegetation. The Aesculapian snake is an excellent tree-climber. When young, it feeds on lizards, as an adult, on rodents, moles and shrews, young birds and eggs. Females lay clutches of 5–8 eggs and the hatchlings from these are $8\frac{1}{2}$–10 in (22–25 cm) long. The snake is named after Aesculapius, son of Apollo and Coronis, mythical founder of the science of medicine, who is usually represented with a large snake coiled around his staff. FAMILY: Colubridae, ORDER: Squamata, CLASS: Reptilia. I.E.F.

AESTIVATION, a term applied to animals which go into a resting or torpid state during the summer, often called 'summer sleep' to distinguish it from hibernation, or winter sleep. It can occur in a wide variety of animals, from snails and insects to fish and mammals, and it is found most frequently among inhabitants of desert regions where the summer season provides high temperatures and periods of drought. Aestivating animals become relatively inactive, the metabolic rate is lowered, food reserves stored in the body are utilized, and the rate of water loss from the body to the surrounding environment is considerably reduced. The African lungfish, *Protopterus,* is noted for its ability to survive for several years in a state of aestivation, when the rivers in which it lives dry up. The fish curls up in a leathery 'cocoon' embedded in a ball of mud in the river bottom. Here it can survive for up to four years, during which time it lives off its own muscle tissue, and becomes shrivelled in appearance as a consequence.

The ability to aestivate is very important in the lives of small desert mammals, such as ground squirrels, pocket mice and gerbils, if they are to survive the long summer season when environmental temperatures are high, and food and water are in short supply. As these warm-blooded animals become inactive, the metabolic rate is lowered, the rate of breathing decreases, and the temperature of the body drops until it is nearly the same as that of the surroundings. For all practical purposes the aestivating mammal is cold-

The adipose fin, typical of salmon-like fishes, lies between the dorsal fin and the tail.

blooded and this has the considerable advantage that the rate of water loss through the lungs during breathing will be markedly less than that in an active animal. These changes in the physiology of aestivating animals are very similar to those produced during hibernation, but whereas the latter state is induced when temperatures drop below 50°F (10°C), aestivation occurs at temperatures around 77°F (25°C). J.A.W.

AFRI, the name used in Arabia for the Dorcas *gazelle.

AFRICAN EYE WORM *Loa loa*, perhaps the most familiar migrant parasitic worm infecting man. It is one of a number of the roundworms which do not live permanently in one site in the body, but have the habit of wandering through various tissues and organs and in so doing may cause considerable damage and discomfort to the host. It belongs to the filariid group of roundworms and is transmitted from person to person by the bite of a blood-sucking fly (*Chrysops*) which acts as an intermediate host in the life-cycle. The adult female worms, living in the subcutaneous tissue of man, liberate microfilariae (see elephantiasis), which are carried around the body in the blood stream. During the day, when the flies are actively feeding, the microfilariae are to be found in large numbers in the superficial blood vessels of the body, but at night they retreat to deeper vessels. Larvae are taken up by the flies as they suck blood and there undergo development in the body of the insect host. When infective to the human host, the larvae escape from the proboscis of the fly during feeding and enter the bite wound.

The adult worms are 1–3 in (2·5–7·5 cm) long and live just below the surface of the skin, moving about from time to time. They cause irritating swellings on the skin, but these usually subside fairly quickly. More painful sensations arise when the worms are in the area of the eyes, their movement across the surface of the eyeball causing irritation, soreness, excessive watering and disturbed vision. However, in this position the worms are most obvious and may be removed surgically. ORDER: Spirurida, CLASS: Nematoda, PHYLUM: Aschelminthes. D.W.

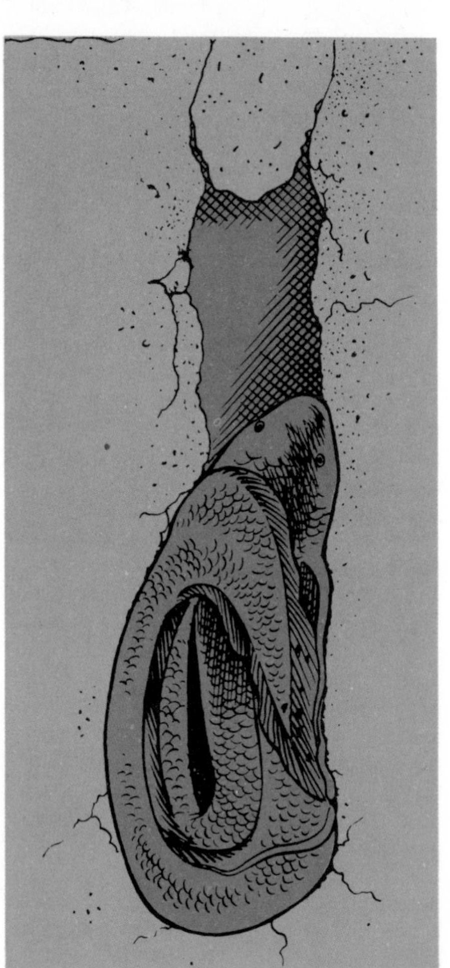

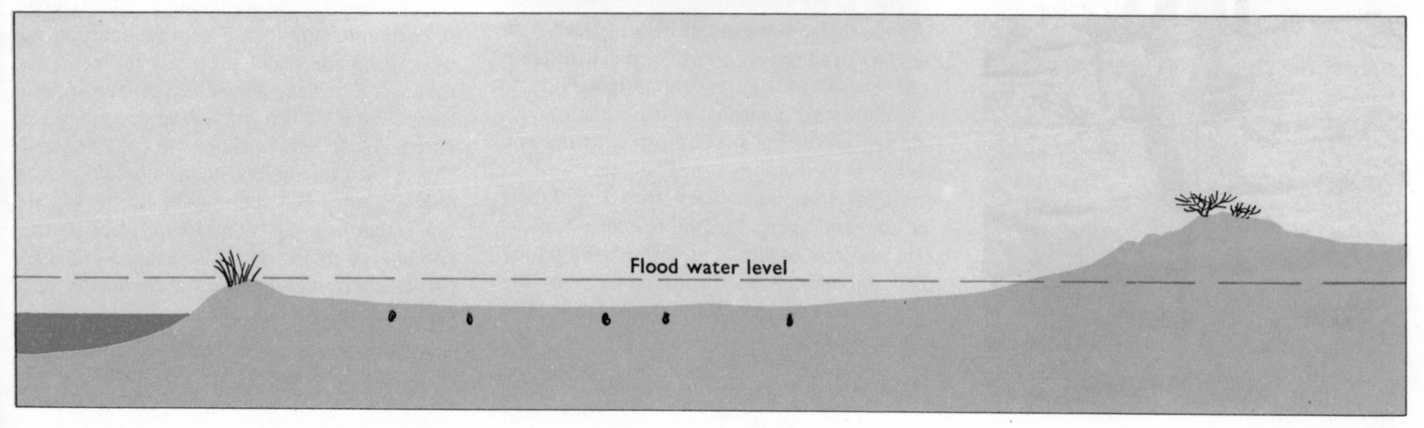

Right: The African lungfish burrows into the soft mud, thus forming a short tube in the mud, at the bottom of which is a larger cavity which enables the fish to turn around and bring its mouth to the top of the cavity. To prevent itself drying out the fish secretes large quantities of mucus which form a cocoon as it hardens leaving an opening where the mouth of the fish lies. The top of the tube is partially closed by a lid, although air can still percolate into the tube to the fish. In this extraordinary state the fish can survive while the lake or pool above completely dries out. As in animals that hibernate, the metabolism of the body slows down to a very low level and the fish is dependent on its reserves of fat for the small amount of energy required to keep it alive. When the lake refills with the onset of the rains the cocoon softens and the emaciated fish is able to leave it and soon recovers from its period of starvation. Fossil lungfishes in cocoons have been found in rocks dating from the Triassic period (180-225 million years ago). Bottom: Cocoons are often found in flood water areas which dry out periodically.

AGAMIDS, a large family of lizards living in the Old World. Agamids differ from most lizard families in their teeth, which are acrodont. That is, the teeth are fixed by their bases on the summit of the ridge of the jaw. The post-orbital temporal line on the skull is complete. The tongue is short, thick and slightly forked. Agamids are small to medium-sized lizards with powerful claws. They live on the ground, in rocks or in trees. Their limbs are fully developed. The scaly skin very often consists of small spines which appear mainly on head and tail. Tail autotomy is completely absent in agamids. The ability to change colour depending on temperature and emotional changes is well developed. Most agamids feed on insects and other small invertebrates. A few are omnivorous, others mainly herbivorous. Nearly all agamids lay eggs, only a few species of the genera *Phrynocephalus* and *Cophotis* being oviparous.

There are approximately 35 genera of agamids with 300 species. The focal point of their distribution is the oriental region but from there they have spread to Africa, the Indo-Australian Archipelago and Australia. They did not reach Madagascar, which is inhabited by the iguanas that are otherwise confined to the New World. Nowhere in the world do agamids and iguanas occur together, as the former always drove out the latter. The agamids only reached the borders of temperate zones in the Old World: in Europe, the hardun *Agama stellio* is to be found in the southern part of the Balkan peninsula and a few species of *Agama* and *Phrynocephalus* are found in the central Asian steppe.

About 60 of the 300 species of *Agama* live in southwest Asia and Africa. With their dorso-ventrally flattened heads and strong limbs the medium sized agamas look like typical lizards. They live on the ground, among rocks or on thick tree trunks. Some of the rock dwellers have taken to living in the walls of houses, like the African *Agama agama*.

The many species of the Toad-headed agamids *Phrynocephalus* live in the deserts and semi-deserts of Central and West Africa. Although the colouration and markings of back and head of these tiny lizards contain some surprising colours they match their surroundings perfectly. Their behaviour also seems to fit their desert environment. They can quickly bury themselves in sand by wriggling their flat bodies from side to side.

The Flying dragons of the genus *Draco* found throughout the Indo-Australian Archipelago are small tree dwelling agamids. On each side of the body which is supported by five or six pairs of extended ribs there is a flap of skin or 'flying skin' that can be spread. This flying skin works like a parachute and enables the Flying dragon to glide from one tree to another, often covering considerable distances. The flying skin and also the erectable throat pouch frequently show striking colours, especially in the males which display them during courtship or in territorial dispute. When taking off from a tree the dazzling colours can be seen clearly and are surprising even to the human eye. The Flying dragons are insectivores, the predominant part of their food being ants that are caught with the tongue and crunched with the teeth.

The Angle-headed agamids *Gonyocephalus* are slightly bigger tree dwelling agamids ranging from Southeast Asia to New Guinea and in Australia and the South Sea Islands. The species of the genus *Calotes* are also tree dwellers and are common in tropical and subtropical Asia. None of these, however, shows any special adaptation to tree living comparable to the Flying dragons. In contrast to ground dwelling agamids the bodies of the tree agamids are slightly flattened from side to side. The change of colour in some of these species is quick and distinctive. The bloodsucker *Calotes versicolor* got its common name from the brilliant red that appears on the head during courtship and territorial dispute. The red colour can change to an unobtrusive brown within seconds if the lizard loses a fight and is ready to flee.

East African agamid lizard

Amongst the most impressive of the agamids is the Water lizard *Hydrosaurus amboinensis*. With a length of about 3 ft (90 cm) it is a giant in its family. On its tail it sports an enormous rigid crest which is supported by the spinal column. Nothing is known of its function. The Water lizard and also lizards of the genus *Physignathus* roam the forest trees in search of food and will drop into the rivers in moments of danger and escape by swimming or walking under water. The Australian Frilled lizard *Chlamydosaurus kingi* is about the same size as the Water lizard. Its skinfold is supported by the tongue bone and can be raised like an enormous cape. This colourful frill together with the wide open mouth are displayed at any enemy. The contrasting colour of the mucous membrance emphasizes this threat posture. Sometimes when fleeing at high speed the Frilled lizard runs on two legs.

Australia has a great variety of remarkable agamids. The Bearded lizard *Amphibolurus barbatus* can inflate its spiny throat pouch and assume a similar threat posture to that of the Frilled lizard. The moloch or Thorny devil *Moloch horridus* of the Australian semi-deserts is protected by big pointed thorn-like spikes that give this little lizard a most bizarre appearance. Contrary to its common name the moloch is a completely harmless lizard that feeds mainly on ants. Relying on its protective colouring a moloch will sit quietly next to an ant trail and pick up a few insects with its tongue from time to time. As it is very dependent on certain types of ants the moloch is probably the most specialized of all species of agamids.

The Spiny-tailed lizards of the genus *Uromastix* from the desert belts of West Asia and North Africa are specialized in a different manner (see mastigures). Spiny-tailed lizards are mainly herbivorous, at least when adult, and search for the sparse flowers, fruits and leaves of the semi-desert. They also feed on dried parts of plants. They are active during the day and spend the nights and unfavourable seasons of the year in burrows which they dig themselves or in crevices in the rock. FAMILY: Agamidae, ORDER: Squamata, CLASS: Reptilia. K.K.

AGASSIZ J. Louis R., 1807–1873. Biologist, geologist and teacher, born in Switzerland, moved to the USA in 1846. He trained under a number of eminent men including Cuvier, whose doctrine of catastrophes he modified, claiming that God had created a series of progressively more advanced forms. He introduced the concept of the ice ages, the Alps having been shaped by the action of glaciers. As a Professor of Zoology at Harvard he did much for American zoology, travelling and publishing widely. In 1859 he established the Museum of Comparative Zoology at Harvard. This was given further substantial support by his son Alexander (1835–1910), a marine zoologist and surveyor of mines.

AGASSIZ, the failure of Louis Agassiz was redeemed to some extent by the success of his son Alexander. He made a substantial fortune as a mining engineer and paid off his father's debts. He also developed an interest in oceanography and took part in an expedition in the Caribbean and Gulf of Mexico. One important practical innovation was the use of the kind of steel cable used in mining for dredging at great depths. Until then stout ropes had been used but Agassiz' cable cut the time of making a sounding by one third. A sounding of 18,000 ft (5,500 m) took Alexander Agassiz one hour.

AGGRESSION, taken by most zoologists to occur between two members of the same species, may involve outright fighting even leading to injury or death, but more generally actual combat is replaced by a ritualized encounter. The attacks made by predators on their prey are not considered as aggression as they are aimed at obtaining food; it is rare for a predator to kill more of its prey than it needs. This distinction may, however, be an artificial one rising from a human evaluation of the situation; there is no evidence that the inner mechanisms for predatory attacks and those for interspecific aggression are different.

Aggressive behaviour is particularly involved in the defence of territory and in the establishment of the social hierarchies typical of birds and mammals. The many scars borne by older male Elephant seals indicate the amount of fighting which takes place among these animals when the bull is defending his harem from other males. (The elongated canines of these animals can inflict considerable wounds.) But such fights are the exception rather than the rule. More typical are the combats of cichlid and other teleost fish. The two animals align themselves parallel to one

Bearded lizard in threat posture, with mouth open and throat pounch inflated, displaying its 'beard'.

Royal terns threatening an intruder.

another, head to tail. At the same time their dorsal fins and tails are fully extended presenting the appearance of an enlarged body to their opponent. They 'fight' by each turning its tail towards the other fish and beating currents of water against its body. These water movements can be detected by the lateral line sense organs of the fish. This behaviour combined with circling round each other continues until one or other swims away leaving the other victor. The impression that the ritual consists of a show of strength is confirmed by observations on other animals. Two male adders will raise the foreparts of their bodies off the ground and intertwine them while pushing against each other. The one that pushes hardest wins, the defeated snake wriggling away. Female Giant iguanas of the Galapagos Islands fight over egg-laying sites by pushing hard against each other, forehead to forehead. This area of the head is heavily armoured. Male stags interlock their antlers and push against each other during the rutting season when they are fighting for position.

Often the gestures of fighting are derived from other behaviour. Thus, the head-down posture of a male stickleback threatening on its own territory seems to be related to the pattern shown when the fish is excavating a hole for its nest. In the threat posture, an animal may be seen to be holding itself ready for attack while refraining from actually carrying it out. A Black-headed gull threatening an intruder into its area characteristically stands with its neck elongated, bill pointed slightly downwards (ready to stab) and with wings raised slightly away from its body (the wings are used in fighting to buffet the opponent). During such an encounter, one gull may peck violently at the ground, uprooting plants and tossing them aside. Both the pecks and the way of pulling at the grasses are similar to movements in actual fighting but the behaviour is directed at the ground, not at the rival. This is typical of 're-directed aggression', where the combat is not going well and the aggression is aimed at an object or another individual. When two higher ranking monkeys are engaged in a fight, for example, re-direction is often towards a lower ranking member of the group. When the possibility of attack is deflected onto an object, the behaviour serves to avoid the dangers of actual fighting.

Threat of real combat may be held off by submissive or appeasement behaviour on the part of the losing animal. These actions 'cut-off' the aggression and seem to lower the intensity of the dominant bird's behaviour. Mutual grooming is a powerful means of reducing aggression. Aggressive encounters between members of a colony may end in one grooming the other, when the aggressors' intensity of behaviour visibly slackens. A female bird may lower a male bird's aggressive reactions to her by preening him, and similar behaviour is also reported in some species of ants.

Injury may follow where the losing animal cannot escape. Thus, a cichlid fish retiring from a combat will be pursued by the victor; if they are in a small tank, where the vanquished cannot move far away, the victor's aggressiveness will not decline as it would with distance from its territory. This results in vicious attacks on the loser which continue until it is killed. The social hierarchies which usually control aggression amongst, for example, a group of primates may well break down if the group is confined. Being amply fed, the need for food seeking behaviour is eliminated thus removing one of the activities taking up the most time under natural conditions. Since the confined animals are often crowded as well, there is constant irritation in the group. Re-direction of aggression leads to other monkeys being involved in a quarrel which at first concerns only the two combatants and there are many reports of violent and continuous fighting lasting many months in groups of rhesus and other monkeys when confined in zoos.

When there is continual social stress of this sort in the place of the peaceful conditions of the wild, other effects come into play. Stress in caged rats and mice has been shown to bring about increased activity of the adrenals and lowered fertility in the females who are also less able to rear their young.

The nature of aggression is still in dispute. The behaviour patterns of aggression can be evoked by electrical stimulation of particular areas of the brain in birds and in mammals, though in general some visual stimulus, for instance, a stuffed 'rival' is necessary to evoke the behaviour fully. Endocrines undoubtedly have their effect as the enhanced aggressiveness of the male cockerels after injection of androgens shows. Aggression has been called a drive essential to life, which requires 'working out'. According to this theory aggression is innate in man as well as in animals and must be deflected into socially acceptable ends. But aggression can also be shown to be the result of the conditions under which an animal is raised, or in which it finds itself, thus crowding evokes massive aggression far beyond the normal. Elucidation of the origin of his aggressive behaviour has obvious importance for the future of man and the assurance of world peace. J.D.C.

AGLASPIDS, the earliest and most primitive order of arachnids. They probably gave rise to both the Horseshoe crabs (order Xiphosurida) and the Giant water-scorpions (order Eurypterida). They were fairly small, mostly between 2 and 6 in (5–15 cm) long, and the body was divided into a cephalothorax (prosoma) and an abdomen (opisthosoma) of 11 or 12 segments which ended in a strong tail-spine. The cephalothorax had a pair of prominent, compound eyes and six pairs of jointed appendages; the first pair, the chelicerae, ended in pincers, the remainder were walking legs. The first few abdominal segments, at least, bore walking legs similar to those of the cephalothorax.

The aglaspids were marine. They first appeared in the Lower Cambrian and seem to have died out towards the end of the Ordovician period; a time range of about 120 million years. ORDER: Aglaspida, CLASS: Arachnida, PHYLUM: Arthropoda.

AGONISTIC BEHAVIOUR, when an

Top: Two Herring gulls fluttering up, jockeying for the dominant position from which to attack. Bottom: Courtship in cichlid fishes begins with a show of strength, an aggressive seizing of each other by the mouth.

animal, on the border of its territory, meets a rival, both attack and escape tendencies may be evoked. There is therefore conflict between the behavioural directions in which the animal may go. The various kinds of behaviour which result have been called 'agonistic'. Thus, the animal may attack or it may flee, it may alternate between these behaviours or a compromise movement may appear.

Such a compromise may show itself in movement such that the two animals do not face each other. A turn so that the animal's flank is towards the rival places it in such a position that it is neither turned towards, in the attacking position, nor turned completely away, in the posture for flight. As both aggressive movements and flight behaviour tend to elicit attack, this sideways-on position is less likely to arouse the rival to attack, as when two Black-headed gulls turn sideways and walk parallel to each other, both showing the threat posture of the head and wings. The element of escape tendency in this behaviour is given by the way in which the gull's head moves back and its feathers become more closely sleek, as the two birds come closer, these being characteristics of the behaviour of a gull preparatory to take-off.

Threat at territory boundaries is not all explicable in terms of a conflict between attack and escape behaviour. Some elements of the signals seem to be direct results of the physiological condition of the animal. Thus, the raised gill covers of a fish, such as *Cichlasoma meeki,* which seem to increase the size of the head may also permit greater ventilation of the gills, so improving the oxygenation of the blood, giving greater energy prior to attack. The intake of air by some birds may also have the same function and may have become ritualized in the great development of conspicuous air-sacs like those of Frigate birds. When puffed out these form part of the threat display of the male birds. Hair erection in mammals is under autonomic control and this by-product of the change in the physiology of the threatening animal may have led to the evolution of special ruffs and tufts of hair whose erection took on the function of signals.

The fact that parts of both escape and attack behaviour can occur together suggests that the relationship of the two behaviours is not a simple one of mutual inhibition. Electro-physiological studies of cats has shown that it is impossible to produce pure attack or escape behaviour by electrical stimulation of distinct areas of the brain. Instead the areas overlap with each other and with those producing a threat. This indicates that the relationships of threat and attack/escape are by no means simple, as the explanation that threat results when attack and escape conflict might suggest.

J.D.C.

Long-eared owl *Asio otus*, of Eurasia, in threat posture appears larger and quite terrifying, by spreading its wings and fluffing out its feathers.

AGOUTI, almost tailless rodents, about the size of a large rabbit but with rather long slender legs. They belong to the genus *Dasyprocta* placed, with the pacas and acushis, in the family Dasyproctidae. They live in a variety of habitats, but are found especially in forest, from southern Mexico to southern Brazil, where they feed on leaves and fruit. Agoutis usually have rather speckled coats. The name 'agouti' is also used by geneticists to describe the banded hairs of the wild form of House mouse in contrast to the mutant colour varieties that are extensively used in genetical research. FAMILY: Dasyproctidae, ORDER: Rodentia, CLASS: Mammalia.

AIR-BREATHING FISHES, species able to breathe atmospheric air directly. In the vast majority of fishes breathing, that is to say the absorption of oxygen and the elimination of carbon dioxide, is accomplished by the gills. The air-breathing habit is known only in the bony fishes (the teleosts) but fossil remains from up to 250 million years ago show that many of the earliest fishes had lungs and breathed air. During the long evolution of the fishes, most groups passed from using the lungs as breathing organs to using them as a hydrostatic organ, that is to say, a swimbladder (see separate entry). The living lungfishes, however, did not lose this primitive air-breathing habit, but in other fishes it was lost and then later regained, this time with structures other than a 'lung' to absorb the oxygen from the air.

Mudskippers, which spend a considerable part of their time out of water, have evolved a fairly simple alternative to strict air-breathing. Before emerging into the air, the fish fills its gill chamber with water so that it can still absorb oxygen with its gills.

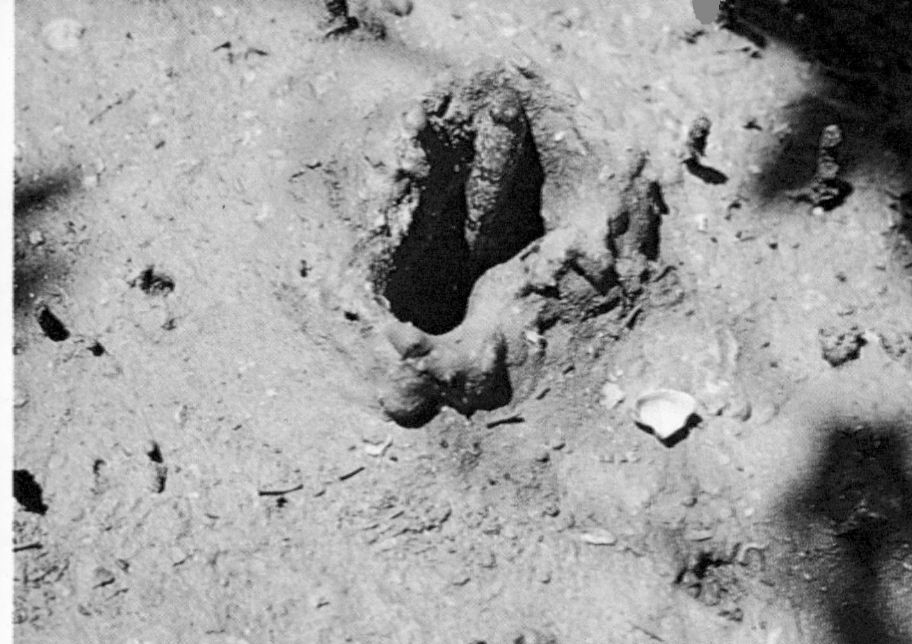

A mudskipper searches for food on a mud-flat uncovered at low tide. These amphibious fish 'walk' with their limb-like forefins.

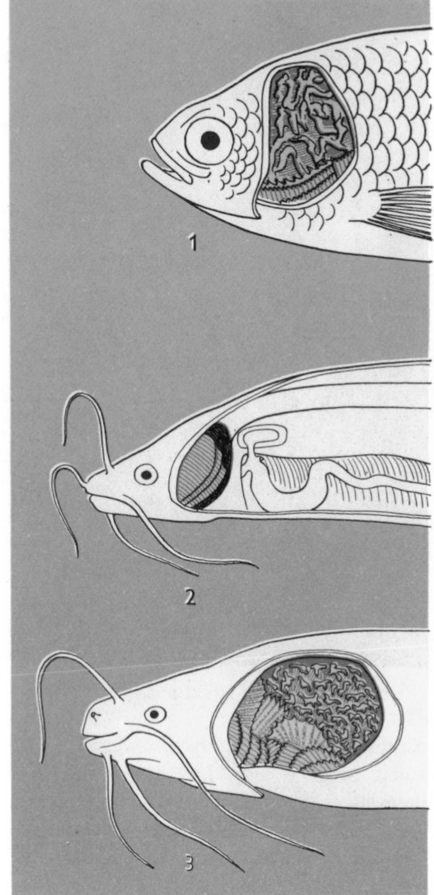

Accessory air breathing organs in: 1. Climbing perch *Anabas testudineus*, 2. Indian catfish *Heteropneustes fossilis*, 3. African catfish *Clarias lazera*.

To increase absorption, there are numerous small blood vessels close to the surface of the skin lining the roof of the mouth and a certain amount of gas exchange takes place there. These vascularizations, or concentrations of fine blood vessels just beneath the surface of the skin, are often found lining the gill covers of certain catfishes.

In one group of catfishes, the Loricariidae or Mailed catfishes, and also in some of the loaches, air is taken in and passed down into the intestine. The walls of a part of the intestine are vascularized and gas exchange can take place here, the used-up air later being voided via the vent.

The anabantid or labyrinthfishes of the tropical Old World have a labyrinthine breathing organ at the top of the gill chamber, hence their common name. Some members of this group are so strictly adapted to air-breathing that they will actually drown if prevented from reaching the surface, a most unexpected failing in a fish! A major problem in using the gills as air-breathing organs is that in air the fine lamellae or plates of the gills tend to collapse. This is overcome in certain catfishes (e.g. some species of *Clarias*) by a stiffening of the gill filaments. In addition, the gills may bear spongy arborescent organs supported by cartilage and these are able to absorb oxygen that has been taken into the gill cavity. Some of the symbranchid eels and the snakeheads have similar air-breathing organs.

Lungs are typically paired structures lying below the alimentary canal, while the swimbladder lies above the alimentary canal and just below the backbone. There are some primitive fishes in which the swimbladder, by its shape and position, is clearly a swimbladder but is used like a lung. Some of the osteoglossids or Bony tongues, the tarpon and certain characins such as *Erythrinus*, use the swimbladder in this manner. The inner lining of the swimbladder is spongy in appearance and this gives a large surface area for the absorption of oxygen and removal of carbon dioxide. Under 'Fishes' it is explained how the modern bony fishes, the teleosts, evolved from a more primitive radiation of the fishes known as holosteans. The few surviving holosteans all have a swimbladder and use it as a lung.

The question arises, why should fishes, which appear to be well adapted to life in water, have gone to such lengths to re-develop organs to enable them to breathe air directly? The answer is that other specializations enabled fishes to explore and colonize a very wide variety of habitats. With growing competition for food and living space there were still some niches that were not yet filled, namely those in which air-breathing was an advantage or even a necessity. Most of the air-breathing fishes live in water where the concentration of oxygen is low, either temporarily or permanently. The snakeheads and symbranchid eels live in small streams

Air breathing catfish *Clarias batrachus*.

Air breathing Dwarf gourami *Colisa lalia*.

running through marshes where oxygen levels become very low and the streams themselves may dry up. The mudskippers are able to skip from one small pool to another within the mangrove swamps when the tide is out. The habits of the lungfishes are worth more detailed discussion and this can be found in the 'lungfish' entry.

AJOLOTE *Bipes biporus*, is one of three species of worm-lizard native to Mexico and southern Baja California. The soft skin of its body is folded into numerous rings and this, with its cylindrical body, gives it a close resemblance to an earthworm. Its eyes are covered with skin but it has two forelimbs each with five toes well equipped with claws. Few specimens were known to science until recently. Nothing is known of its breeding habits. FAMILY: Amphisbaenidae, ORDER: Squamata, CLASS: Reptilia.

ALARM BEHAVIOUR varies with experience. A young animal often takes cover at a loud noise or on seeing an object move in an unaccustomed way. Gradually, if these phenomena are not accompanied by harm to the animal, it becomes habituated to them, (see habituation) and ceases to respond. Birds get used to a scarecrow but any novel stimulus, such as changing the position of the scarecrow, renews their alarm. By contrast, there is evidence that young birds have to learn which are their predators.

Habituation may occur at different rates to different stimuli. For example, the tube-dwelling fanworm *Branchiomma* will withdraw into its tube when the light intensity above it is reduced. Although habituation to such a decrease occurs rapidly, habituation to shadows is very slow. Shadows would seem to be token stimuli of possible predators and therefore the reaction is the protective one of escape from potential danger. Nevertheless, even here there is discrimination. The fanworm withdraws into its tube only when the shadow falling on it is moving at a certain speed. Shadows moving at other speeds do not evoke this protective response. This behaviour does not wane on repetition. Thus a particular group of stimuli, likely to arise from a fish feeding on these worms, is singled out for a permanent alarm response.

The pattern of response to danger varies greatly among animals. The fanworm withdraws into its tube thus sheltering its head tentacles which might be bitten off by a fish. The chemical stimuli from a starfish cause a scallop to swim away by vigorously closing its shells and squirting water out on either side of the hinge, in a form of jet propulsion. Night-flying moths are hunted by bats which use their sonar to locate them. A bat emits a series of very high-pitched squeaks locating the insect by the echoes of these squeaks being bounced from its body. But these moths can pick up the sound of the squeaks and when they do so they often react by fluttering to the ground. They respond in this way to tape-recordings of bat squeaks as well as to those from real bats.

Response to danger will often be complete immobility for very frequently predators locate their prey only when it is moving. When stillness is combined with cryptic colouring, the effect of the camouflage is greatly enhanced.

A special kind of response to danger is the distraction display. A squid releases a puff of ink when it is alarmed. At one time this was interpreted as a smoke screen behind which the squid could swim away, but it seems likely that the very obvious mass of ink actually deflects the predator's attack by distracting its attention while the squid escapes. Distraction displays are particularly well developed among birds, especially when they are nesting or have young. The display usually takes the form of an exaggeratedly conspicuous performance by the adult that draws a predator's attention away from the relatively inconspicuously coloured chicks, who either remain still or scuttle for cover. The adult 'feigns injury' with unusual and apparently unco-ordinated actions making it obvious to the attacker. A. A. Saunders, an American naturalist, was by a lake shore when he saw a Wood duck with nine young on the water. A Red-shouldered hawk came down to attack them. The ducklings swam quickly in all directions, but the mother stretched out her neck, turned on one side, flapped a wing in the air and paddled in circles as though she were crippled. The hawk turned and dived again aiming at the duck but collided with some bushes which the duck had just managed to reach. The hawk flapped away and perched on a nearby tree. When the duck reappeared, the hawk attacked again but again was unsuccessful. Even when two of the ducklings left cover and scurried across open water, the hawk took no notice of them, it was so attracted by the mother bird. In the end it flew off and the duck gathered her brood around her again.

The behaviour of one alarmed animal may be a warning to others, which then take cover. The white tail of a rabbit which is frightened becomes a conspicuously moving signal, and other rabbits seeing it are alerted. Sometimes one rabbit, alarmed at the sight of an intruder, thumps on the ground with its hindfeet. All rabbits within earshot respond by bolting for cover. Many birds have special calls by which they warn not only members of their own species but others as well of the presence of danger. A wandering cat will rouse a blackbird to scold it in a garden. All birds in the vicinity take to the wing, the safest way of escape from a ground predator. The same blackbird reacts to a hawk with a high-pitched call. Other birds react by moving into cover for protection against aerial attack. The alarm call of a chaffinch shows many of the characteristics of this type of high-pitched call. It is mainly on one note, unlike a territorial call, and this note is of a frequency which seems to make its source most difficult to locate. So, whereas any other notes might lead the predator to the bird giving the warning, the attacker will have the greatest difficulty in locating the bird that is using a high-pitched call. In this way the bird giving the alarm does not sacrifice itself for the sake of others. Alarm calls are particularly interesting examples of communication, for they are signals whose understanding is not restricted to one species. All the passerines in the area will respond to a chaffinch's alarm notes, as they will to a blackbird's, and even rabbits learn to recognize them and bolt for cover.

Chemical substances alert some animals in much the same way as sounds alert birds. A minnow attacked by a pike releases a chemical into the water from its injured skin. This causes other minnows to swim away. It will also affect a few related species although it does not have the universal effect of a songbird's alarm call. Scent substances which cause alarm in others are produced by ants from different glands according to the species. In *Pogonomyrmex*, the substance is effective over a distance of 1–2 in (3–5 cm). Other ants will approach if it is present in low concentrations but will retreat from the spot when the concentration of the scent is high

J.D.C

ALBACORE, a name given to certain large Tuna-like fishes with long dorsal and anal fins in adults

Eyed hawkmoth *Smerinthus ocellatus* at rest (top left) shows only cryptycally patterned wings. Alarmed (top right), the hindwings are parted revealing a pair menacing 'eyes', which are sufficient to scare away a bird.

A Praying mantis (below) in the normal relaxed attitude will assume a most grotesque posture (right) when alarmed, calculated to inhibit a predator's attack.

Prairie dogs feeding. Individuals sitting on the burrow craters will by their alarm cries act as sentinels, on sighting a coyote, sending all within earshot scuttling into their burrows.

ALBATROSSES, 14 species of large, long-winged, gliding seabirds comprising the family Diomedeidae, one of the families of *tubenosed birds. They vary in length from 28–53 in (17–135 cm) but in flight they seem much larger because of their long wings. The largest, the Wandering albatross *Diomedea exulans,* has the broadest wing-span of any living bird, up to $11\frac{1}{2}$ ft (3·5 m). The wings are very narrow in proportion to their length, so have a very high aspect ratio, which is an adaptation to gliding flight. High aspect ratio wings are aerodynamically very efficient but they are difficult to flap and require a relatively high air speed to function efficiently. Albatrosses are therefore found particularly over the windiest parts of the oceans and are quite at home in the 'Roaring Forties' which blow almost continuously from west to east over the southern oceans. The winds were of great importance to sailing ships on their passage to and from Australia, but have been of equal or greater importance to the southern albatrosses for much longer time. With their help the albatrosses circumnavigate the world with greater ease than any clipper.

The word 'albatross' is derived from the Spanish and Portugese 'alcatraz', which for long has been the name given to large seabirds, particularly pelicans, in Iberia and parts of the West Indies. 'Alcatraz' seems to have come, in turn, from the Arabic 'al-cadous', adopted from the Greek for a water pot or bucket and refers to the capacious pouch of the pelican. When Portuguese seamen first penetrated the South Atlantic in the 15th century they encountered numbers of albatrosses for the first time and gave them the same name that they gave to other large seabirds. The word was used equally indiscriminately among the early British navigators and it has been variously spelt alcatraze, algatross, albitross, and albatros, only recently settling to the now generally-accepted 'albatross'.

Albatrosses are stoutly-built with a white or brown plumage, often marked with darker brown on the wings, back and tail. The head is large and carries a strong, hooked bill, with nostrils opening through horny tubes, as in all species of the 'tubenosed' order. The legs are short, the hind toe is rudimentary or missing entirely, and the other three toes are webbed. The sexes are externally similar, except in the Wandering albatross, where the female has more dark markings, while the fully adult male—it may take 10 years to become fully mature—is pure white except for black wing tips.

There are only two generally-accepted genera of albatrosses: *Diomedea* with 12 species, and *Phoebetria* the Sooty albatrosses with two, differing in a number of structural features including the length of the tail. Most albatrosses live in the southern oceans, but the Galapagos or Waved albatross *D. irrorata,* breeds on the equator, and three species, the Short-tailed albatross *D. albatrus,* the Laysan albatross *D. immutabilis,* and the Black-footed albatross *D. nigripes,* breed on islands in the North Pacific. Otherwise, albatrosses only appear north of the equator as vagrants.

The very long wings and the short legs of albatrosses make them rather clumsy on land. If there is no wind they cannot take flight. Sometimes when attempting to take flight in low wind speeds, or when molested, albatrosses, like other tube-nosed birds, vomit their stomach oil. At other times, particularly on their breeding grounds, they seem to take human intrusion with equanimity, even when slaughtered in their thousands. For these reasons, and probably also because their facial characteristics give the impression of a somewhat fixed, almost human 'expression', albatrosses have long been regarded as rather stupid birds. Thus the name given by seamen to a number of species is 'gooney' which, like 'goon', is derived from 'goney', the old English word for a rather stupid person. Other species are known as 'mollies' or 'mollymawks', possibly from the Dutch word 'mallemok'—a stupid gull. An alternative suggestion as to the derivation of 'mollymawk' and its many variants is that it comes from the Dutch 'malle-mugge', the tiny flies which swarm round lighted lamps. The vast

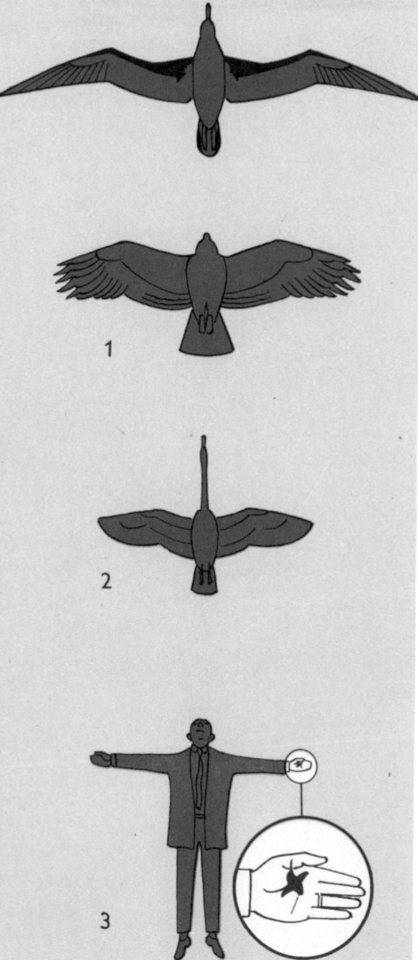

The wingspan of the Wandering albatross compared with 1. the Golden eagle, 2. Grey lag goose and 3. a man holding the smallest bird, a Bumblebee hummingbird, in his hand.

flocks of fulmar petrels so resembled these insects that the Dutch whalers gave them the same name, and the name became transferred to albatrosses. But the 'stupid gull' derivation, at least, is probably correct because in Japanese waters albatrosses have been known as 'bakadori', or fool-birds, for centuries.

Albatrosses tend to be gregarious and, except for *Phoebetria,* are colonial nesters. When not on the breeding grounds they spend most of their time in flight over the open oceans, covering enormous distances in their prospecting for food. They usually feed while sitting on the water but they will also pick up things in flight or may dive shallowly. They take most kinds of marine animal which can be found at the surface and are fond of squid. The bill covering of albatrosses, composed of separate horny plates, and particularly the hooked tip of the upper mandible, are eminently suited for grasping the slippery prey. Albatrosses are very catholic in their tastes and have been known to take most of the edible materials the sea provides, from the gelatinous floats of the Portuguese man-o'-war, with its trailing stinging tentacles, to the circles of blubber and fibrous material cut out of whales' flukes for the attachment of towing chains. They are especially fond of fatty or oily foods and in a number of areas have benefitted considerably over the years from the enormous amount of blood and offal from whaling factories.

Observations on the feeding habits of albatrosses have suggested that they may have a well-developed sense of smell. This is supported by the great development, for a bird, of their olfactory organs and associated brain areas, a development shared by other tubenosed birds and possibly linked with the tubular arrangement of the nostrils.

The *Diomedea* albatrosses breed in colonies of many hundreds or thousands of individuals, mostly on remote oceanic islands. Nests vary from a simple scrape to a conical mound 1 ft (30 cm) or more high made of turf or soil and with a nest cup in the top lined with feathers and grasses. There is one egg, white often speckled with red-brown, particularly around the large end. The sexes share incubation which lasts from about 65 days in the smaller species such as the Laysan and Black-footed albatrosses to 70–80 days in the larger species such as the Wandering albatross and the Royal albatross, *D. epomophora.*

Albatrosses have elaborate courtship displays involving mutual bowing and wing-flapping and, in the various species, a wide variety of calls—screams, groans, croaks and braying sounds. Sounds are also produced by clattering the mandibles of the bill together. The birds of a mated pair continue their mutual displays throughout the breeding season and frequently preen each other.

Black-browed albatross *Diomedea melanophrys*.

The map shows the direction of prevailing winds used by albatrosses in crossing the southern oceans.

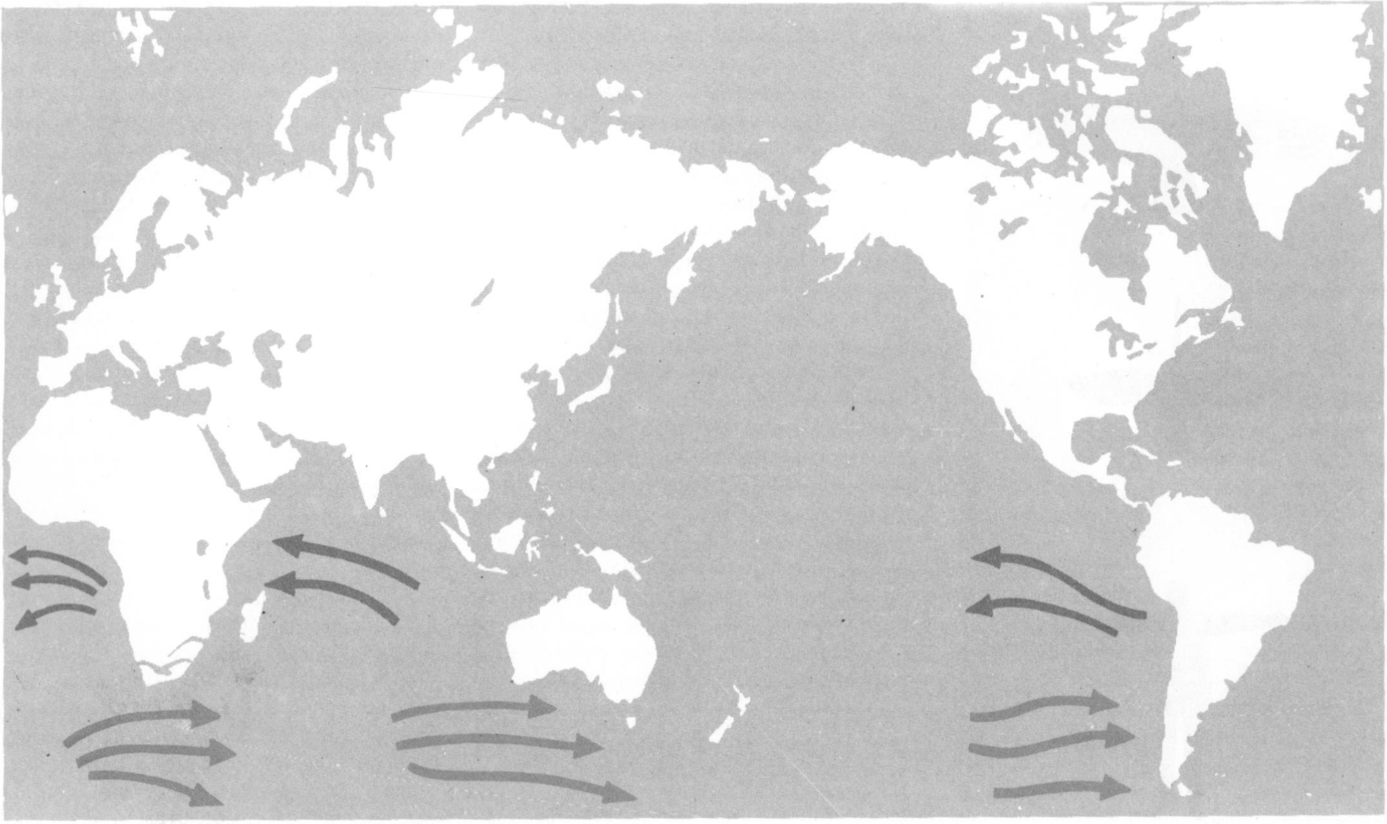

All the albatrosses except the Waved albatross lay their eggs between September and January, the southern spring. Even the North Pacific species do this, although there is no obvious reason for it, except perhaps as a retention of an ancestral habit, these species having probably originated in the southern hemisphere. Without any significant pressures upon them to change their time of breeding they have retained their ancestral pattern. It may also be that the summer temperatures on the islands where they now breed would be too hot for their comfort.

The Waved albatross of the Galapagos, the only exclusively tropical species, lays during May and June. Perhaps this is connected with the relative abundance of food at that time of the year. The Waved albatross, like the Galapagos penguin has probably only been able to colonize the archipelago by virtue of the cold Humboldt current. This sweeps up the west coast of South America and out towards the Galapagos, producing a boundary of cold and warm water near the islands, where there is a high production of plankton and therefore of fish. The Waved albatross seems to fly southwards to feed in this area.

The nestling period of the albatross is very extended, so much so that the larger species are not able to breed every year. The period from hatching to first flight of the young in the smaller species is $2\frac{1}{2}$–3 months but in the larger species it is as long as 8–9 months. A fledging period of 243 days (over $8\frac{1}{2}$ months) is recorded for the Royal albatross, for example. Both sexes feed the chick, by regurgitation, regularly for the first week or so, then with decreasing frequency, leaving the chick to its own devices for increasing periods. For example, one marked Wandering albatross, known to be still feeding its chick, was seen 2,640 miles from its nest. Such a distance is not far for an albatross, and this is probably not an isolated example. Like other large, long-lived birds, albatrosses lay only one egg per season and have a high life expectancy once the vulnerable fledging period is passed. This is reflected in the apparent readiness with which the adults will travel long distances while their chicks are still in the nest. They must have a high likelihood of returning, for an albatross chick with only one parent would probably starve.

Black-browed albatross on nest.

The greatest danger the albatross chick has to face is predation by skuas when its parents are away. This is a common hazard in seabird colonies, and does not usually do excessive harm, although skuas and Giant fulmars were reported to have killed 95 out of a hundred Wandering albatross chicks on Gough Island in the South Atlantic in 1895. This was, however, probably exceptional.

The Wandering albatross begins to lay at the end of December, though some individuals may not have eggs until February. After hatching the growth of the chicks is very rapid, their weight increasing by up to $3\frac{1}{2}$ oz (100 gm) per day, and after about six months they weigh as much as the adults. They are then left for increasing periods of time through the southern winter and around October begin to move about in the colony and try their wings. The young then have to make way for another generation, but stay in the vicinity of the colony for some time while they develop their independence and powers of flight. By the time the chicks are old enough to fend for themselves it is spring once more and too late for the parents to nest again. They, therefore, abandon the colony until the following spring and so the Wandering albatross only lays in alternate years, about one half of the population laying each year.

The two species of *Phoeberia,* the Sooty albatross *P. fusca* and the Light-mantled sooty albatross *P. palpebrata* also breed on oceanic islands but not in large colonies. They are found characteristically in the temperate subantarctic latitudes of the South Atlantic and Indian Oceans. Their nests are 6 in (15·3 cm) or more in height, forming shallow, truncated cones with a nest cup in the top. Even so the fully-grown chick overflows the nest. Unlike other albatrosses the *Phoebetria* species build their nests on inaccessible cliff shelves and edges, showing one of the few examples among albatrosses of a change in behaviour following human interference.

Wandering albatross at its breeding ground.

Greyheaded albatross *Diomedea chrysostoma.*

The *Phoebetria* albatrosses may be distinguished from the *Diomedea* albatrosses by their almost uniformly dark plumage, an incomplete white eye-ring, and particularly narrow wings, as well as the elongated tail already mentioned. Their general proportions contribute to an outstanding mastery of the air, as R. C. Murphy noted in his classic two-volume work *Ocean Birds of South America*: 'In a family of supreme fliers, the Sooty Albatrosses occupy a special pinnacle of excellence'. The great ornithologist Gould also noted how their delicacy of structure contributes to the gracefulness of their flight. The two species are similar in size and appearance and are equally gifted in flight, being more manoeuvrable and generally lighter on the wing than the other albatrosses. They stay poised over ships much more frequently than the other species, and occasionally even pass between the masts.

The outstanding aerial abilities of Sooty albatrosses are doubtless partly connected with their occupation of inaccessible nest sites. The nests are frequently on cliff ledges overlooking the sea with a vertical drop beneath. Not only must the chick remain closely attached to the nest for the long weeks of its development, but when the time comes must be able to launch itself into the air without the lengthy practice indulged in by the *Diomedea* species. In the Light-mantled sooty albatross this is especially so.

Most species of albatross are migratory, sailing over the whole of the Pacific and Southern oceans, largely following the trade winds, when not breeding. For navigation purposes they could make use of prevailing winds, but it seems that, like other birds, they have a well-developed ability to navigate by the sun or stars independently of the earth's surface. One Laysan albatross for example, carried experimentally some 4,000 miles from its nest returned home in 32 days.

How albatrosses sail the winds.

Clearly, that which makes albatrosses unique among birds, even among seabirds, is their faculty of sustained sailing, gliding flight. This is dependent on a high air speed, and is one of the primary reasons for albatrosses being found in the windiest oceanic regions. Albatrosses' wings have the highest aspect ratio (proportion of length to breadth) of any bird, from 20 to 25 compared with around 5 for gamebirds such as pheasants. This is the shape which is pre-eminently adapted to gliding, for drag is inversely proportional to aspect ratio. The albatross in fact is admirably adapted for 'dynamic soaring', which is the method of flight evolved for making use of the difference in speed between winds at sea-level and those at some height above the surface, normally up to 50 ft. The wind is usually in the same direction at the different heights, but near the surface of the water it is slowed by friction. The albatross makes use of this by gliding downwind at an angle, gathering speed in relation to the sea surface. Just before hitting the water the albatross turns about into the wind, sometimes cutting the water with a wing tip. The momentum gained from its rush downwind carries the albatross up but it is taken up to its original 50 ft level by the lift imparted by the increasing speed of the wind. In this way the albatross can travel for miles by a series of glides and climbs with never a wingbeat. It may also glide along the wave troughs, using the up-draughts from wave crests to assist it. The shape and relatively small area of the wing results in albatrosses,

Laysan albatross chick.

other than *Phoebetria,* having no great manoeuvrability, only enough for its normal requirements. In still weather, albatrosses are 'grounded', but as they have few predators this is unimportant.

Albatrosses versus airfields.

The albatrosses, as a group, have suffered considerably over the years as a result of human activities, particularly in the 19th and 20th centuries. From early times man has used the bird for food, for both its flesh and eggs are palatable. But they do not seem to have suffered mass slaughter in early times as did the penguins and others. And some minor taboos against killing them even developed, as indicated by Coleridge's *Ancient Mariner,* written at Wordsworth's suggestion after the latter had read, in a book of exploration, an account of the consequences of killing an albatross.

Albatrosses began to suffer severely in the latter part of the 19th century when their plumage came much into demand for millinery purposes and for bedding. The three North Pacific species were worst hit and many nationalities were involved in the slaughter, including Americans and Canadians and, particularly, the Japanese. The Short-tailed albatross, which is basically a bird of the western Pacific, suffered particularly badly and was almost completely exterminated when volcanic eruptions decimated the last remaining colony on Torishima in 1939 and 1941. Since then, however, protection by the Japanese Government has proved effective, and birds which must have been at sea during the eruptions have started the colony again.

The other two Pacific species suffered badly also, but their populations were bigger and protection was instituted earlier. The largest albatross colony was on Laysan Island, some thousand miles west of Hawaii, and the slaughter there was so enormous and so publicized that in 1909 President Theodore Roosevelt had Laysan and other Leeward Islands established as wild-life reservations. Even so, a lessening of demand for the feathers and growing public sentiment against such killing was needed before the decline of the population was checked.

The Second World War was a great threat to many albatross populations in the Pacific. Hundred of thousands of birds were killed as a side-effect of normal warfare, and on one island at least the starving Japanese garrison ate the whole colony.

The history of the relationship between the Laysan albatrosses and man on Midway Atoll has been a checkered one. In 1935 Midway was established as a staging post for planes crossing the Pacific. To begin with birds and humans survived pretty well together, but during the war, and since then, use of the aircraft runways has increased considerably and the birds have become a hazard—especially to jet planes, for a bird can totally destroy a jet engine if sucked in. Unfortunately the runways were built across the traditional breeding grounds of the albatrosses, and it is very difficult to change the basic habits of these birds. At one time it was suggested that the whole population of albatrosses on Midway should be destroyed, but this would have meant the elimination of a third of the world's population of the Laysan albatross (the total population being some million and a half). Fortunately the operation was never carried out. However, various attempts at population control have involved the destruction of many thousands of birds although very few, if any, planes have been lost through bird strikes.

About half the surface of Sand Island in the Midway Atoll has been covered with metal paving for planes to land and to eliminate albatross breeding habitat. In the process of this paving the land has been bull-dozed flat

Left: Gliding flight of an albatross travelling down wind. Right: Gliding is also aided by updraughts created by wave action.

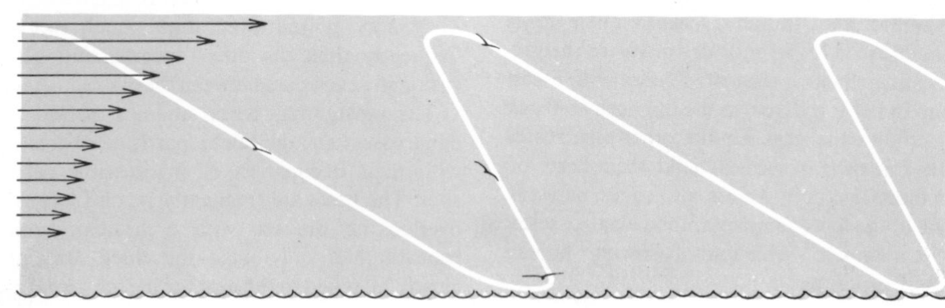

Courtship display of Wandering albatross.

and much of the vegetation has been removed. In addition to the elimination of breeding sites, attempts at control have involved the destruction of all albatrosses over an area at least 750 feet from the centre of operational runways. In 1959–1960 the 'control kill' was some 15% of the breeding population, totalling about 34,500 pairs. But the percentage of breeding birds eliminated does not give a complete picture of the effect on the colony, for bereaved birds, it has been found, are not likely to nest the following year. Moreover, it is not known how many potential breeding birds have been lost as embryos or chicks, though the total must be some hundreds of thousands at least.

Unfortunately, one of the reasons for the flattening of the runway areas on Sand Island, the elimination of updraught conditions used by the birds, does not seem to have been a correct solution to the problem of birds crossing the runways, for albatrosses continue to cross, but now at a lower, more dangerous level. A better solution would be to encourage vegetation, including trees, as close as is feasible to the runways, keeping the birds above the level of the planes landing and taking off. This would also be much preferable from the general ecological point of view.

Clearly, it is very difficult for albatrosses and aeroplanes to use the same terrain without considerable inconvenience to one or the other, or both. This is exemplified by the situation on the other Midway Island, Eastern Island, where a veritable forest of cables supporting radio masts may eliminate as much as a sixth of the world's population of the Laysan albatross. In the 1964–65 breeding season the total population of this species on Eastern Island was under 30,000 pairs. The number of albatrosses killed by crashing into the cables between 15 November, 1964 and 22 May, 1965 was around 3,000. As we have noted, albatrosses are not particularly manoeuvrable and they depend on the winds for their flight. Under certain conditions they cannot avoid flying through the radio mast area, with death as the likely result. After a storm, the direction of which forces the birds to fly through the mast area, hundreds of dead albatrosses litter the ground. Sooty terns *Sterna fuscata* also die in thousands.

Radio masts are not the only hazards which seabirds have to cope with as a result of man's activities. Millions of birds of hundreds of species die at the world's lighthouses every year when they crash into them on their night migrations, dazzled by the light. But the problem of the Midway radio mast cables would seem to be more easily soluble than that of the lighthouse deaths. Unfortunately, officialdom, like the law, is often an ass. We may note this comment by Prof. H. I. Fisher, the distinguished American biologist who has made a detailed study of the Midway albatross problem: 'A request to put streamers on a single cluster of guy cables, as a test installation to check their effectiveness was denied. The engineers felt the narrow strips of thin plastic would offer too much resistance to strong winds and might cause a cable to snap. It would seem, however, that the effect of the streamers would be considerably less than the impact of a seven-pound albatross hitting a cable at 60 miles per hour. And no cables have ever been broken by any one of the thousands of birds which have hit them.' The story of the Laysan albatross of Midway Atoll illustrates the difficulties and complexities of conservation in the modern world.

Although there are currently millions of albatrosses in the North Pacific, very few penetrate into the North Atlantic and none breeds there. It has not always been so, for a fossil albatross *D. anglica* has been found in both Britain and eastern North America. This find is only outshone by *Gigantornis* from the Eocene of Nigeria, a possible albatross which had a sternum twice the size of that of the largest living albatross. It would seem that at one time the albatrosses were able to move north from the southern oceans almost as easily into the North Atlantic as into the North Pacific, but today the windless equatorial doldrums form an effective barrier. Only 2 or 3 birds are reported per year on the eastern Atlantic seaboard, but at least they are now welcome and not persecuted as they were in historical times. One famous example is the female Black-browed albatross *D. melanophrys,* which visited the gannet colony on Mygennaes in the Faeroe Islands from 1860 until 1894, when it was killed. Another of the same species has been resident in the gannet colony on the Bass Rock off eastern Scotland during the summers of 1967, 1968 and 1969. With further protection, albatrosses may become established in the North Atlantic again.

Wandering albatross at nest, with egg.

One further feature of albatrosses that must be mentioned is their habit, in common with other tubenosed birds, of vomiting the oily contents of the stomach when molested, particularly when they are young. Most, if not all species of albatross have this habit which is probably derived from the common vertebrate alarm reactions which empty the gut in an emergency. Presumably this reduces the animal's weight and thus promotes escape. In the albatrosses the oily gut contents are particularly unpleasant to most other animals, and as they can be ejected with force and with a fair degree of accuracy they are an effective deterrent to intruders. FAMILY: Diomedeidae, ORDER: Procellariiformes, CLASS: Aves. P.M.D.

ALCYONARIANS, corals (Cnidaria, Anthozoa) which include the soft corals like the Sea fans, Blue corals and Precious coral. Many are brightly coloured and occur in clean shallow warm seas. Their skeletons are horny or made up of calcareous spicules, never hard and stony as in reef corals.

ALDER FLIES, four-winged insects of the suborder Megaloptera of the order Neuroptera. They are represented in Britain by only two species, *Sialis lutaria* which occurs in ponds and lakes and *Sialis fuliginosa* which is usually found in running water. They are stout-bodied, brown in colour, have long filamentous antennae and fold their wings along the back in the form of a ridged roof. The adults are commonly found among aquatic vegetation and reeds in May and early June. They are weak fliers and frequently fall onto the water surface where they form a ready source of food for fishes. They are common in both stony and muddy-bottomed streams and the fisherman's artificial fly, the 'alder' is modelled on them. The eggs are laid in large batches on reeds and other emergent water vegetation. The larvae on hatching crawl or fall into the water where they live at the bottom as active predators, feeding on worms, other insect

Alder fly *Sialis*, found near rivers and lakes in Europe, form food for fishes.

larvae and small molluscs. The larva has a pair of long bristled lateral appendages on the abdomen which give it the appearance of being ten-legged. The larvae of the British species grow to about $1\frac{1}{2}$ in (4 cm) in length but those of the American Dobson fly *Corydalis* are commonly over 3 in ($7\frac{1}{2}$ cm) long and have enormous scissor-like mandibles which are retained by the male in the adult life.

Closely related to the Alder flies are the Snake flies (Raphidioidea) which are by contrast wholly terrestrial and in which the posterior region of the head is drawn out into a long 'neck'. The larvae are found under loose bark and on vegetation where they are active predators on other soft-bodied insects. FAMILY: Sialidae, SUBORDER: Megaloptera, ORDER: Neuroptera, CLASS: Insecta, PHYLUM: Arthropoda. R.C.F.

ALEWIFE *Alosa pseudoharengus*, a herring-like fish of the western north Atlantic and related to the shads of Europe. Two explanations have been given for its common name: it may be a 17th century corruption of the American Indian name for the fish *Aloofe*, or it may be derived in some way from the French word *Alose* meaning a shad. The alewife is a silvery fish resembling a herring but with marked striations radiating across the gill cover. It rarely reaches 12 in (30 cm) in length. It is found both in the sea and in freshwaters, the populations often migrating back and forth. Normally they live in deep water but in June or July they come into the shallows or feeder streams to breed. Alewife are also found in Lake Ontario, from whence they migrated via the Welland Canal into Lake Erie in 1931. Since then the Lake Erie population has grown considerably. The alewife plays a fairly important part in fisheries along the Atlantic coast of the United States and in the lakes. FAMILY: Clupeidae, ORDER: Clupeiformes, CLASS: Pisces.

ALFONSINOS, a common name for members of the Berycidae, a family of primitive fishes in many ways intermediate between the soft-finned fishes and the more advanced spiny-finned groups of the super-order Acanthopterygii. The earliest berycids, from rocks of the Cretaceous period 70–135 million years old, are little different from the modern alfonsinos, so that the latter are of great interest to students of fish evolution.

The alfonsinos are ocean-living fishes of moderately deep waters down to 2,500 ft (750 m) and are found in the Atlantic and Indo-Pacific regions. *Beryx splendens* is world-wide and *B. decadactylus* is not uncommon off the continental shelf of the North Atlantic. Both have silvery bodies with reddish fins and forked tails. As in the acanthopterygians, the first ray of the pelvic fins is spiny but there are many more soft rays (up to 13). The body is deep and compressed and the eyes are large. These fishes are rarely used for food except in Japan where *Beryx splendens*, which reaches 2 ft (60 cm) in length, is a popular table fish. FAMILY: Berycidae, ORDER: Beryciformes, CLASS: Pisces.

Alfonsino, earliest spiny-rayed fish in fossil record.

ALIMENTARY CANAL, is basically a tube of varying diameter in which food is processed. It is generally considerably longer than the body-space in which it lies, the human alimentary canal for instance being nearly 30 ft (9 m) long, and so is thrown into loops or coils which can move over each other to some extent. Associated with it are glands which produce substances to digest the food.

ALLEN'S RULE, propounded by J. A. Allen in 1877, that the colder the climate the greater the tendency towards smaller extremities. Allen gave as an example the variation in size of the ears of Jack rabbits. The Jack rabbit *Lepus campestris*, of Arizona, for example, has long ears, that of Oregon has shorter ears. Farther north, the related Varying hare *L. americanus*, has even shorter ears and the Arctic hare *L. arcticus*, has ears only half the size of those of the Arizona jack rabbit. Another example is seen in the ears of the Fennec fox *Fennecus zerda*, of North Africa and Arabia, the Red fox *Vulpes vulpes*, of Europe, and the Arctic fox *Alopex lagopus*.

The ears get progressively smaller from the tropics to the polar regions. Experimentally, it has been found that mice reared at lower temperatures have shorter tails than those reared at high temperatures. The rule does not apply in comparing two segments of a population one of which migrates and the other does not, since the development of muscles for migration tends to counteract the effect of the cold.

Loss of body heat is linked with the ratio between surface area and volume of the body. The smaller the animal the greater the loss because the surface area is proportionately greater than the volume of the body. The decrease in the surface area of the extremities substantially reduces the rate of heat loss. See Bergmann's rule.

ALLIGATOR GARS, see 'garpikes' for which it is an alternative name.

ALLIGATOR LIZARDS, about five species of *Anguid lizard living in Central America and the southern part of North America.

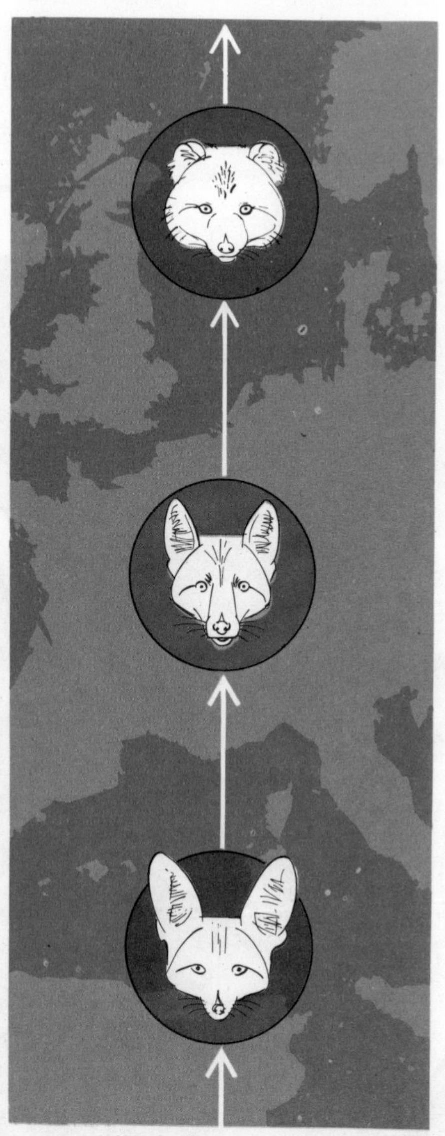

ALLIGATOR SNAPPING TURTLE *Macroclemys temmincki,* the largest freshwater turtle in the United States and one of the largest in the world. Reaching a weight in excess of 200 lb (90 kg) it is sluggish and heavily armoured, frequenting the bottoms of lakes and rivers. It is unique in possessing a built-in fishing lure: a fleshy appendage on the floor of the mouth that resembles a twitching worm. Fishes, attracted by this lure enter the mouth and are swallowed by the turtle. The ruse is enhanced by the dull colouration and rough shell, which is usually heavily covered with algae and serves to render the turtle invisible. FAMILY: Chelydridae, ORDER: Testudines, CLASS: Reptilia.

ALLIGATORS, an ancient, relict group of crocodilians comprising only two species out of a total of over 30 forms in the order Crocodylia. They are distinguished from crocodiles by the pattern and arrangement of the teeth, and, not so reliably, by the shape of the snout. In the alligator the lower row of teeth project upwards into a series of pockets in the upper jaw so that when the mouth is closed, the only teeth exposed to view are the upper teeth. This gives the alligator an appearance of 'smiling' when viewed from the side. The crocodile, on the other hand, normally has both rows of teeth exposed when the jaws are closed, and the teeth intermesh with one another. Particularly prominent is the enlarged tooth fourth from the front which may even extend above the line of the upper jaw giving a constricted appearance immediately behind the nostrils. So the crocodile's 'smile' resembles a toothy leer.

Alligators are found only in two widely separated parts of the world: the upper Yangtse River valley in China and the southeastern United States. One theory is that the less aggressive alligator—which will run away from man—was once almost world-wide in distribution. but the more recent crocodiles have successfully weeded out the alligator throughout its range to where it is now found only in two relict 'islands'.

The more efficient crocodile, faster growing and consuming more food, but not as long-lived as the alligator, may have been simply a keener competitor for food. However, the alligator can withstand cold more successfully than the crocodile. When water temperatures drop below 65°F (18°C) an alligator still surfaces for air, whereas the crocodile when exposed to cold water sinks and drowns. This explains the occurrence of the alligator in relatively colder regions. In North America, the American crocodile has successfully survived in extreme southern Florida, but its numbers are severely affected by cold spells. Alligators, however, range from southern Florida, north into the Carolinas and west to Texas.

Although the crocodile is now the most numerous and widespread of the crocodilians throughout the tropics, the alligator family has come up with perhaps an answer to the crocodile: the caiman. Caimans are even smaller than crocodiles and a number of species occupy the northern regions of South America and appear to be spreading out in a slowly radiating pattern into the regions occupied by crocodiles. With an appetite and temperament to match that of the crocodile, it is conceivable that these 'new-comers' may eventually replace a large number of the crocodiles over a great part of their range.

Man, however, has had a crushing effect on the populations of all crocodilians, primarily regarding hide-hunting. During the period 1880 to 1894, for example, $2\frac{1}{4}$ million alligators were slaughtered. Although the alligator is protected in the USA by most of the states in which it is found, it has been illegally hunted and its hides sold to markets in northern states in such numbers that it is doomed to extinction unless efforts are taken to curtail this smuggling and poaching.

American alligator *Alligator mississipiensis.*

The Chinese alligator is protected by the government of China but there is no recent word on whether its numbers are increasing. In fact, it has been said that the Buddist priests hold the alligator in high regard, and will quietly liberate captured specimens if they have the opportunity.

The name 'alligator' is thought to be derived from the Spanish word *el lagarto,* meaning 'the lizard'. In Latin America, many smaller forms of crocodilians are called *lagarto.* The larger forms are called *cocodrilo.*

In years past, baby alligators were gathered by the thousands and sold in pet stores in the United States. This resulted in a rapid decline in alligator populations, whereupon many states in the south began protecting small alligators or at least controlling their

Allen's rule, as demonstrated by members of the fox family, in which the ears become progressively smaller as we travel north: Desert fennec *Fennecus zerda* of Africa (bottom), European common fox *Vulpes vulpes,* Arctic fox *Alopex lagopus* (top).

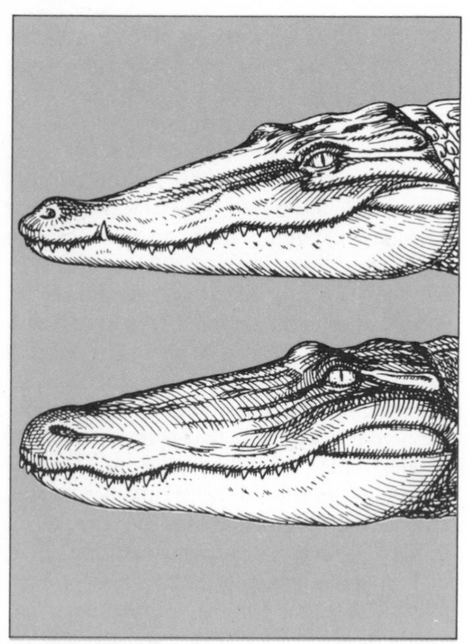

The crocodile (above) has both rows of teeth exposed when the jaws are closed, including the enlarged fourth tooth from the front, giving it an appearance of leering. In the alligator (below) the lower row of teeth projects upwards in the upper jaw, including the fourth tooth, and the only teeth exposed to view are the upper teeth, giving it an appearance of smiling.

export. Although baby alligator traffic has been halted, baby Spectacled caimans have been sold by pet stores in even greater numbers, with the result that some South American countries have become alarmed at this drain on their natural populations of caiman and are gradually placing these species under protection and control.

Crocodilians of any kind make poor pets. They are usually unpredictable in temperament, especially if their enclosure is heated to the extent where they can efficiently digest food. Normal household temperatures are generally too low for proper assimilation of food by the baby crocodilian, and although it may be quite lethargic and unaggressive in this state, it will usually develop and grow quite unnaturally, resulting in deformed jaws, a humped back, or even death within a few months. Even zoological parks have difficulty in providing necessary heat requirements, food with the proper balance of nutrients and minerals, exposure to adequate dosages of the proper lighting and necessary space for adequate growth.

Alligators will feed on practically anything moving that wanders close enough to be snatched up and will conveniently fit into their mouths. They are strictly carnivorous, and prefer to gulp down food in smaller, whole portions. However, if necessary, an alligator can dismember a larger animal by thrashing the victim back and forth or suddenly rotating over and over several times to 'unscrew' a portion. Typically, baby alligators feed on insects, worms, crustaceans and small fish. Later they take frogs and perhaps small rodents. Four-foot (1·2 m) long individuals feed on larger fish, lizards, baby turtles, and rat-sized rodents. Eight-foot (2·4 m) alligators feed on rodents, some larger fish, and an occasional unwary bird. Larger individuals may even be lucky enough to snatch up a small wild pig or stray dog, although their food consists primarily of large rodents in the wild. Alligators play an important part in controlling rodents in such out of the way areas as swamps and canals where they would otherwise destroy vegetation and water levels in areas even far removed from the alligator's habitat. The stomach of an alligator also contains stones, pebbles, and even hard, man-made objects that aid in breaking down food particles for digestion, much like the gizzard in a bird.

Alligators, in the wild construct underground dens at least portions of which are filled with water. In fact, one method used by collectors for locating alligators is to probe with a long pole into the soft earth along a river bank. It is easy to tell when the pole enters a large, open cavern and contacts an alligator. At egg-laying time in the spring, a female American alligator constructs a large mound of mud and vegetation about 5–7 ft (1·5–2·5 m) wide at the base. 20–70 hard-shelled eggs $3\frac{1}{3}$ in (8·5 cm) by $2\frac{1}{2}$ in (6·5 cm) are laid in a cavity in this, and are then covered with more debris and sealed in by the restless activity of the mother. The peeping of hatching young after approximately 10 weeks of natural incubation will encourage the female to tear open the nest and help release the eight-inch (20 cm), brightly coloured black and yellow young which will then make for the nearest water and are then given some protection by the female for the next few months. They grow by about 12 in (30 cm) a year during their first few years.

Alligators have been known to attain large sizes in the past, and some records claim individuals over 20 ft (6 m) in length (in which case, such individuals probably weighed well over half a ton). A 19 ft (5·8 m) specimen was shot in Louisiana a generation ago. Today, 10 ft (3 m) specimens are a rarity, and 8 ft (2·4 m) individuals are uncommonly hard to find in the wild.

Chinese alligators are not known to exceed a length much over 6 ft (1·8 m).

Except in moments of danger or when seizing prey alligators are slow-moving. Even their bodily processes work slowly, which is perhaps why they have been known to reach the age of 75 years. Crocodiles, on the other hand, are not known to live much beyond 30 years.

In contrast with true crocodiles, the two

American alligators in water.

Young alligators look almost benign.

ribs on the first cervical vertebra (the atlas) of an alligator diverge only a little. Moreover, alligators have bony plates not only on the back but also on the belly beneath the large horny scutes. Whilst with true crocodiles there is generally only a single transverse series of occipital scutes and not more than six nuchal scutes, these are usually far more numerous in alligators.

True alligators of the genus *Alligator* are characterized by having the nasal cavity longitudinally divided by a bony septum. This septum is also visible in the living animal because the hump of the nose exhibits a clear longitudinal sub-division. The other genera of alligators (in the broader sense) which do not have this bony septum are referred to by the collective name 'caiman' although they probably do not form a natural group like the genus *Alligator*.

The typical characteristic of the Mississippi alligator is the relatively long but very flat and broadly rounded snout. On the top, a few rudimentary bony ridges extend parallel to one another from the base up to the hump of the nose but the front corners of the eyes are not interconnected by a transverse ridge. In the midline of the back there are generally eight longitudinal rows of large scutes. The keels of the two central longitudinal rows of scutes along the top of the tail run parallel to one another right up to the end and do not curve outwards.

A very sad part is played by commercial interests. Since the skin of the belly of the Mississippi alligator is only sparsely ossified, it is well suited for the manufacture of bags and other leatherware; even coats are made of alligator leather. A rather ingenious souvenir industry has caused the slaughter of countless young animals in order to prepare them and, with tasteless paintwork and ornamentation, sell them as souvenirs. The author of this article even saw at an American airport two small alligators which had been dressed up as a bridal couple, the male in tails and tophat and the female in a wedding dress and veil! FAMILY: Alligatoridae, ORDER: Crocodylia, CLASS: Reptilia. R.P.

ALLIGATOR. The Chinese alligator was made known to scientists nearly 100 years ago. The fact that there was a species of crocodilian in China was suspected by a priest, Father Fauvel, from sketches and illustrations he found in old Chinese literature. It was not until the year 1879, however, that Fauvel succeeded in proving its existence and accurately describing it.

ALLIGATORS, baby alligators have long been popular pets, so much so that their collection is one of the strongest pressures on the populations around the Caribbean. The advantages of a small alligator as a pet is that it feeds on insects, water fleas and tadpoles and is, usually, quite docile. Unfortunately large numbers that are sent to pet shops arrive dead and those that do not die often survive for only a short time or are abandoned when they grow too large. The abandoning of pets is quite a common practice and results in the countryside becoming populated with semi-wild dogs and cats, apart from exotic animals. At one time the craze for pet alligators reached such a peak that there were stories circulating that the sewers of New York were infested with alligators feeding on rats and scaring sewermen. The stories survived the denials of officials but authentic reports are few. An 8 ft (2·40 m) alligator was found in a storm drain near the Harlem River and a 2 ft (60 cm) baby alligator was found in a trash can on the subway in Brooklyn.

ALLOPATRIC SPECIES, two or more closely related species of which the areas of distribution are neighbouring without overlapping. See Sympatric Species.

ALPACA *Lama pacos,* a camel-like domesticated animal of the high Andes. It stands 3 ft (90 cm) at the shoulder, its long fleece, often reaching the ground, is of uniform black, reddish-brown or even white, as well as mixed colours, but piebalds are much rarer than in llamas. There is a tuft of hair on the forehead. The alpaca inhabits the high plateaux of Bolivia and, particularly, Peru. The principal centre of breeding from time immemorial has been on the high plateau of Lake Titicaca in the Departments of Puno, Cuzco and Arequipa. The alpaca thrives best at altitudes between 13,000 and 16,000 feet (4,300–5,300 m) with low air humidity, except in the rainy season. At lower altitudes the animals are often rachitic and their wool is poorer. The alpaca has very sensitive feet and prefers the soft moist ground with tender grasses of the 'bofedales', where there are many pools and puddles in which they like to wallow. A lack of ground moisture is said to produce a fatal foot disease and in rainless years the mortality rate is higher than at other times. Alpacas are more fastidious feeders than llamas.

The Alpaca, domesticated for its wool.

Alpacas are divided up into different herds (puntas), according to age, sex and uses. They often consist of several hundred animals, free to graze all day and driven at night into stone-walled enclosures or corrals. The mares are put to stud at the age of two years, the stallions at three years. In many ranches the stallions, which graze apart from the mares on higher-situated pastures, are only allowed to join the mares every eight days in the rutting season (December to April), since they pursue the mares very violently and much damage can be done if they are not carefully watched. The stallions not wanted for breeding are castrated at the age of 1–2 years.

The period of gestation is 11 months. The mares foal in the rainy season. From the age of seven onwards alpacas are used only for meat production. At the present time the quality of alpaca wool is only slightly lower than that of the vicuña and is being even further refined by crossing with vicuñas. The suri, a breed of alpaca with finer, thicker and longer hair, provides up to 11 lb (5 kg) of wool per annum, but shows a greater susceptibility to parasitic diseases. Shearing takes place every 2 years before the rainy season in November or December, when temperatures are fairly uniform. It is done with ordinary knives or with shears. The Indian women can divide the wool into seven classes just by feeling it. Black alpacas are particularly in demand owing to the heavy coat of hair. There are numerous large commercial farms, but most of the alpacas are owned by Indians. In Peru the number of alpacas is estimated at over 2 million and in Bolivia at about 50,000.

The alpaca, like the llama, was already known in 200 B.C., but nothing precise is known about when they were domesticated. The Incas were already breeding these wool-bearing animals when the Spaniards arrived. They were the sole property of the Government. The alpaca, however, had less religious

Except that it lacks a hump, the alpaca clearly shows its relationship to the camel.

significance as a sacrificial animal than the llama. FAMILY: Camelidae, SUBORDER: Tylopoda, ORDER: Artiodactyla, CLASS: Mammalia. H.G.

ALPINE CHAR *Salvelinus alpinus*, a member of the large salmon family, often referred to merely as char. In Great Britain the populations of Alpine char are entirely land-locked in the deep and cool lakes of Scotland, Northern England, Wales and Ireland. Off Greenland, however, the fishes feed in the open sea but return to freshwater to breed, a habit commonly found amongst the Salmonidae.

During the final cold period of the Ice Age, the Alpine char became isolated in lakes as the ice sheet receded. As often happens, this isolation has led to slight differences in body form between the populations in the various lakes, which encouraged zoologists of the last century to refer to each lake population as a different species. It is now recognized, however, that all the British char belong to the same species.

Alpine char are fairly large fishes, a good specimen from British waters weighing up to 3 lb (1·4 kg), but they are caught by British anglers more by accident than design. The flesh is most delicate, however, and they are actively fished for in northern Norway when they leave the deep waters of the lakes and make their way into the feeder streams to breed (a relict of their former migratory habit). One of the most attractive features of the Alpine char is its beautiful colouring. During the spawning season the males assume a bright breeding dress of intense scarlet on the belly and flanks while the back becomes jet black. FAMILY: Salmonidae, ORDER: Salmoniformes, CLASS: Pisces.

ALTERNATION OF GENERATIONS, a remarkable feature of most plants and many of the lower animals, in which the parent reproduces sexually and the offspring, which are different in form, reproduce asexually. The third generation resembles the first generation in form and reproductive method. Such generations alternate, there being rarely more than two forms.

A typical example is in *Obelia*, a Sea fir, in which one generation consists of colonies, 1–2 in ($2\frac{1}{2}$–5 cm) high, of polyps. At intervals on the stems of the polyps arise rods of tissue from which minute jellyfishes or medusae are budded off, asexually, to swim freely in the sea. These medusae represent the second, or sexual, generation, which shed ova and sperm into the water. The fertilized ova give rise to planula larvae which settle on the seabed and grow into new polyps.

The Common jellyfish *Aurelia aurita* also has an alternation of generations. From its fertilized ova arise planula larvae which settle on the bottom of the sea and grow into polyps, each known as a scyphistoma. After settling the scyphistoma withdraws its tentacles and its body becomes repeatedly constricted until it looks more like a pile of saucers. Each 'saucer' becomes detached in turn and swims away as a minute medusa which grows into an adult jellyfish 1 ft (30 cm) in diameter, and the cycle is then repeated.

In various forms an alternation of generations is found in other Cnidaria than *Aurelia* and *Obelia*, and in the Foraminiferida, Liver flukes, tapeworms, Platyhelminthes and Nematoda.

AMBERJACKS, marine fishes related to the Horse mackerels, scads and pompanos. They have fairly deep, compressed bodies, slender and crescentic tail fins. Unlike many other carangid fishes, they lack bony scutes along the lateral line. A typical species, *Seriola dumerilii* is found on both sides of the tropical Atlantic including the Mediterranean and the West Indies. Its back is a violet-blue, the flanks reddish-gold and the fins yellow but the juvenile has brilliant vertical bands of gold down the body. Amberjacks live in shoals and are voracious fish, especially when after mackerel. They can be caught by trolling with a spoon or whole mackerel and can provide considerable sport since they grow to over 100 lb (45 kg). FAMILY: Carangidae, ORDER: Perciformes, CLASS: Pisces.

AMBROSIA BEETLES, wood boring beetles closely related to the weevils. They burrow into solid timber making a main gallery from which branch numerous short galleries or cradles. The excavation of these tunnels is usually by the females who make them of a constant diameter, which distinguishes them from the tunnels made by many other wood boring insects.

The unusual feature of these beetles is that they cultivate a certain type of fungus on the walls of their galleries which they use as food. It is thought the adult beetles re-inoculate each new gallery by either regurgitating spores from their crop, by defaecating viable spores or by carrying spores stuck to their body hairs. Possibly different species use one or more of these different methods to start their cultures. However, it is known that the spores are carefully nurtured on a substrate of larval excrement or wood chips and that other competitive species of fungus are 'weeded' from the ambrosia fungus *Monilia candida* by the adult beetles. The adults feed the young larvae in the cradles with the fresh succulent tips of the fungal fruiting bodies (conidia). The older larvae and the adults graze the entire fungal mat which is capable of regrowth.

The fungus probably grows on sap released during the tunnelling activities of the beetles. FAMILY: Scolytidae, ORDER: Coleoptera, CLASS: Insecta, PHYLUM: Arthropoda. P.F.N.

AMBUSH BUGS, a small group of predacious insects, so named because of their habit of concealing themselves and lying in wait for their victims, in the flowers of various herbaceous plants, notably members of the Compositae. Like all true bugs, their mouthparts form a pointed beak used to pierce the tissues and suck the juices of their prey. Other insects attracted to the flowers are seized in the massive, raptorial forelegs of the Ambush bug, and subsequently killed. The bodies of these bugs are generally flattened and coloured so that they blend with their surroundings and remain unnoticed by the prey until it is too late. FAMILY: Phymatidae, ORDER: Hemiptera, CLASS: Insecta, PHYLUM: Arthropoda.

Alternation of generations: (above) life-history of the Common jellyfish, (below) life-history of the Sea fir *Obelia*.

AMBYSTOMATIDS, North American Mole salamanders, are sturdily built broad-headed, medium-sized salamanders. They include the Marbled salamander *Ambystoma opacum* which may attain a length of 5 in (12·5 cm) and is terrestrial. It lives on hillsides near streams from New England to Northern Florida and westwards to Texas. Breeding takes place in autumn, fertilization is internal and the eggs are laid in shallow depressions on land, usually guarded by the female until the next heavy rain, when they hatch. In very dry conditions they may not hatch until the following spring. In most other ambystomatids, such as the Spotted salamander *Ambystoma maculatum*, which has the same range as the Marbled salamander, courtship takes place in water with an elaborate ritual. The sperm are released in a packet, or spermatophore, which the female picks up with her cloaca. The Spotted salamander breeds in the early spring when it may be seen in fairly large numbers making their way to the breeding ponds. After breeding they return into 'hiding' until the next spring and for the rest of the year they are secretive and rarely seen. The eggs hatch in 30–54 days releasing larvae of ½ in (1·25 cm) long. After 60–110 days the external gills are resorbed, metamorphosis is complete and the animal becomes terrestrial at a length of 2–3 in (5–7·5 cm). Adults grow to a length of 9 in (22·5 cm).

The Tiger salamander *A. tigrinum* may grow to 13 in (32·5 cm) which makes it amongst the largest of the terrestrial salamanders. It derives its name from the yellow or light olive bars on its upper surface. It has a similar distribution to the Marbled and Spotted salamanders except that it is a lowland form. Its eggs are laid in deep-water ponds, metamorphosis is completed quickly.

Another familiar Mole salamander is the Frosted flatwood salamander *A. cingulatum,* 4½ in (11·25 cm) long, named for the greyish dorsal markings on a black background which suggest frost on leaves. The second part of the name refers to distribution of the species in the wire-grass flatwoods between North Carolina and northeast Florida.

The Ringed salamander *A. annulatum* is generally only found in the mating season after heavy rain when it may be seen in shallow pools, from Central Missouri to West Arkansas and Eastern Oklahoma. For the rest of the year it is difficult to find despite its comparatively large size of 8 in (20 cm).

The majority of salamanders, including the ambystomatids, are usually voiceless. A notable exception is the Pacific 'giant' salamander *Dicamptodon ensatus*, which occurs in the moist coastal forests from British Columbia to Northern California and may reach a length of 12 in (30 cm). It makes a low-pitched bark or scream, especially when disturbed. As its name suggests this is a large

Tiger salamander, largest terrestrial salamander, one of the so-called Mole salamanders.

species. In contrast to the slender, graceful appearance of the other ambystomatids this form has a clumsy build, yet it can apparently climb well and has been found several feet above the ground in small bushes or on sloping tree trunks. Almost all ambystomatids have well developed lungs but the Olympic salamander *Rhyacotriton olympicus,* 4 in (10 cm) long, has extremely small lungs. It inhabits mountain streams of the coastal forests of Oregon and Washington.

The genus *Rhyacosiredon* is known from four species which occur at the southern edge of the Mexican plateau.

Neoteny (breeding in the larval state) is not uncommon in the Ambystomatidae, the best known example being the axolotl, the permanent larva of *Ambystoma mexicanum.* It is found around Mexico city and keeps well in captivity. Some species of salamander are habitually neotenous in one part of their range and not in another. For example, in the eastern subspecies of the Tiger salamander metamorphosis takes place within a few months, but in the western subspecies metamorphosis often fails to take place, the animals breeding as larvae. The major factor which contributes to the neoteny is a lack of iodine in the water.

The ambystomatids (family Ambystomatidae) together with the plethodontids (family Plethodontidae) form the suborder Ambystomatoidea, the largest group of tailed amphibians with some 27 genera and in excess of 200 species. FAMILY: Ambystomatidae, ORDER: Caudata, CLASS: Amphibia. R.L.

AMERICAN BROOK TROUT *Salvelinus fontinalis,* strictly speaking not a trout but a char. Its native home is America and Canada, where it inhabits the eastward-flowing rivers and grows to 14 lb (6·4 kg) in weight. It is an attractive fish, with the fins and body mottled and barred. Because of its appearance and edibility, it was introduced into Europe in 1889 as a sporting fish. The introductions have generally been successful except in Great Britain, where the fishes usually escape to the sea and are lost to sight or, if in lakes, fail to thrive. They are strongly cannibalistic and great care must be exercised if a fishery is to be maintained. FAMILY: Salmonidae, ORDER: Salmoniformes, CLASS: Pisces.

AMERICAN BUNTINGS, relatively small finch-like birds of North America belonging to the two subfamilies Pyrrhuloxiinae (=Richmondeninae) and Emberizinae of the family Emberizidae. Those Pyrrhuloxiinae called buntings comprise six species of small, highly coloured and attractive birds in the genus *Passerina,* e.g. the Indigo bunting *P. cyanea,* the Lazuli bunting *P. amoena,* the Painted bunting *P. ciris* and the Varied (or Beautiful) bunting *P. versicolor.* Those species of North America Emberizinae popularly called bunting are the Lark bunting *Calamospiza melanocorys,* the Snow bunting *Plectrophenax nivalis,* its close relative McKay's bunting *P. hyperbore* and the Rustic bunting *Emberiza rustica,* a straggler from Asia. One species of North American longspur, the circumpolar Lapland longspur *Calcarius lapponicus,* is known as the Lapland bunting in Europe. All the European Emberizinae are called buntings, so collectively the term may be applied to all species of American Emberizinae, including the juncos, the American 'sparrows', towhees and brush-finches. See also buntings, cardinals and Song sparrows. FAMILY: Emberizidae, ORDER: Passeriformes, CLASS: Aves.

The Marbled salamander, smaller than the Tiger salamander, is sometimes found on hillsides.

AMERICAN WOOD WARBLERS, a New World family of small perching birds. This family is a part of the great adaptive radiation in the Americas of songbirds with nine primary wing-feathers which includes the tanagers, troupials etc. There are about 113 species, varying from 4–7 in (10–18 cm) long, found from Alaska and northern Canada south to southern South America. Many species are found only on islands in the Caribbean, and many genera breed only in North America or Central America or tropical South America. In general they are brightly coloured birds with striking patterns of orange, yellow, black and white plumage. Some, however, have dull, uniform grey or brown plumage while others have bright plumage with blue or red markings. Sexual and seasonal differences in plumage-pattern are common in the more brightly coloured of the northern species, but in many of the tropical ones females are also brightly coloured and they keep their bright plumage all the year round.

The majority of the Wood warblers inhabit areas of woodland or scrub, but some have adapted to marshes and swamps and even to open fields and the sparse vegetation of the edges of deserts. The northern species are nearly all migrants. Leaving the northern forests they often travel southwards in mixed flocks, providing an impressive spectacle to bird-watchers in the United States as they pass through in waves at migration time. Most of the species live in trees and vegetation and feed on insects caught among the foliage. Some that have developed wide, flat bills and pronounced bristles around the gape live by hawking flies and other airborne insects from a perch, as do the European flycatchers. A few species, including the North American Black-and-white warbler *Mniotilta varia,* creep up tree trunks and boughs, picking food from the bark like treecreepers. Correlated with its change of habits the Black-and-white warbler has developed long claws on the toes and short, stout legs to enable it to cling to tree-bark more efficiently.

Most Wood warblers build cup-shaped or domed nests in bushes or trees, or on the ground concealed by vegetation. The ovenbird *Seiurus aurocapillus,* and some of the other terrestrial members of the family, build large dome-shaped nests on the ground with small side-entrances. These ground-living species are also unusual in that they move about on the ground by walking, while the species adapted to life in vegetation hop on the ground. Like many birds of tropical America, the Wood warblers in this area usually lay clutches of only two or three eggs, but their northern counterparts lay from three to five eggs. The eggs are incubated by the female alone, but both parents feed the young until after they fledge. The eggs of most species are white with brown or grey spots, but some tropical species have immaculate white eggs, especially those that have domed nests where there is no need for the eggs to be concealingly marked.

The genus *Dendroica* with 27 species is primarily a North American group, with five species restricted to islands in the Caribbean. Most of these species are predominantly yellow, with red-brown caps or heads and dark streaks on the breast. The Myrtle warbler *D. coronata* is a familiar bird in many parts of North America and is unusual in feeding on fruit and berries for much of the autumn and winter. A large species, the Kirtland's warbler *D. kirtlandii* has a remarkably restricted breeding range. It breeds only in an area about 60 miles by 80 miles (95 ×130 km) in central Michigan and then only in jack pine trees forming dense stands, 3–18 ft (1–5½ m) tall. Other members of the genus have interested biologists studying the importance of competition between the feeding of similar bird species. Eight or nine species differing only in their songs and the patterns of their plumage breed over large areas of spruce forest in Canada, their breeding territories often overlapping to a considerable extent. Several ornithologists have studied these species and found that they take similar insect foods (mainly the larvae of the Spruce budworm moth) from similar places in the spruce trees. This poses the question of how they can co-exist without any one species being more successful than the others and ousting them by taking increasingly larger shares of the food available. Another interesting problem is why the numbers of several of these species, notably the Cape May warbler *D. tigrina,* fluctuate so widely. In most years these species are scarcer than their relatives, but whenever the Budworm moth populations increase to plague proportions the numbers of these warblers rapidly increase to the point where they outnumber the hitherto more common species many times over, only to decline again as the plague of Spruce budworm larvae decreases.

Several members of the genus *Dendroica* have been recorded as rare vagrants to Europe. For a long time it was thought that these were escaped cage-birds, as it was considered impossible for such small birds to fly so far across the open ocean, but evidence that these are often genuine wind-blown strays is accumulating. Some, however, certainly arrive on the decks of ocean-going liners.

Related to *Dendroica,* the 11 species of the genus *Vermivora* are similar in many ways. Two of the species, the Golden-winged warbler *V. chrysoptera* and the Blue-winged warbler *V. pinus* regularly hybridize over a wide zone of the eastern United States where their ranges meet, including the suburbs of several large cities. Two distinctive forms of hybrid are produced which were considered to be separate species for a long time, and were called the 'Brewster's' and 'Lawrence's' warblers. These hybrid populations have been closely studied by many ornithologists living in the zones of hybridization.

Yellow warbler *Dendroica aestiva,* an American wood warbler.

Another large genus is *Basileuterus* found from Mexico south to Argentina. These are mainly yellow birds with grey or brown markings, but some species are dull-coloured with no striking markings. Many of the species are little known, but there is evidence that the dull-coloured species such as the Buff-rumped warbler *B. fulvicauda* spend more time feeding on the ground and less in trees than the brightly coloured species of the genus, such as the Golden-crowned warbler *B. culicivorus.*

One monotypic North American genus contains the aberrant Prothonotary warbler *Protonotaria citrea.* It is a brightly coloured bird, yellow-bodied with blue-grey wings and is found in the swamp scrub of southeast of the USA. It is remarkable in being the only member of the family that nests in tree-holes, all the others building nests in the open.

A widespread group of small, closely-related warblers, the yellowthroats of the genus *Geothlypis* are found in scrub, marshes and the undergrowth of boggy places. They are nearly all green-backed and yellow below, with a black face mask of varying extent. Several of the species of this genus are confined to the islands of the Caribbean and several genera are confined to the Caribbean islands, two of them only being found on single islands of the Lesser Antilles. The very rare Semper's warbler *Leucopeza semperi* is confined to St Lucia and the nearly-black Whistling warbler *Catharopeza bishopi* is confined to St Vincent.

The largest member of the family is the Yellow-breasted chat *Icteria virens* which is a long-tailed, stout-bodied and heavy-billed species resembling the mockingbirds and thrashers of the family Mimidae more than the more typical Wood warblers. A North American species, it breeds south to central Mexico. Another species the affinities of which with the rest of the wood warblers have been questioned is the Olive warbler *Peucedramus taeniatus* of the southern USA and central America. Thought at one time to be related to the genus *Dendroica,* studies of its internal structure and behaviour have suggested that it is perhaps better classified with the large group of Old World insect-eating birds in the family Muscicapidae.

Another group of birds, the honeycreepers of the genus *Coereba,* were until recently included in a family Coerebidae with some bunting-like birds to which they bear a marked superficial resemblance. Their true position as aberrant Wood warblers has now been recognized, despite the well-marked changes in structure resulting from the adoption of a diet of nectar instead of insects. They have tubular tongues for nectar sucking and are brightly coloured with shades of blue, green and black. One member of this genus, the bananaquit *Coereba flaveola,* is an extraordinarily successful species that has come to live in close association with man in the West Indies. See also honeycreeper. FAMILY: Parulidae, ORDER: Passeriformes, CLASS: Aves. D.T.H.

AMINO ACID, the basic chemical unit from which proteins are synthesized in the animal body. Over 20 amino acids are known, thus a very great variety of combinations to form proteins are possible. Animals cannot synthesize amino acids from the basic elements but depend upon plants for their supply. They can, however, make certain of them by re-combination from others. There are nevertheless 10 amino acids which cannot be formed in the animal body and are therefore known as essential amino acids, since they must be contained in the diet for healthy life.

AMMONITES, group of extinct cephalopod molluscs. Very little is known about their soft parts, but their shells are often well preserved and are quite common in certain geological formations. Living cephalopods are classified chiefly according to the number of gills and arms or tentacles. This information is not available for fossil forms because the soft parts have decayed, so they are classified according to shell structure. They may for convenience be divided into three major groups: the subclasses Nautiloidea, Ammonoidea and Coleoidea. The nautiloids contain the living Pearly nautilus *Nautilus* and a diverse group of related extinct forms. The coleoids contain the extinct belemnites and the living octopuses, squids and cuttlefishes. The Ammonoidea used formerly to be divided into three groups, the goniatites, the ceratites and the ammonites, so that strictly speaking the term ammonite refers only to those ammonoids having a particular type of shell construction. With more detailed knowledge these old divisions have lost most of their original significance and 'ammonite' is now often used rather loosely to include all Ammonoidea.

The ammonite shell had the same basic layers as other mollusc shells and in life consisted mainly of aragonite, a form of calcium carbonate, although this has generally been altered during the process of fossilization by the addition of, or replacement by, other substances. Ammonite fossils are often heavy, but this is due to the cavity of the shell having become filled with deposits and not to the weight of the shell itself, which was usually fairly thin. In most ammonites the shell is coiled in a flat spiral. Less common shapes include helical coiling, like a snail shell, and forms with an initial flat spiral followed by a straight or even hook-shaped terminal portion. Some grew to a considerable size, one coiled Cretaceous species *Pachydiscus seppenradensis* reaching over 3 ft 6 in (1 m) in diameter, equal to an uncoiled length of more than 35 ft (10 m).

The ammonite shell starts with a small, globular chamber called the protoconch, thought to have been formed by the embryo before hatching. The first whorl is generally quite narrow, often smaller in diameter than the protoconch; succeeding whorls increase steadily in size to the aperture of the shell. New whorls may completely cover the earlier parts of the shell so that only the

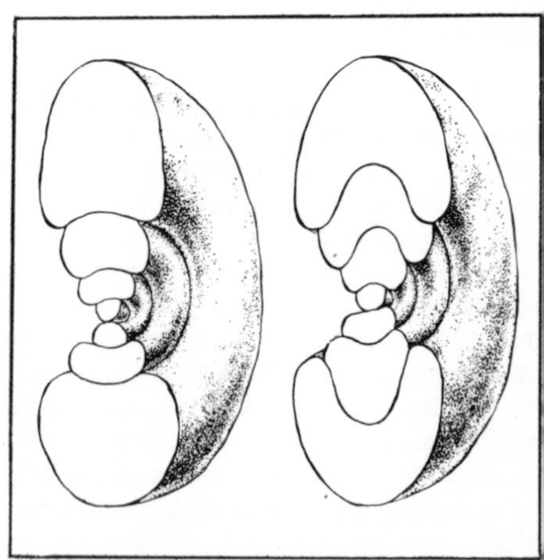

Sections through ammonite shells showing the difference between evolute (left) and involute coiling.

Ammonites have been found which were over 3 ft (1 m) in diameter. This specimen is typical of examples found on boulders on beaches of the south coast of England.

outermost whorl can be seen (involute coiling), or may merely be attached along the outer edge of the preceding whorl so that all the whorls are visible (evolute coiling). The external surface of the whorls may be smooth, or they may bear raised ribs, or knob-like projections or both. Growth-lines may be visible, but these should not be confused with the seams or suture-lines described below. As the animal grew it produced new shell material around the opening, also moved forwards, and secreted internal cross-partitions or septa at intervals behind it so cutting off the older parts of the shell. A fully-formed shell is therefore made up of the embryonic protoconch and a long, coiled portion or conch consisting of an older part (the phragmacone) divided by transverse septa into a number of chambers and the most recently formed part, called the body chamber or living chamber which contained the bulk of the animal and into which it could retreat. This last part usually occupies from $\frac{1}{2}$ to $1\frac{1}{2}$ whorls. Running from the inner end of the animal to the protoconch was the siphon, a slender cord of soft tissue. This perforated the septa and in between them was supported in a narrow, thin-walled tube of shell material called the siphuncle. The first few septa to be formed are gently curved and their edges meet the inner surface of the shell in a simple suture. Later septa become increasingly more folded and frilled especially towards their edges and the suture-lines become correspondingly complicated. Septa, and hence suture-lines, are also present in nautiloids where they remain simple.

Because each septum is attached to the inner surface of the shell the sutures are not visible in an intact specimen, but it is simple to expose them and they are often visible in slightly worn shells without any preparation. Some ammonites could close the shell opening by means of either a single horny plate or else a pair of calcareous plates. These appear to have been attached to the soft part of the animal and not directly to the shell as they are only rarely associated in the fossil. The aperture of the shell is usually damaged to some extent but in some well preserved specimens a small, rounded notch can be seen in the edge farthest from the previous whorl. This is thought to mark the position of the hyponome, a funnel-like organ used in living cephalopods to squirt water in a form of jet propulsion.

Apart from the presence of the siphon and hyponome and a few muscle impressions on the interior surface of the body chamber, nothing is known of the soft parts. Because of the general similarity between ammonite shells and those of the living Pearly nautilus, ammonites have usually been considered to have possessed two pairs of gills and numerous tentacles but there is in fact no direct evidence for this, although there can be little doubt that they possessed the same general type of organization as other cephalopods.

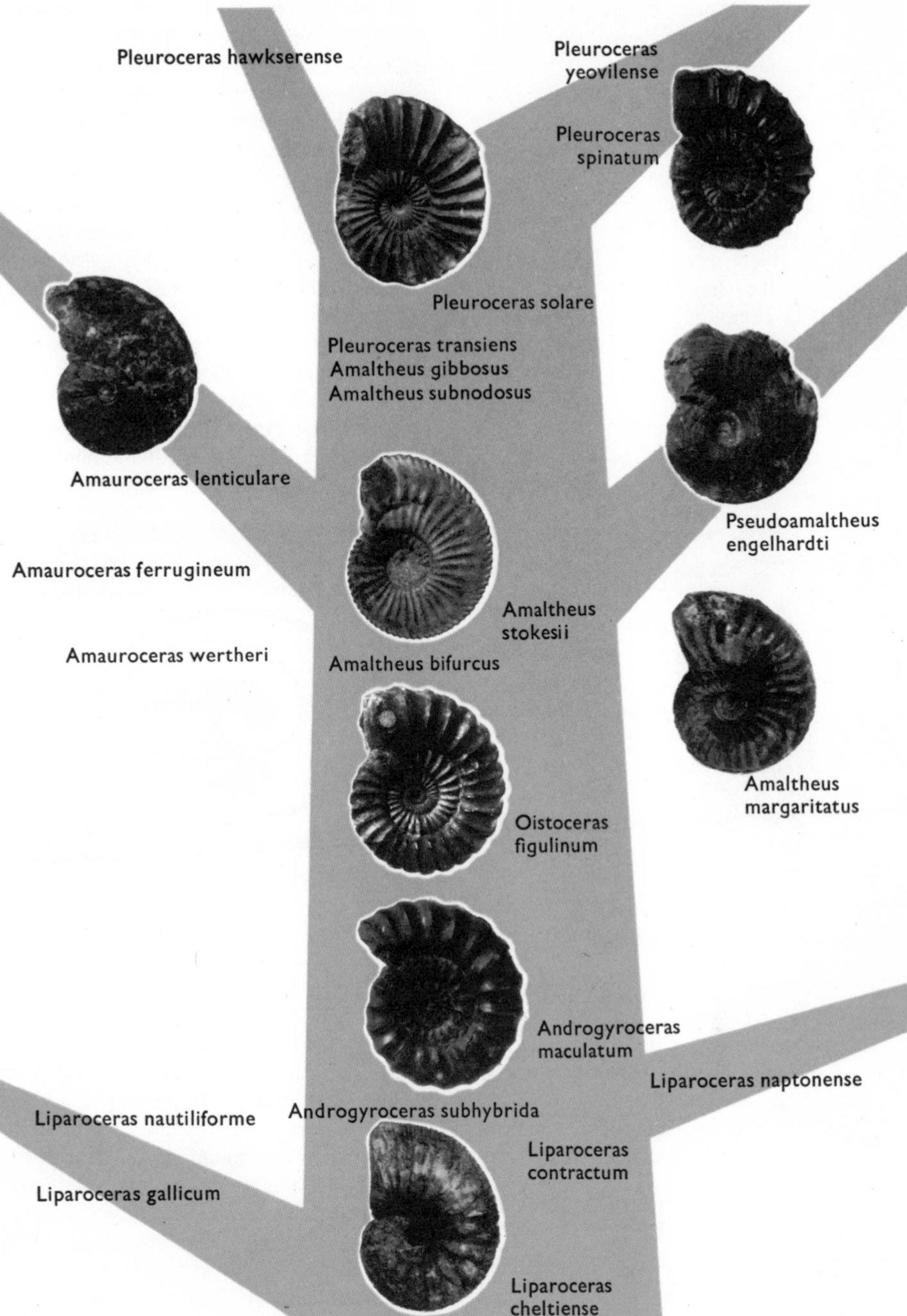

Lines of evolution of the ammonites in successive strata in the Lias (Jurassic), showing how the shape changed from an involute form (at bottom) to various evolute forms of coiling, with varying ornamentation or none at all (top left).

Ammonoids first appear in the Lower Devonian but these forms had relatively simple suture-lines. Forms showing the complicated ammonite sutures, that is true ammonites, are present in Permian formations and these became common and widespread in the Triassic and remained so during the Jurassic and for most of the Cretaceous. Shortly before the end of the Cretaceous ammonites fairly rapidly became extinct, their place being taken by the coleoids.

Like living cephalopods, the ammonites seem to have been entirely marine and never colonized fresh water. Their shells were fairly light and there are good reasons for supposing that the overall density of the animal was further reduced to roughly that of sea water by the secretion of gas into the chambers of the phragmocone. The majority seem to have been fairly good, active swimmers. Those with streamlined, involute shells were probably active, open-water forms. Species with less streamlined, evolute shells were less efficient swimmers and may have spent some of their time on or near the bottom. A small number with relatively heavy shells were probably mainly bottom-living.

There is some confusion as to the exact number of species known but it is probably more than 5,000. Because ammonites were marine, underwent rapid evolution with speedy and widespread dispersal of new species, existed in large numbers and had a hard shell, which improved their chances of fossilization, they have been of great use to geologists in comparing the relative ages of marine deposits, and the Permian, Triassic, Jurassic and Cretaceous systems are subdivided mainly on the basis of their ammonite faunas. SUBCLASS: Ammonoidea, CLASS: Cephalopoda, PHYLUM: Mollusca. Jo.G.

AMMONITES, shells that have pride of place among fossils. They are extremely abundant and their numerous forms allow the geologist to arrange them in series showing the course of their evolution or to assist dating the rocks in which they were found. The abundance of ammonites also makes them easily found by casual collectors. They can be found lying free on the shore after a storm, so doing away with the necessity of chipping them out of rocks. Their pleasing shape is enhanced by their sometimes being fossilized not in rock but in other minerals such as iron pyrites. A Dutch geologist even found a silver ammonite.

The abundance of ammonites led to their being called snakestones in one part of England where the legend has it that there was a plague of snakes and the Abbess of a nearby convent cursed them so that they curled up and died. The name ammonite is derived from Ammon, an Egyptian god with coiled ram-like horns.

AMNIOTES. Vertebrates can be classified into two groups, the anamniotes and amniotes. The former comprises fishes and amphibians, the latter the reptiles, birds, and mammals. The feature which separates the two groups is the type of embryonic development. The typical anamniote embryo forms within a simple gelatinous egg capsule and a moist environment is essential for development. Consequently, even the most terrestrial frogs and salamanders must return to water to breed or at least ensure moist surroundings in which to lay their eggs. The typical anamniote egg has a moderate amount of yolk as a food store and a feeding larval stage is necessary for the completion of development. In contrast the amniote egg of reptiles, birds, and egg-laying mammals can develop on land under the most arid of conditions and the larval stage is eliminated. The egg is covered by a calcareous or leathery shell porous enough to allow the gaseous exchange essential for embryonic respiration but resistant to egg desiccation. Furthermore the amniote embryo develops three extra-embryonic membranes: the yolk-sac enclosing the large food store vital for protracted growth and the elimination of a larval stage, the allantois which is an organ of respiration and excretion, and the amnion which forms a protective shelter over the embryo. The cavity between embryo and amnion is fluid filled so that the embryo carries its own aquatic environment within the egg and the need for a moist external environment is removed.

The first amniotes were the primitive reptiles which evolved in the Carboniferous period. It is likely that the amniote egg evolved at this time as a means of assuring a predator free environment for incubation rather than in association with a general trend towards terrestrial life. In the early Carboniferous the fresh waters abounded with carnivorous fishes and amphibians whereas the land was essentially free of predators apart from the relatively small number of semi-terrestrial amphibia. The aquatic amniote could therefore temporarily leave the water to lay its eggs on land and incubation could continue in comparative safety. Today for similar reasons many completely aquatic frogs leave the water to construct elaborate nests on land away from severe egg and larval predation. Being anamniotes, however, a moist nest is essential for development.

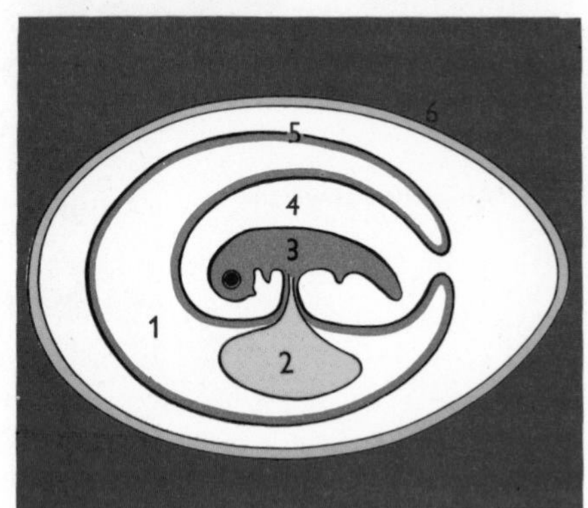

Amniotic egg with parts shown diagrammatically: 1. allantoic cavity, 2. yolk sac, 3. embryo, 4. fluid filled amniotic cavity, 5. amnion, 6. shell.

The reptiles, the birds and the egg-laying monotreme mammals demonstrate the basic pattern of amniote development and freed from the necessity of a damp environment for embryonic development they have dispersed widely. In the higher mammals, where the egg is retained in the maternal uterus, the extra-embryonic membranes become variously modified to unite with maternal tissue to form a placenta. The marsupial mammals represent an intermediate grade between the egg-laying monotremes and the higher mammals for in the great majority of species a placenta is lacking and precocious young are born which must continue their development within the parental marsupial pouch. J.A.

AMOEBAE, single-celled animals characterized by their mode of movement which is by means of pseudopodia—outpushings of cytoplasm. The amoeba pushes out a broad tongue of cytoplasm and then flows into it, a process known as amoeboid movement. The amoebae have been recognized since 1755 but considerable confusion exists concerning the status of the various members of the group. The amoeba seen in 1755 by Rosel von Rosenhof was a large freshwater form which was first called 'der kleine *Proteus*' and later a variety of names including *Chaos* and *Proteus*. Whatever this organism was it was not the organism known today as *Amoeba proteus* which was described in 1878. The problem is that there are a number of large freshwater amoebae which differ considerably from one another but these differences were not recognized a century ago. Any historical review is clouded with confusion and it is best to begin with the situation as it exists today. The best known of the large freshwater amoebae is *Amoeba proteus* which is the protozoan commonly studied in schools. *Amoeba proteus* lives in bodies of permanent water and occupying similar habitats are two other amoebae, *A. discoides* and *A. dubia*. All three of these amoebae possess a single nucleus. There are also a number of large amoebae which possess numerous nuclei, for example *Pelomyxa*. As well as these large freshwater amoebae there are also a number of smaller amoebae which occur in ponds and streams. The existence of all these different kinds of amoebae has led to considerable confusion as parts of the life-cycle of one form have been interpreted as belonging to another.

An amoeba reproduces by dividing into two equal parts. It begins by becoming spherical, then the nucleus divides into two. The two halves of the nucleus move apart, the cell then splits down the middle giving two separate amoebae each with a nucleus. This process is known as binary fission and it takes less than an hour to complete.

Some amoebae can reproduce in a different way. The nucleus divides into hundreds of small ones and each becomes surrounded by a little of the cytoplasm and this secretes a tough wall, all within the original cell. The 'cysts', as they are called, are able to survive even if the water they are in dries up. Cysts can be dispersed, by the wind or carried on the feet of animals, to found new populations. Larger cysts are often formed without reproduction taking place, when the whole cell surrounds itself with a thick wall. Some amoebae also reproduce sexually but *Amoeba proteus* has never been seen to do so.

Amoeba proteus lives either on the bottom

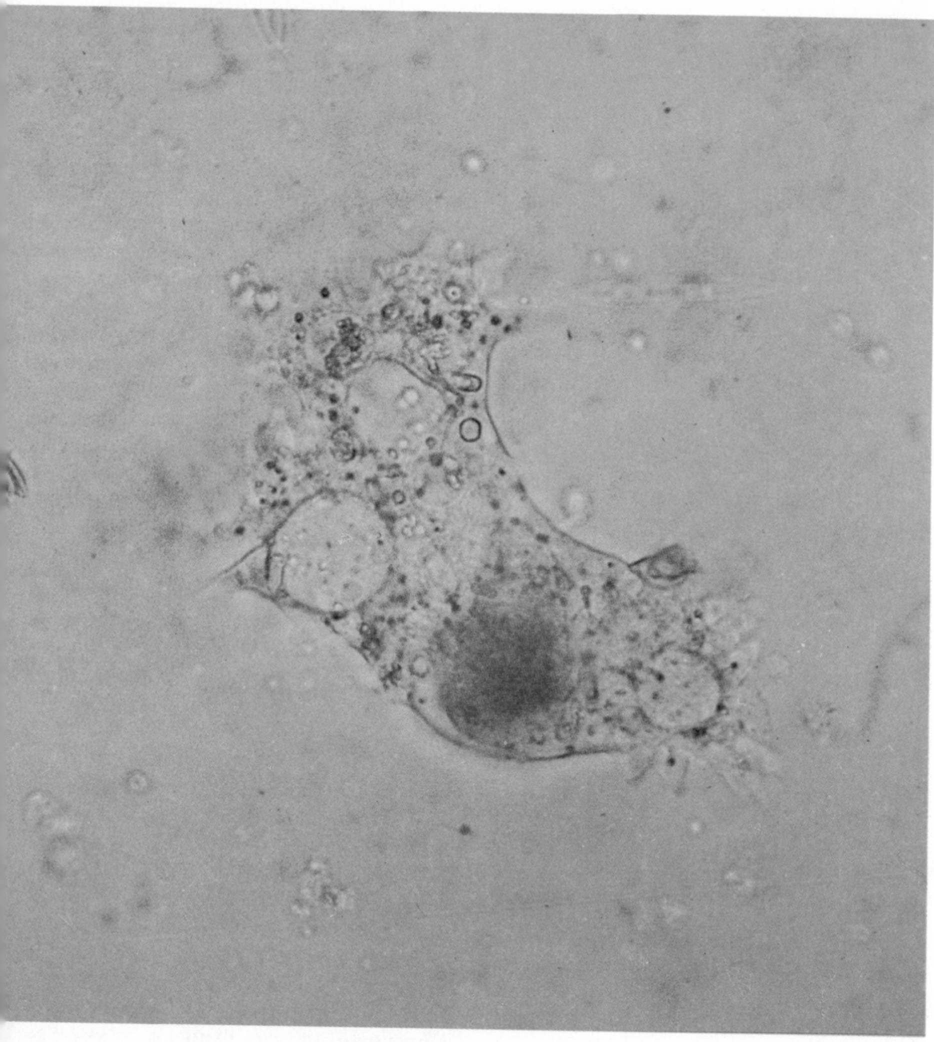

Amoeba viewed under the microscope. The nucleus (the large dark spot), vacuoles (lighter areas, sometimes communicating with the surrounding water), pseudopodia, and dark particles of food, are clearly visible.

of ponds, in the surface film or moving across leaves and other debris. It is a large amoeba measuring over $\frac{1}{2}$ mm in length and moving through a single broad pseudopodium. Its movement is directional and at the posterior end there is a rough region known as a uroid where excretory products accumulate. As *A. proteus* moves it can be seen to be ridged along its length. Somewhere in the amoeba there is a plate-like nucleus. The cytoplasm is of two kinds. The bulk is granular in appearance and is known as endoplasm while at the end of the pseudopodia and elsewhere under the surface of the amoeba there is a clearer layer known as ectoplasm. Within the cytoplasm there is a contractile vacuole, a number of food vacuoles and many crystals.

The amoeba feeds by phagocytosis, that is, it surrounds its food with its pseudopodia and engulfs it. The main food of *A. proteus* consists of ciliates, flagellates and other small organisms such as rotifers and algae. Under laboratory conditions *A. proteus* takes in liquid food substances by a process known as pinocytosis but this probably has no significance in the lives of these amoebae. As it lives in freshwater, *A. proteus* has to deal with the continual problem of getting rid of excess water which it takes in passively by osmosis. Water accumulates in small vacuoles which eventually pass their contents to the contractile vacuole which discharges the water to the outside. It is possible, although unlikely, that the contractile vacuole is concerned in the excretion of waste products, but these are more probably passed out all over the body surface.

Amoeba discoides is very similar to *A. proteus,* but is a little smaller and the body and pseudopodia are not ridged. *Amoeba dubia* is the smallest of the three and differs from them in that the amoeba flows through a number of pseudopodia at the same time. These differences, though slight, are sufficient to allow the expert to distinguish between these amoebae. *Pelomyxa palustris* is quite different. It varies considerably in size, from 0.1–3 mm and contains a large number of nuclei and also numerous food vacuoles usually filled with algae. *P. palustris* moves by means of cytoplasmic waves rather than by pseudopodia which it forms only rarely. It often looks black, but this is not a diagnostic characteristic. Another multinucleate amoeba, *Pelomyxa carolinensis* or *Chaos carolinensis,* the Giant amoeba, measures up to 5 mm in length. It moves by means of pseudopodia which are ridged like those of *A. proteus* and this similarity, which is really a very superficial one, has contributed to much of the confusion existing among students of this group. None of these large freshwater amoebae is known to form cysts and any reports of cyst formation are due to confusion with other amoebae.

A quite separate group of amoebae is known collectively as the Limax amoebae. These are all very small and move by means of a single pseudopodium. All these amoebae form thick-walled cysts. They are found in freshwater and in the soil. The best known Limax amoeba is *Naegleria* which has a flagellated stage in its life-cycle. When the soil is moist it lives as an amoeba, if the soil becomes flooded it grows two flagella and swims in the water, and if the soil dries up the flagella are withdrawn and the animal forms a cyst. Another genus, *Acanthamoeba,* a soil amoeba, has been shown to be pathogenic to mammals if inhaled. This is obviously a case of chance parasitism.

The true parasites belong to the family Endamoebidae. There are a number of genera and species which live in the intestines of invertebrates and vertebrates where they usually live harmlessly and form cysts which are later passed to the exterior and ingested by fresh hosts. The most important member of this family is *Entamoeba histolytica* which causes amoebic dysentery in man.

All amoebae move by means of pseudopodia in a manner known as amoeboid movement, although a few use it rarely (see *Pelomyxa palustris,* above). This kind of movement has received considerable attention because it is common to many cells, for example leucocytes and cancer cells. *Amoeba proteus* has been studied intensively as a model for cell motility, although it has become more and more clear that there is no single kind of amoeboid movement. *A. proteus,* when moving through a single pseudopodium, can be regarded as a tube of cytoplasm in which the central part of the cytoplasm is more fluid than the outer part. The inner part is known as plasmasol and the outer as plasmagel. As *A. proteus* moves the fluid plasmasol squeezes forward to spread out at the anterior end like a fountain. This is the so-called fountain zone. Here the fluid plasmasol becomes less fluid plasmagel and flows backwards. At the posterior end of the amoeba the reverse occurs. These facts are accepted by the majority of investigators in this field, the question as to where the motive force for this movement comes from is still

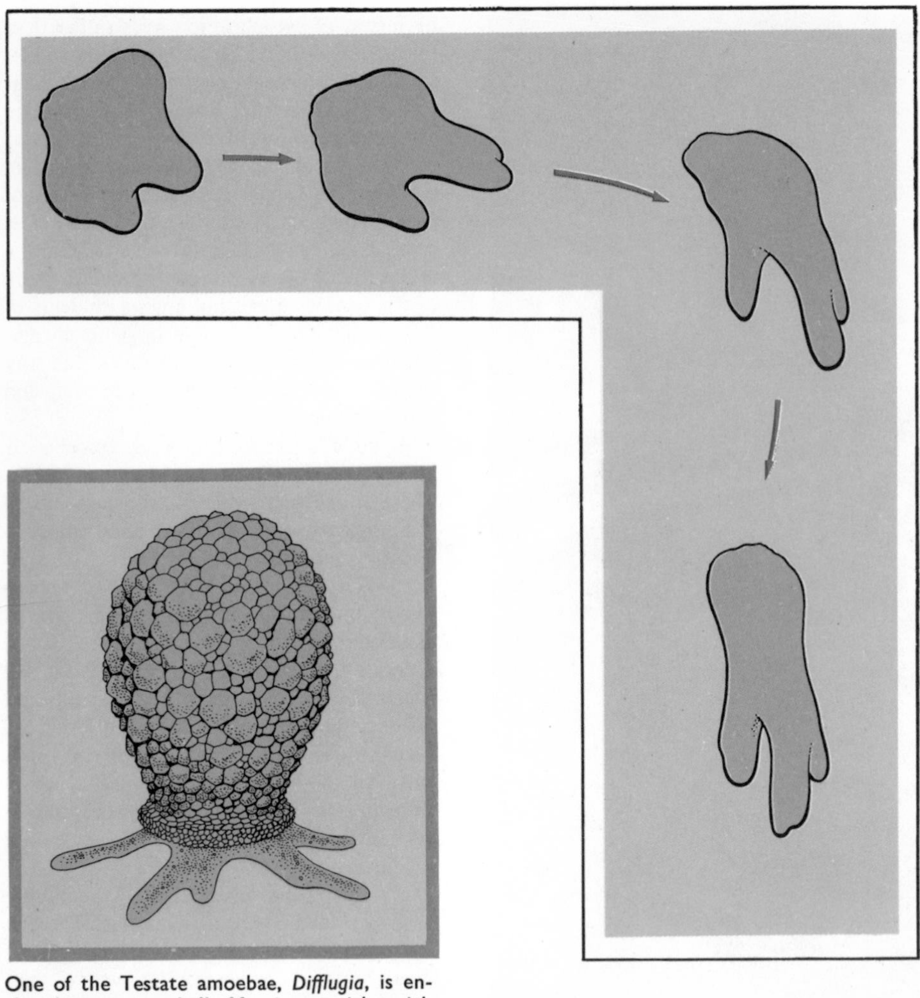

One of the Testate amoebae, *Difflugia*, is enclosed in a test or shell of foreign particles with the pseudopodia protruding through the opening at the bottom.

(Top) Flow of cytoplasm as visualized by fountain stream theory of movement. Bottom left illustrates the theory which assumes that the cytoplasm contracts pulling the animal forwards. (Bottom right) The molecular rachet producing movement which rotates the animal forward.

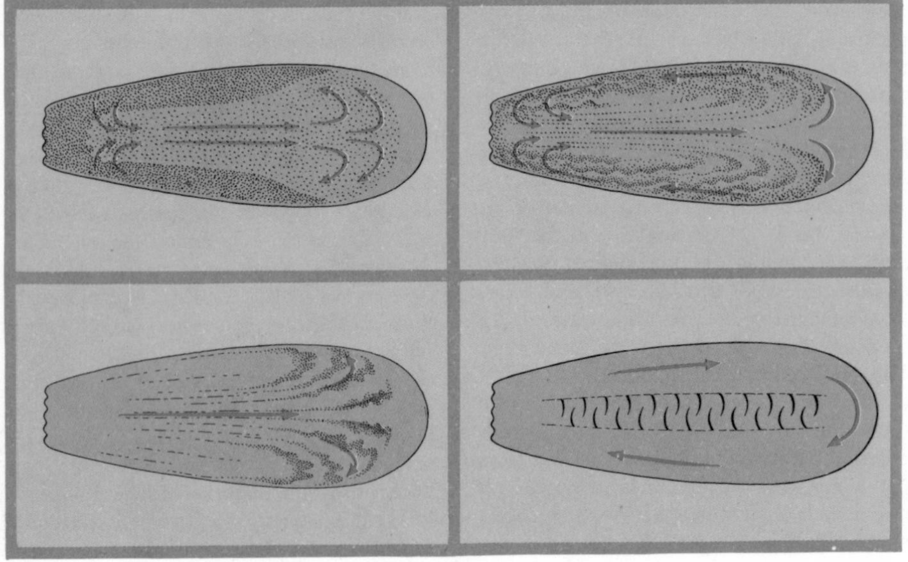

open. The oldest and most widely held theory maintains that the plasmasol consists of folded molecules which straighten out in the fountain zone to fold again at the posterior end of the amoeba. This theory implies that the motive force comes from behind and drives the core of plasmasol forward. Critics of this theory maintain that an amoeba must work from the front and the major alternative theory holds that the plasmasol is pulled forward by the contraction of the plasmagel at the anterior end. Other theories include the possibility of a shearing mechanism which causes the inner molecules to pass forward on chemical ratchets as in muscle contraction. No theory has yet won universal acceptance. ORDER: Amoebida, CLASS: Sarcodina, PHYLUM: Protozoa. F.E.G.C.

AMOEBAE, TESTATE, bottom-dwelling single-celled animals found in freshwater and in damp places such as sphagnum moss. A few are marine. They divide asexually and form cysts under adverse conditions, which allow them to survive periods of drought. They possess a shell, consisting of a single chamber, which distinguishes it from the shells of the Foraminiferida which typically have several chambers. Some shells consist of a pseudochitin secreted by the amoeba itself, as in *Arcella*, but in others the substance produced by the amoeba may be impregnated with foreign substances such as sand grains or other similar particles, as in *Difflugia*. In one genus, *Euglypha*, the shell consists of siliceous plates secreted by the animal itself. ORDER: Testacida, CLASS: Sarcodina, PHYLUM: Protozoa.

AMPHIBIA, a class of vertebrates which contains the newts, salamanders, frogs, toads, and caecilians. The word means 'double life' and refers to the fact that typically these animals spend part of their life in the water and part on land. They are distinguished from the reptiles, their closest relatives, in having a soft moist skin which lacks scales and in having an egg which has no hard shell to prevent it from drying up and which must therefore either be laid in water or in some other way kept moist. They are descended from the first vertebrates to venture onto the land in the Devonian period some 350 million years ago. There are 3,000 species of living amphibians, divided into three orders: Apoda, the caecilians, legless burrowing animals which spend most of their life underground in the tropics; Caudata, amphibians with tails, including the salamanders and newts; Anura, amphibians which lose their tails as they become adult and are adapted for jumping, including frogs and toads.

Black-spined toad *Bufo melanostictus*, with its vocal sac extended.

White's treefrog *Hyla caerulea*, an Australian species, pulls its eye-balls in to aid it in swallowing a mouse.

Amphibians are found throughout the world. The Apoda are found in all tropical countries except Australia, the Celebes, Madagascar and the West Indies. The Caudata are an essentially temperate group particularly well represented in North America. They have penetrated the tropics in South America as far as the Andes but are absent from Africa. The Anura are found all over the world except in permanently frozen areas and on oceanic islands. They are particularly abundant in the tropics.

Amphibians are cold-blooded and most of them become sluggish at low temperatures. Those in temperate regions hibernate during the winter, many frogs burrowing into the mud at the bottoms of ponds while toads usually burrow into moist earth. During hibernation they do not feed and what little respiration is necessary occurs through the skin.

All adult amphibians are carnivorous, most, by virtue of their size, feeding on insects and other invertebrates although large frogs will eat mice. In their turn amphibians form the diet of many animals, snakes and birds being the worst enemies of the adults while many fish and large aquatic insects feed on the eggs and tadpoles.

Respiration. One of the most important changes which must occur for an animal to move from an aquatic to a land-living existence is in its method of respiration, that is, the way it exchanges oxygen and carbon dioxide with the medium around it. Fish breathe by gills and reptiles, birds and mammals with lungs. Amphibians use both these methods and in addition use the skin. The tadpole, for instance, living in the water, has gills. When it changes into the adult and just before it leaves the water the gills are lost and as an adult it breathes by means of lungs as well as through the skin, including the skin of the mouth, the combinations in which these three ways are used varying with the species.

In the Lungless salamanders (Plethodontidae) the adult does not develop lungs and breathes entirely through the skin. The mudpuppies (Proteidae) and the sirens (Sirenidae) develop lungs, but also continue to use gills.

The extent to which frogs and toads use the skin for respiration depends on the kind of life they lead. The Tailed frog *Ascaphus truei* lives in fast-flowing streams containing a lot of dissolved oxygen, so it respires mainly through its skin and its lungs are small.

An important feature of the use of lungs by the amphibians is that they are filled not by movement of the ribs, as in reptiles, birds and mammals, but by movements of the mouth. The floor of the mouth, which contains a plate of cartilage, is raised and lowered by muscles. At the same time the nostrils are opened and closed and air is alternately forced into the lungs and then allowed to escape, pushed out by the elastic nature of the lungs. This is an inefficient way of breathing since only one mouthful of air can pass to the lungs at a time. It may have been the adoption of this method which made it necessary for the ancestral amphibians to develop the use of the skin for respiration. It also helps to account for the relatively small size of the group Amphibia. Those land animals which developed the use of ribs gave rise to the enormous variety of reptiles, birds and mammals—ample evidence of the superiority of the method.

The eye. Another structure which must be modified to allow an animal to live on land is the eye. The outer transparent layer of the eye must be kept moist and amphibians have glands which produce a fluid that continuously bathes the eye and movable eyelids which can cover it completely.

The eye is unequally developed among the amphibians. Many caecilians are blind and in some salamanders which live in caves the eyelids are drawn together and the eye has degenerated. Most amphibians rely on their vision to find their food and to warn them of approaching danger. A frog's eyes are prominently situated on top of its head where they can survey a wide angle. Those frogs which jump at their prey such as Tree frogs can apparently see farther than those foraging at ground level, and these can see farther than toads, which stalk their prey. Those frogs which feed at night often have large eyes and show an expansion of the pupil in the dark in the same way that a cat's eye does.

The voice. Some amphibians have a voice. The caecilians are voiceless and the salamanders also lack vocal cords although some of them can manage a faint squeaking sound. The vocal powers of frogs and toads are, however, well known. The nightly chorus during the breeding season is one of the most

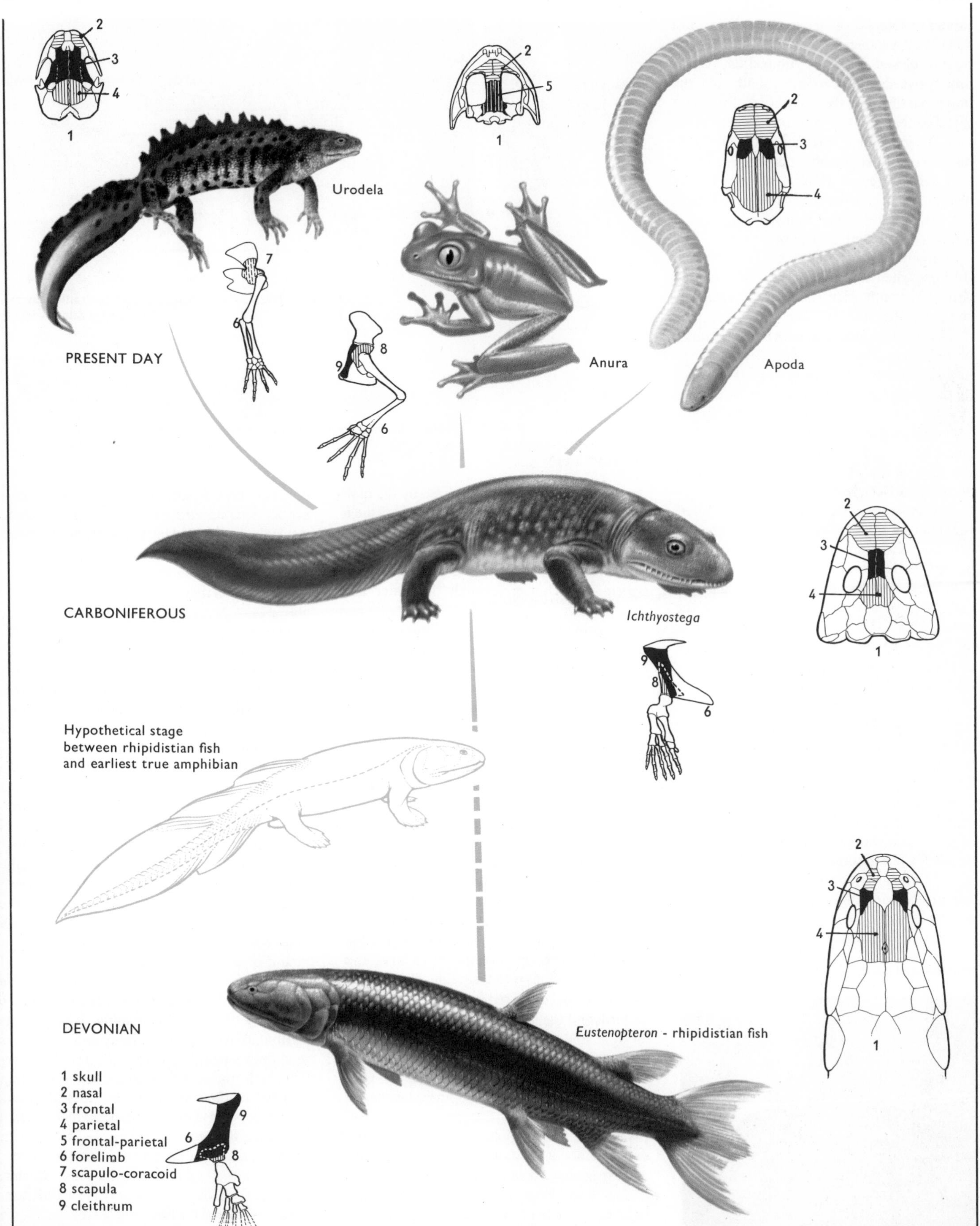

PRESENT DAY

Urodela

Anura

Apoda

CARBONIFEROUS

Ichthyostega

Hypothetical stage
between rhipidistian fish
and earliest true amphibian

DEVONIAN

Eustenopteron - rhipidistian fish

1 skull
2 nasal
3 frontal
4 parietal
5 frontal-parietal
6 forelimb
7 scapulo-coracoid
8 scapula
9 cleithrum

During the evolution of Amphibia there have been two major events, the evolution from rhipidistian fish of a form, *Ichthyostega*, able to walk on land, and the separation of the three well defined groups living today. The main structural changes in the skull and forelimb which accompanied these events are shown.

familiar sounds of tropical regions. The sound is produced with the mouth and nostrils closed and air is pumped backwards and forwards between the mouth and the lungs, passing over the vocal cords. Frogs can therefore call equally well underwater as on land. There is great variation in the pitch and duration of the sound and most species have a very distinctive call which is a useful clue in identification. In most species only the male is able to call, the sound being used to attract females during the breeding season.

Many frogs have another kind of cry which they use when startled or seized. It is uttered with the mouth wide open and is usually a shrill squeal or scream.

The ear. In connection with the importance of the voice the ear is well developed. In frogs and toads the ear drum is on the surface of the body and can usually be seen as a circular area of the skin, usually lightly coloured, just behind the eye. Salamanders have no ear drum and can only detect vibrations transmitted to the skull through the bones of the front legs.

Reproduction. One of the most characteristic features of amphibians is their method of breeding. Most are able to breed for only a limited period each year. Usually this is controlled by the seasons. In temperate regions frogs and salamanders breed in the spring while in the tropics most frogs breed at the beginning of the rainy season. In some forms it may be more closely controlled by the weather. The Spadefoot toad *Scaphiopus* of dry desert regions in North America and the water-holding frogs of the Australian deserts are able to breed whenever the infrequent and irregular rainstorms have formed temporary pools.

Among the frogs and toads the female is usually attracted to the male by his croaking. In some salamanders the female is attracted by smell while in some, the European Smooth newt *Triturus vulgaris*, for example, the brightly coloured male performs a courtship display in front of the female.

The eggs are usually laid in the water. In frogs and toads they are fertilized by the male after they have left the female's body. This is accomplished by the male clinging onto the female's back, known as *amplexus. As the eggs are released by the female the male ejects sperm which swim through the water and fertilize them.

In primitive salamanders fertilization is also external but in most others it is internal. The male deposits the sperm on the bottom of the pond inside little protective packets or spermatophores. The female picks these up with the lips of her cloaca. Inside the cloaca the protective coat dissolves and the sperm fertilize the eggs as they pass to the outside.

Amphibian eggs are protected in the water by a thick layer of jelly either round a large mass of eggs or round each one. The number of eggs laid varies with the size of the animal and according to whether they are laid in sheltered or exposed places. Many frogs lay as many as 20,000 eggs at a time. In general, salamanders lay fewer eggs than do frogs.

The development of amphibians occurs in two stages. The egg develops into a larva and the larva develops into the adult. The egg has little yolk, as compared with that of a reptile or bird, and the larva must find its own food. In frogs and toads the larva or tadpole looks very different from the adult while in salamanders it is similar in appearance. The time the different stages of development last varies considerably. In the European frog *Rana temporaria* the tadpole hatches out of the egg after about 14 days and changes into an adult frog after about 3 months.

The Rain frogs *Breviceps* of Africa lay their eggs on land and the tadpole stage is passed within the egg, young adult frogs emerging after about five weeks. In the Spadefoot toad, whose eggs are laid in temporary pools, the tadpoles hatch after only two days. In some European newts of the genus *Salamandra* the eggs are retained inside the female and the larvae do not emerge until they are almost ready to change into adults. Amphibians are usually able to start breeding when they are from one to four years old.

The life span of most amphibians is not known with certainty. Common toads of Europe *Bufo bufo* have lived in captivity for 36 years and Tree frogs for 22 years although they probably do not live as long as this in the wild.

The skin. Like the fish and other vertebrates the skin of amphibians is composed of two parts, an outer epidermis and an inner dermis, but unlike that of a fish the outer part of the epidermis is composed of a layer of dead cells which on land helps to prevent the loss of too much moisture. As the animal grows this outer dead skin is cast off in the same way that snakes and other reptiles shed their skin, the difference being that the skin of amphibians is without scales except for the minute ones embedded in the skin of some caecilians.

The skin contains two kinds of glands. There are the mucous glands, which are distributed over the whole body and supply a clear fluid which keeps the skin moist. It is this which makes a frog slimy to the touch. Modified mucous glands on the toes of Tree frogs produce a sticky substance which helps them cling to vertical surfaces. In the Lungless salamanders (Plethodontidae) the male has a patch of glands on the chin which produces an odour that attracts the female to him at the start of the breeding season.

The second kind of gland is the poison glands which are particularly common in terrestrial amphibians. The so-called 'warts' of toads are in fact masses of these poison

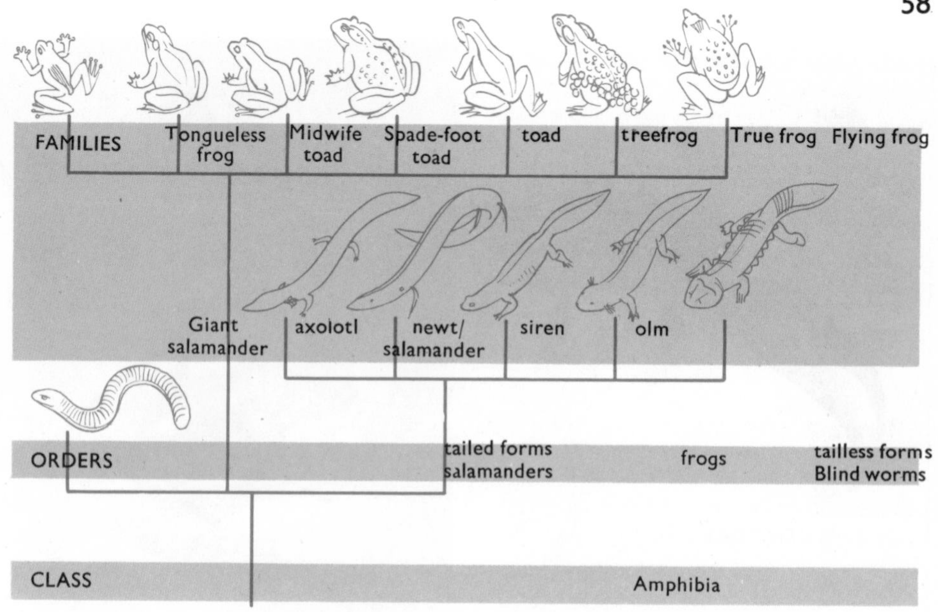

Geneological tree of the Amphibia. From the ancestral *Ichthyostega*-stock have diverged three main branches: the limbless caecilians (right), the tailed salamanders and newts, and the tailless frogs and toads (top).

Male Crested newt, *Triturus cristatus*, of Europe.

glands. When the animal is frightened they produce a milky fluid which is poisonous to other animals. A dog which has seized a toad in its mouth usually drops it quickly and shows signs of discomfort for some time afterwards. Many amphibians which are poisonous are also brightly coloured, thus warning other animals of their unsuitability as food. The most poisonous frogs belong to the family Dendrobatidae. They are found in the forests of South America and are used by the Indians to obtain poison for the tips of their arrows.

Many amphibians are brightly coloured and the different colours are produced by different arrangements of three kinds of pigment cell or chromatophore in the skin. Many frogs, particularly Tree frogs, are able to change colour quite rapidly. This is brought about by some of the chromatophores expanding and spreading the pigment through the skin while others contract. The European Tree frog *Hyla arborea,* which is usually pale green, can vary from almost white to very dark green.

The tongue. Most amphibians possess a well-developed muscular tongue while fish do not. It is usually attached at the front of the mouth with the main part folded back. It is kept sticky by glands in the mouth and can be flicked out rapidly to catch the prey. A tongue is of little use in the water and some aquatic salamanders have only a fleshy fold on the floor of the mouth, while some toads which spend most of their life in water have lost the tongue altogether.

Skeleton. Although salamanders are similar in general appearance to ancient forms, having a long body with four small limbs and a large tail, this resemblance is superficial. The skeleton has undergone many modifications. For example, the bones of the skull are reduced and in parts of the skeleton bone is replaced by cartilage. The number of bones in the backbone varies, being greatest in those salamanders which never leave the water and least in those which spend most of their life on land.

The edible frog, of Europe.

The natterjack or running toad of Europe.

The Apoda have a thin worm-like body adapted to their burrowing mode of life. The limbs and their girdles are completely missing and the tail is very short. The skull is heavily built and protects the brain from damage as the head is pushed into the ground. The backbone consists of a large number of vertebrae, in some species there are as many as 200–300 bones, which makes the body very flexible.

The skeleton of the frogs and toads is well-adapted to their jumping habits. The tail, which would be in the way when jumping, is lost and the hind limbs, which provide the propulsive force, are lengthened. The hip girdle is firmly attached to the backbone which is very short and rigid, having only nine vertebrae. The forelimbs and the shoulder girdle are strengthened to withstand the shock of landing.

It can be seen that it is incorrect to think of modern amphibians as being intermediate between fish and reptiles. They are very different from their ancestors which formed the actual link.

Fossil amphibians. The group from which the earliest amphibians developed was the Crossopterygii. These were freshwater fishes which gave rise to several different groups from the Devonian period onwards. In one of these, the Rhipidistia, can be found all the characters necessary in an amphibian an-

A pair of brilliantly coloured frogs *Atelopus varius* of tropical America.

cestor. For instance, the fins had fleshy lobes whose skeleton had essentially the same arrangement of bones as is found in tetrapod limbs while the bones of the skull were also comparable with those of the earliest amphibians.

The oldest known fossil which can definitely be classified as amphibian is *Ichthyostega* from the Devonian deposits in Greenland. This was about 3 ft (90 cm) long and in some ways resembled a fish, in others an amphibian. Nearly half the body comprised a large tail with a fish-like fin. The limbs, however, were well developed, rather short but certainly capable of supporting the animal.

It is not known why these earliest amphibians ventured onto the land. It is suggested it was to crawl to the next pool when the one in which they were living dried up. Having done this they would perhaps stay on the land for longer and longer periods until eventually they only returned to water to breed.

Ichthyostega is contained in the Labyrinthodontia, one of the two groups into which the extinct amphibians are divided. Most labyrinthodonts were large sprawling animals probably resembling crocodiles. They flourished in the Carboniferous and a few survived into the Triassic. It was from labyrinthodonts that the reptiles evolved.

The second group was the Lepospondyli. These were generally smaller animals and several forms had lost the limbs and were snakelike in appearance. They survived until the beginning of the Permian period and probably gave rise to the modern amphibians although since fossils of modern types of amphibians have not been found earlier than the Triassic there is a gap in the fossil record and the actual ancestry of the modern forms cannot be determined.

As far as man is concerned amphibians are a very inoffensive group. None of them is dangerous or poisonous to man and none of them carries disease. They are not pests of crops or in the house and, in fact, are useful in the enormous number of insects they eat. They have little commercial value. In some countries the back legs of some large frogs are eaten as a delicacy, and the platanna or Clawed toad *Xenopus laevis* is well-known for its use in pregnancy testing. M.E.D.

AMPHICOELA, a suborder of amphibians with amphicoelous vertebrae, considered to be primitive. The vertebrae, which are quite unlike those of any other amphibian group, are concave at each end. There is only one family with two genera, *Leiopelma* from New Zealand, with three species, and *Ascaphus* of the North American and southwestern Canada known only from a single species. All are small seldom exceeding 2 in (5 cm) in length. They live in cool places. Archey's frog *Leiopelma archeyi* lays its eggs under stones and its larvae develop within the egg capsule, so there is no free-swimming tadpole. The young hatch as miniature frogs, require no surface water but move around in the damp earth and vegetation. Hochstetter's frog *L. hochstetteri* lays its eggs in small tunnels close to or sloping into water. Usually the male stands guard over the eggs. The embryos

Diagram illustrating the life-history of a frog. 1) Eggs laid in water release tadpoles with external gills (3). These are later lost and limbs grow out, first the hindlimbs, then the forelimbs (4-6). The tail is gradually absorbed as the tadpole changes to the froglet (6-7), which emerges onto land (7) where it will take three years to reach sexual maturity.

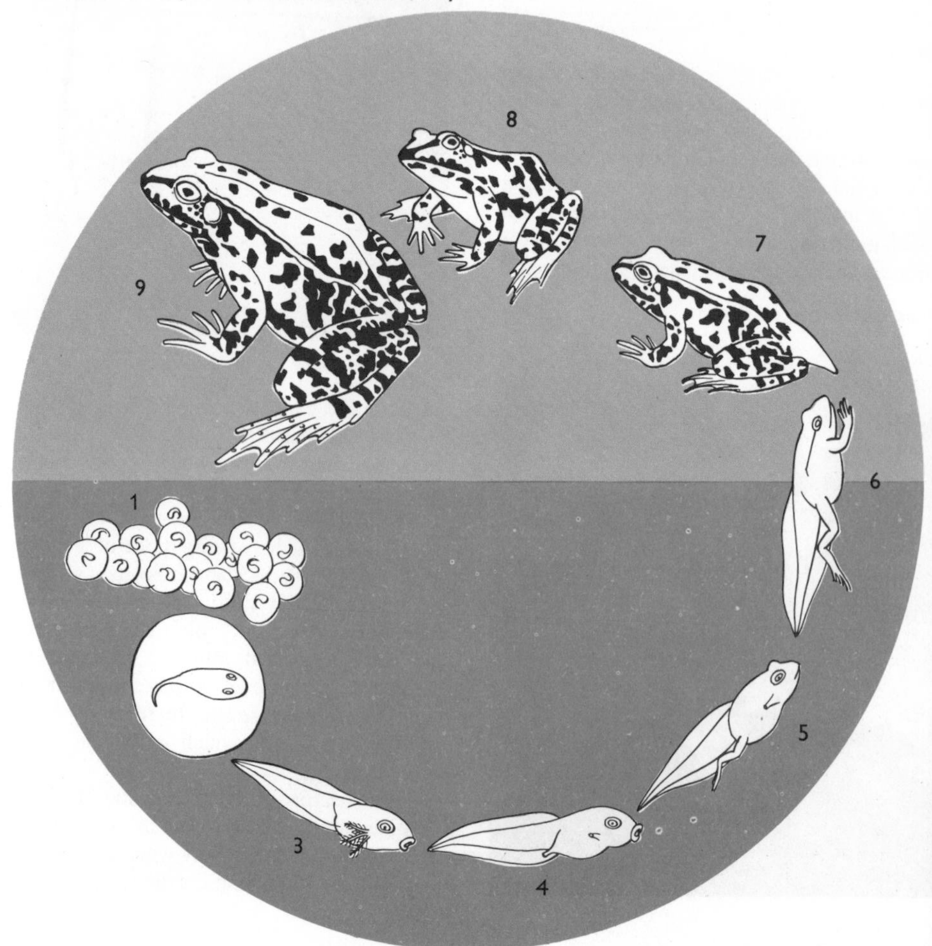

develop a long tail which is used to rupture the egg capsule and allow the larva to escape. The larva respires through the skin of the abdomen and the tail until the lungs develop sometime after hatching.

The Tailed frog *Ascaphus truei* is so called because it has a posterior projection which superficially resembles a tail. It is, however, part of the cloaca, the chamber into which the gut and urino-genital systems empty, so it forms a common exit for both reproductive and excretory matter. The cloacal projection in the Tailed frog is used to insert the sperm into the female during mating, which is unique among frogs. Tailed frogs are voiceless and this is correlated with their life in swift-moving streams where a call would be unheard because of the noise of the water. The tadpoles become attached to rocks soon after hatching by a triangular adhesive organ which prevents them from being carried away by the swift currents. Tailed frogs can endure cold and are usually found in areas where the water temperature does not exceed 40°F (5°C) even on a summer's day. In captivity they need to be kept in a refrigerator. FAMILY: Ascaphidae, ORDER: Anura, CLASS: Amphibia. R.L.

AMPHIOXUS, another name for the *lancelet, the scientific name of which was originally *Amphioxus,* which became anglicized. The lancelet is now named *Branchiostoma*. It is a primitive chordate living in shallow seas throughout the world, and it probably resembles an early stage in the evolution of vertebrates.

A typical caecilian, legless amphibian.

The Striped salamander *Salamandra salamandra.*

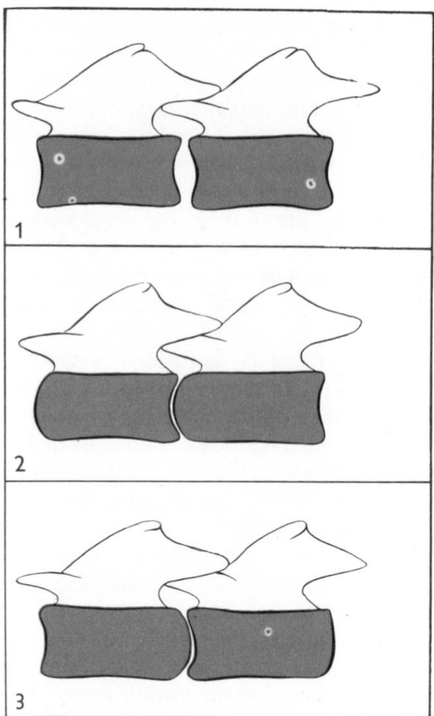

The vertebrae of Amphibia are of three types: 1. amphicoelous (Greek *koilos* = hollow) in which the centra (in red) are concave (or hollow) each end; 2. opisthocoelous, concave behind; and 3. procoelous, concave in front.

AMPHIPODA, with over 3,600 species from the seas and fresh waters of the world, the order is one of the most successful and dominant of the Crustacea. They are essentially marine *benthic organisms ranging from the upper intertidal areas to a depth of over 5,000 fathoms (9–10,000 m) in the *abyssal trenches of the Philippines and Tonga. A number have adopted a truly pelagic existence in the open waters of the seas and oceans. The benthic forms extend through estuaries into freshwater and are abundant in streams, rivers, pools and lakes to an altitude of 13,000 ft (4,000 m). A remarkable population occurs in Lake Baikal in Siberia with over 300 species which have not been found in any other locality. Other freshwater forms are found in deep wells and caves; they are blind and colourless.

The amphipods are, like the Isopoda to which they are distantly related, peracaridian (superorder Peracarida) forms in which the female develops the young within a brood-pouch beneath the thorax. They are regarded as having evolved from a malacostracan ancestor (subclass Malacostraca) at an early period to give a wide variety of form between the four suborders Gammaridea, Hyperiidea, Caprellidea and Ingolfiellidea.

The suborder Gammaridea contains over 3,000 species distributed over 57 families indicative of vast diversity of form. The morphological range, however, is small so that the differences between species, genera and families are often based on a number of apparently trivial characters. These small differences are associated with ecological and habitat differences which indicate fundamental physiological differences. The Gammaridea are regarded as the typical amphipods. The body which is without a carapace, shows the usual division into head, thorax and abdomen. The first thoracic segment is fused to the head leaving seven free thoracic segments. The six abdominal segments are also distinct and the body terminates in a free and independent last segment. The body is usually flattened from side to side so that in section it is deeply arched and ventrally grooved. The development of this groove and deeply arched body means that the thoracic legs cannot extend sideways to support the body in a vertical position, as they do in isopods. The legs hang vertically downwards and give no stability for a vertical stance. Thus amphipods lie on their sides and drag themselves over the substratum by the last five pairs of legs assisted in water by the pleopods of the abdomen. The weak powers of walking are often compensated by adoption of methods of living which involve little walking. Thus some climb and scramble over seaweeds, others burrow into sand or mud or live in permanent burrows, others become pelagic. *Chelura tenebrans* is a woodborer.

The head carries a pair of sessile eyes and well-developed antennules and antennae which may show sex differences. The mouthparts consist of biting mandibles, a pair of well-developed maxillules and generally reduced maxillae. The maxillipeds of the first thoracic segment are fused at their base and are closely applied to the other mouthparts and function with them. Typically feeding is on large particles but various methods are found.

The first two pairs of thoracic legs are generally modified for prehension and referred to as gnathopods. They are variously modified for many functions, often assist in the feeding process and are better developed in the male being also used in copulation. Of the remaining five pairs, which are ambulatory, the first two, like the gnathopods, point forwards with backwardly directed terminal claws and the last three pairs are directed backwards with forwardly directed terminal claws. Each of the last six pairs of legs carry from their most basal joints thin flat lamellar expansions which function as gills. Each shows afferent blood channels receiving de-oxygenated blood from a ventral sinus and returning oxygenated blood along efferent channels direct to the heart. The legs of segments three to six also carry the flat lamellar oostegites in the female which by overlapping form the brood-pouch.

The abdominal appendages fall into two distinct groups. The first three pairs are typical pleopods (Gk *plein*—swim; *pous*—foot) fringed with long setae. Each pair is linked together with coupling hooks and successive pairs beat in a metachronial rhythm in which the beat of each pair occurs earlier than that of the one behind it and later than the one in front of it. The result is the creation of a current of water through the ventral groove. This current enters the groove from directly in front of the body over the mouthparts and also laterally from openings between the limbs. The current aerates the gills for respiration and also the developing embryos in the brood-pouch of the female. In some forms it carries particles of food on to the mouthparts. It is also the main propulsive force in swimming. The last three pairs are the uropods (Gk *oura*—tail) which are directed backwards. The first two pairs particularly are stout appendages and, by pushing against the substratum, can assist in locomotion. The third pair may also assist in this way but they may be modified to act as rudders. The body of a typical gammarid is flexed between the third and fourth thoracic segments. It can be suddenly extended into a straight line by muscular action for forward spurts through the water or held extended for swimming. Some amphipods, e.g. *Haustorius,* swim on their backs and steer with the last pair of legs.

The feeding methods of amphipods show great variety. Fundamentally they may be regarded as macrophagous, e.g. the common species of *Gammarus* of intertidal shores which pick up pieces of organic detritus, mainly seaweed, and rasp off portions with their mouthparts. They are scavengers, either vegetarian or omnivorous. *Corophium volutator* which builds U-shaped tubes in the fine soils of estuaries is a selective deposit feeder. When feeding on the surface of the soil it scoops up the mud with its gnathopods and from it selects particles of organic matter for transfer to the mandibles. When feeding in its burrow the respiratory current through the tube also functions as a feeding current carrying with it small particles of organic matter which are filtered off by a fringe of setae on the second gnathopods. The species of *Bathyporeia* which burrow into the sands of the sea shore select sand grains from those carried in suspension in the respiratory current as it passes over the mouthparts. Each grain is rapidly revolved over the mouthparts and any organic matter on its surface, e.g. harpacticid copepods, removed and passed to the mouth. In *Haustorius* which is also a sand-burrower the maxilla has been secondarily developed to produce a current of water and to act as a filter for minute particles which are removed by the maxillipeds and passed to the mouth. It can also feed by picking up large particles. *Haploops tubicola,* which builds tubes of mud particles on the sea floor in shallow waters, extends its antennae, which form a meshwork acting as a filter, into the water. The meshwork is always directed to face the current. Other species of amphipods show many modifications of the general methods described above.

The breeding of amphipods is typically peracaridian. In species in which reproduction has been observed the male lies across the body of the female and passes sperm into the brood-pouch. The pair separate and the female immediately lays eggs into the pouch. Fertilization follows immediately. Embryonic development gives a young larva which is a miniature of the adult. The number of eggs in each brood is very variable in the many species; figures from 2–750 have been recorded usually with smaller numbers in fresh-water than in marine forms. It is usual for more than one brood to be produced each year. The first brood in the spring arises from overwintering young females. This brood matures to give further broods throughout the summer and an autumn brood which survives the winter.

A succession of species living in fully marine to freshwater conditions may be traced through estuaries. At low water and in the infra-littoral *Gammarus locusta* occurs which can withstand a salinity range of 35–28%. In the intertidal area *Marinogammarus obtusatus* occurs in the lower half of the area and is a markedly stenohaline form intolerant of brackish-water conditions. *M. marinus* is a mid-tidal form with a salinity range of 35–10% and thus tolerates brackish water. *Gammarus zaddachi salinus* is found over a range of 31–4% but will not tolerate freshwater. *G. z. zaddachi* and *G. duebini* will tolerate freshwater and may be found in rivers. They have a salinity range of 15–0%. *G. pulex* is entirely adapted to freshwater. It rapidly excretes the water which it inevitably absorbs. It also shows an enlarged excretory organ compared with marine forms which is probably associated with the re-absorption of ions to maintain ionic equilibrium.

The Hyperiidea containing over 300

The sandhopper *Orchestria gammarella,* nearly twice natural size, lives among small red seaweeds and tiny pebbles.

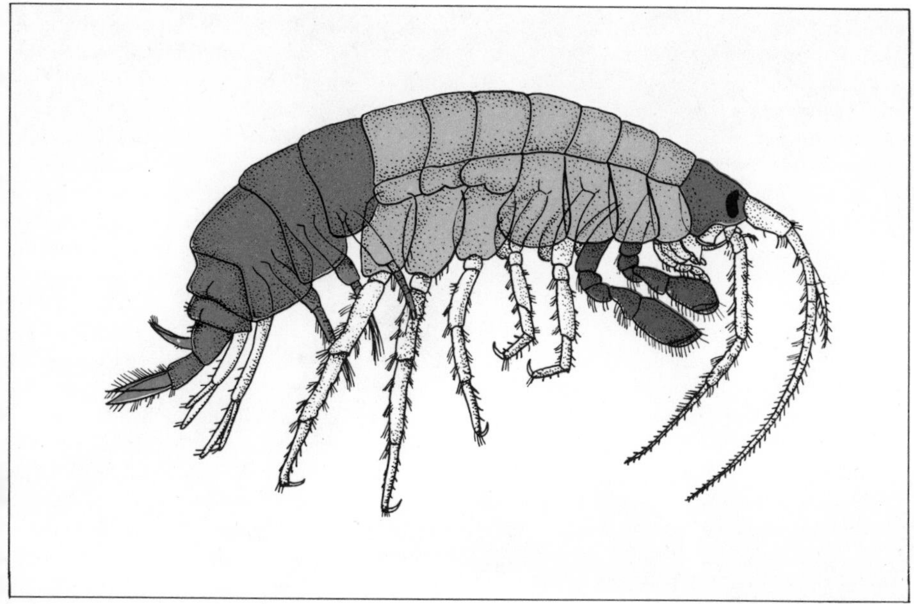

A typical amphipod showing the main divisions of the body: head (red), thorax (yellow) and abdomen (brown), with thoracic limbs (purple) and abdominal limbs (blue).

species are characterized in most forms by the extensive development of the eyes which take up the sides of the head. The eyes are usually divided into two parts for vision into the water below, as well as into the water above, the body. This may aid predation. The gnathopods are small and there are well-developed claws on some of the other legs which are all otherwise prehensile. They are pelagic forms with oily bodies which are rich in vitamin A. They occur in enormous numbers in the oceans of the world and are a source of food for fishes, seals and whales. As is well known for pelagic macroplankton in general, the hyperids perform vertical diurnal migrations. They begin to rise to the surface waters at nightfall and to return to deeper waters at daybreak. The propulsive mechanism to raise them upwards is the repeated flexure of the abdomen against the water. This migration has been shown to occur in *Parathemisto gracilipes* which is a neritic water form and *P. gaudichaudi*, over 1 in (30–35 mm) long, an oceanic species of the colder waters of the northern and southern oceans. These two species, as hyperids in general, are carnivorous, feeding on the other living species of the macroplankton which they are well adapted to capture. Another hyperid *Hyperia galba* with jade green eyes may often be found in the sub-genital pits of jellyfish, e.g. *Rhizostoma octopus*. It feeds by rasping the tissues of the pit. The remarkable *Phronima sedentaria* is found inside the empty test of salps, e.g. *Pyrosoma*. It eats the living zooids retaining the dead test which functions as a protective cover. By movements of the pleopods and abdominal flexure a current of water is drawn through the test which carries with it particles of living food. The female, after release of the brood, leaves the test but continues to push it through the water as the young larvae develop.

The Caprellidea contain the caprellids and the cyamids. The caprellids, e.g. *Caprella*, are often referred to as the Skeleton or Ghost shrimps. They depart from the gammarid form by having two thoracic segments fused to the head, and by considerable reduction of body parts. The coxal plates are absent and in many genera the legs on the fourth and fifth segments. The abdomen is very reduced and unsegmented with reduced or vestigial appendages. They have lost the power of swimming and the typical ventral groove. They are found in large numbers scrambling about on hydroids and seaweeds. Here they feed in any opportune way. They capture live copepods by lying in wait and recognize a passing animal by the water currents it creates. The caprellid has a sense organ on its antennule which is sensitive to small water movements and it is probable that it can see it with its well-marked eyes. The second gnathopod is shot out to capture the prey, which is held in front of the mouthparts and portions are bitten off by the first gnathopods. Some forms also feed on diatoms, dinoflagellates and detritus which they scrape up from the substratum. They respire through the usual amphipodan gill and brood their young in pouches.

The Ingolfiellidae are a small group of seven species within one genus. They are small and blind, with elongated bodies in which only the fourth and fifth pairs of abdominal appendages are developed. The seven species are remarkable in their wide geographical distribution and habitat. They range from shallow water in coral sands and the temperate waters of the English Channel to ocean depths and cave pools. CLASS: Crustacea, PHYLUM: Arthropoda. E.E.W.

AMPHISBAENIDS, or worm-lizards represented by some 125 species in Africa, South America and Mexico. One species of the genus *Blanus* is found in Europe; one *Rhineura* in the United States and several in the West Indies. Three species of *Bipes*, found in Mexico and Lower California, are unique among the amphisbaenids in having diminutive, but well developed forelegs. With this exception all worm-lizards present essentially identical features. They closely resemble earthworms in their long and cylindrical body, with the integument arranged in rings separated by shallow grooves. Their movement, unlike that of snakes or legless lizards, is in a straight line and the animal can move backwards or forwards with equal ease. There are no external ear openings, the eyes are covered with scales and, when visible, appear as dark spots. Only the left lung is present. The exact relationships of worm-lizards are not clear. Although long grouped with reptiles, there is considerable doubt whether these animals actually are lizards or, for that matter, reptiles.

Amphisbaenids are inoffensive and spend their lives in underground burrows, beneath forest litter or in the nests of ants and termites. Association with ant colonies is common, and in parts of South America, the local peoples (which believe the animal to be a venomous snake) refer to it as *mai das saubas* or 'mother of ants'. Little is known of the feeding habits of these animals, examination of the stomach contents revealing little other than ants and termites. Captive examples of the large, tropical American species *Amphisbaena alba*, however, readily accept from a dish shreds of meat mixed with beaten raw egg yolks. The same species will also actively chase and consume live crickets. *Rhineura* feeds on small spiders and earthworms.

Both oviparous and ovoviviparous species are known, but the majority of species probably lay eggs, live births being recorded for only a few African species.

Completely defenceless when exposed, worm-lizards resort to a ruse, often used by animals, of imitating something else. Thus, several species raise the tail from the ground and by waving it about give a reasonable impression of an alert snake. Such behaviour is apparently successful for many native peoples consider the animals venomous or at least aggressive.

Modern worm-lizards appear to have remained essentially unchanged since they first appeared many millions of years ago. The fossil record dates to the Eocene. Then as now, most of them were small animals, seldom more than 1 ft (30 cm) in length. Several species attain a greater size, however. *Amphisbaena alba*, previously mentioned, reaches a length of 18 in (46 cm) as does *A.*

Amphiuma, North American salamander, almost legless.

fuliginosa, also from South America. *Monopeltis,* an African genus, is considered to be the largest known, attaining a length in excess of 2 ft (60 cm). FAMILY Amphisbaenidae, ORDER: Squamata, CLASS: Reptilia. J.M.M.

AMPHIUMAS, among the largest amphibians in the world, also called 'Conger eels', 'Congo eels or snakes', 'Ditch eels' or 'Lamper eels' depending on the region and individual whim. The same names are applied without much discrimination to other elongated aquatic animals, whether they be true eels, sirens, or true lampreys. To avoid confusion, the scientific name Amphiuma is used as the common name.

The amphiumas are elongated salamanders. The three very similar species are distinct enough from all other salamanders to be placed in a separate family Amphiumidae. Superficially they resemble eels in size, proportions and colour and it is easy to understand how the two could be confused, particularly if seen moving through a mass of weeds. The movements, however, are different. Amphiumas are more apt to crawl slowly and thrash wildly when disturbed. They lack the smooth grace of true eels.

Amphiumas have a cylindrical body, averaging about 24 in (60 cm) and may reach 46 in (116 cm). The tail, if undamaged, is approximately $\frac{1}{4}$ the total length and tapers to a point. The most distinctive anatomical feature is the presence of two pairs of small legs, with 1–3 toes according to species, which are totally useless for propulsion. The head is long, pointed and compressed from the top. The colour is dark, uniformly brownish grey or slate grey above and lighter below. In contrast to the eel, there are no gill openings or fins behind the head, and no external gills as in the sirens. Vision is probably very poor, the eyes being very small.

Because of the close similarity of all amphiumas they were formerly considered to belong to one species *Amphiuma means.* Now three species are recognized. The least known is the One-toed amphiuma *Amphiuma pholeter* which was described only in 1964. This is the most degenerate of the family, being the nearest to becoming blind and legless. It does not seem to attain as large a size as the other two. The head is shorter, more rounded, with even smaller eyes. The limbs are proportionally shorter, and have only one digit. It is brownish grey, with little difference in shade from top to bottom but usually there are lighter mottlings. It is presumed that the range of the One-toed amphiuma extends through the swamplands of Florida's west coast. The Two-toed amphiuma *Amphiuma means,* with two toes on each limb, is larger, up to 36 in (90 cm) long. Its dark grey colour changes gradually to the lighter grey below. It ranges along the coasts from Virginia through all of Florida and west through Southern Mississippi. The Three-toed amphiuma *Amphiuma tridactylum,* up to 40 in (100 cm), is usually brownish grey above and lighter grey below, with an abrupt transition between the two. It has three toes on each limb. Its range extends up the Mississippi Valley to the southern border of Illinois and west into eastern Texas.

Amphiumas are found in warm, weedy, quiet bodies of water in the lowlands of southeastern and gulf-coastal plains of the United States and into the Mississippi Valley as far north as Missouri. They are mostly active at night searching for small aquatic animals. Besides soft-bodied prey like worms and insect nymphs, their powerful jaws enable them to crush snails and subdue crayfish. An occasional frog or fish is caught with a surprisingly fast strike. They may occasionally come out on land on wet nights.

Little is known of the reproductive habits, courtship if any and mating procedures being unrecorded but fertilization is internal. In the Two-toed amphiuma fairly large elliptical eggs, $\frac{1}{3}$ in (8 mm) in diameter, are extruded like a row of beads connected by a continuous gelatinous string. The eggs may number 48 or more and are sometimes guarded by the female who stays with them in a sheltered hollow during the long incubation period of several months. The eggs hatch in about five months into 2 in (5 cm) long larvae which metamorphose and lose their external gills when 3 in (7·5 cm). During growth the legs, which start off well developed, fail to keep pace with the rest of the body.

Amphiumas adapt well to captivity, being long-lived and hardy and learning to feed readily from the hand even during the daytime. Nevertheless, they are not very popular either as public exhibits or as pets. They hardly ever move but tend to fight each other and other animals and occasionally bite when handled. The natural enemies of the amphiuma are the Rainbow snake *Abastor erythrogrammus* and the Mud snake *Farancia abacura*. Both are found in the same area as the amphiuma, the distribution of the Mud snake in particular being practically the same as that of the amphiuma and it may largely depend on amphiumas for food. FAMILY: Amphiumidae, ORDER: Caudata, CLASS: Amphibia. E.L.J.

AMPLEXUS. In mating the male frog or toad clasps the female with the forelegs around her body. The two are then said to be in amplexus. As the male clings on the female's back this brings his cloaca above hers, so that as her eggs are laid he fertilizes them. He clasps her either just in front of her hindlimbs, in the more primitive families, or behind the forelimbs in the other families. The amplexus is a reflex action and during the breeding season a male will automatically clasp anything that moves, such as a fish or another male. In most species the male gives a grunt or buzzing sound if another male tries to clasp him. It signals it is a male. If a female which has laid her eggs is clasped again the hold is not usually maintained because the female's body is not swollen with eggs—an important factor in causing the male frog to remain in amplexus.

The male in most species has a patch of spines on the first finger which swells during the breeding season and helps him retain his grip. In some species there are similar patches on the upper arm or on the chest. The forearm muscles of male frogs are larger than those of females.

Male and female of the Common frog *Rana temporaria*, of Europe, in amplexus.

ANACONDA *Eunectes murinus*, the largest of the non-venomous snake family Boidae. One of the more aquatic boas, it inhabits swamps and slow moving rivers in the northern parts of South America to the east of the Andes. It is the largest of living snakes, for although its length is a little less than that of the Reticulated python of Asia it is proportionately much thicker.

Its reputation as a man-eater is largely undeserved. A large anaconda may be capable of devouring a child but such occurrences are rare. It generally shuns human habitations and preys chiefly on birds and small or medium-sized mammals such as rodents and peccaries. Fish and caimans are also included in its diet.

Like all boas the anaconda is ovoviviparous, the female giving birth to as many as 72 living young, each measuring about 3 ft (1 m) in length. FAMILY: Boidae, ORDER: Squamata, CLASS: Reptilia.

ANACONDA. The size of a moving animal is always difficult to judge so it is not surprising that incredible lengths have been reported for the giant snakes, the anacondas and pythons. Even a relatively small snake seems almost unending as it crawls through undergrowth so with a little embroidery about adventures in remote corners of the earth the record length claimed for an anaconda attained 140 ft (42 m).

Such a record can easily be dismissed but it is not easy to establish what is the greatest length to which an anaconda will grow. Experts on snakes give differing figures, for two reasons. They have different standards as to when a record can be considered reliable, one expert rejecting a record that another accepts, and, most important, it is very difficult to measure even a dead snake as its body stretches so easily that even pulling it into a straight line distorts it. The current record for anacondas seems to be $37\frac{1}{2}$ ft (11·4 m) placing the anaconda just ahead of the Reticulate python in record length.

Stories of man-eating anacondas are also difficult to prove and even the most reliable accounts leave room for doubt.

ANADROMOUS FISHES, term applied to fishes which ascend rivers from the sea in order to breed. The term is also commonly used for those which inhabit large lakes and ascend the affluent rivers only during the breeding season. Fishes that perform the reverse, descending to the sea in order to breed, are termed catadromous.

The most striking examples are the salmons, the sturgeons, the Beaked salmons (Galaxiidae) and the shads.

Movement between salt water and freshwater poses considerable problems to the fish in the delicate balance between salts and water entering and leaving its body, that is to say in the osomotic balance. Briefly the body fluids of fishes are less salty than sea water but more salty than freshwater. As a result, marine fishes tend to lose water and must drink frequently, ridding themselves of the excess salts thus taken in, excreting them mainly through the gills. Freshwater fishes, on the other hand, tend to absorb water and must excrete copious amounts of urine. The way in which anadromous fishes adjust from one environment to the other and back again is a remarkable but only partly understood aspect of physiology.

The anadromous fishes appear to have evolved in freshwaters and to have later used the sea as a feeding ground. Apparently it proved easier for the adult fishes to adapt to life in salt water than for the eggs and young. The parents are therefore obliged to return to their ancient breeding grounds to spawn successfully.

ANAEROBIOSIS, the ability to live in conditions devoid of oxygen, involving respiring anaerobically. Anaerobic respiration is the process of obtaining energy from food substances without using oxygen to do so. Examples of such processes are the breakdown of glycogen to lactic acid in vertebrate muscle (glycolysis) and the breakdown of glucose to ethyl alcohol and carbon dioxide by yeast (fermentation). The conversion of glycogen or glucose to lactic acid (or some similar end-product) often occurs in animals living in temporarily or permanently deoxygenated conditions and also in some tissues (such as muscle) when the supply of oxygen is inadequate for aerobic respiration to occur (the Krebs cycle and its associated processes, which normally follow glycolysis).

Respiratory processes transfer some of the energy inherent in the substrate molecules to molecules of ATP (adenosine triphosphate), which is the convenient source of energy used to run the cell's activities. The yield of energy from glycolysis is far less than that from the Krebs cycle, for the number of high-energy molecules of ATP obtained by respiring a given amount of glucose is much smaller during anaerobic respiration than during aerobic respiration.

The glycolytic pathway of anaerobic respiration involves a long series of reactions but may be represented, in essence, thus:

$$\underset{\text{glucose}}{C_6H_{12}O_6} \longrightarrow \underset{\text{lactate (lactic acid)}}{2CH_3.CHOH.COOH}$$

Fermentation, on the other hand, may be shown thus:

$$\underset{\text{glucose}}{C_6H_{12}O_6} \longrightarrow \underset{\text{ethyl alcohol}}{2C_2H_5OH} + 2CO_2$$

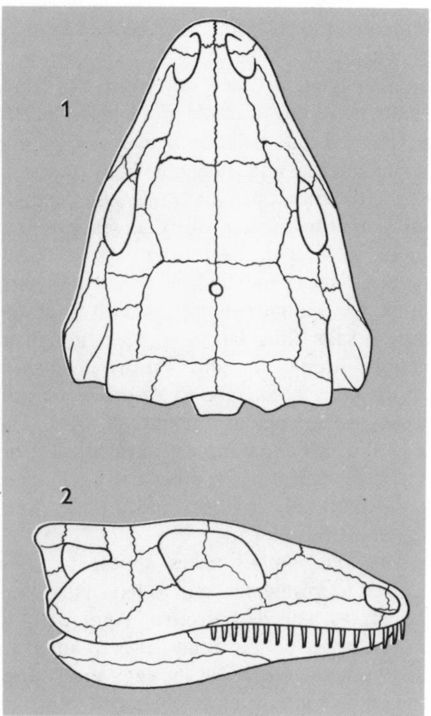

1 Dorsal view and 2 side view of anapsid skull showing the solid skull roof without perforation behind the eye socket.

During a period of anaerobic conditions lactic acid may accumulate, and become oxidized when oxygen is again available. Consequently, after a period of anaerobic conditions, when oxygen is again available, the consumption of oxygen may be at a higher rate than usual while the lactic acid which accumulated during the period of anoxia is being oxidized. This is known as incurring, and repaying, an 'oxygen debt'. It is a characteristic feature of the physiology of many anaerobically respiring animals, and also of muscle tissue during and after a period of very high activity.

Some animals are obligate anaerobes, being only found in conditions free of oxygen. There are relatively few such species, but there are many which are facultative anaerobes, being able to survive short or long periods without oxygen interspersed among the more normal periods of oxygen plenty. Many parasites rely almost exclusively on anaerobic respiration. Some do so because there is no alternative, as the environment is deficient in oxygen (e.g. parasites of the gut or body cavity). Other parasites respire anaerobically even though oxygen is available, because glucose is present in such abundance that glycolysis is an adequate process for them in spite of its relatively low energy yield (e.g. some protozoan parasites of the blood).

Environments which are generally oxygen deficient part or all of the time include coastal and estuarine muds, the bottoms of certain lakes and ponds, and similar situations. The oxygen lack is usually due to the activities of certain micro-organisms and the presence of readily oxidizable chemicals. See also respiration. A.E.B.

ANAPSIDA, subclass of the Reptilia comprising two orders: the Cotylosauria and the Testudines. The diagnostic anapsid feature is the presence of a complete roofing of bone on the skull behind the orbits. In all other reptilian groups the skull in this region is variously perforated for the passage of jaw muscles. This group includes the oldest and most primitive of all reptiles, the cotylosaurs or 'stem reptiles'. From them all other reptiles evolved. The cotylosaurs are first found as fossils in the Carboniferous and became extinct in the Permian. The tortoises, turtles, and terrapins constituting the Testudines, although preserving the anapsid skull pattern, are separated on many features from their cotylosaur ancestors. The oldest chelonian is of Triassic age.

ANASPIDS, an order of fossil jawless fishes (Agnatha). These fishes had a slender, cigar-shaped body covered by small bony plates resembling scales. Larger bony plates covered the head, but the general impression is of fishes with fairly flexible bodies capable of active swimming. The axis of the tail was directed downwards, with the fin set on top, the reverse of the situation found in most fishes (but resembling a transitory stage occurring in the ammocoete larva of the lamprey). There was a single median nostril, as in the modern lampreys and hagfishes. A series of pores behind the head appears to have been the external gill openings like those found in the lamprey. See also article fossil fishes and the accompanying classificatory table. ORDER: Anaspida, SUBCLASS: Monorhina, CLASS: Agnatha.

ANCHOVIES, a family of usually small and silvery fishes allied to the herrings and found in temperate and tropical seas with a few species passing into freshwater or with permanent populations in rivers. Anchovies can be immediately distinguished from any small herring-like fishes by the pointed snout that overhangs the mouth and the long and slender lower jaw. The body is slender, more or less compressed depending on the species, there is a single soft-rayed dorsal and anal fin and the tail is forked. The silvery scales are often easily shed. The majority of species are small, usually growing to 4–6 in (10–15 cm), but a few species may reach 12 in (30 cm). The anchovies, of which about a hundred species are known, are essentially tropical fishes with a few species in temperate waters. The best known of the latter is the European anchovy *Engraulis encrasicolus,* an elongated, round-bodied species that forms large shoals and is found from Norway southwards to the Mediterranean and the west coast of Africa and forms the basis for large fisheries. A very similar fish is found off the American Atlantic coast and in the Caribbean, as well as off the coasts of South Africa, Japan and southern Australia. It forms one of the three principal species in the great 'Iwashi' fisheries of Japan. Along the Pacific coasts of the Americas *Engraulis mordax* in the north and *E. ringens* in the south are also of considerable economic importance, the catches off the Peruvian coasts at one time being the highest for any single species of fish in the world (not excepting the famous menhaden of the American Atlantic). The anchovies of the tropical New World all have smooth bellies without the series of saw-edged scutes found in herrings and in the anchovies of the Indo-Pacific region. The anchovies in the latter area show a number of curious specializations. In some species of *Thryssa* the body is greatly compressed, the anal fin is very long and the principal bone of the upper jaw, the maxilla, is extended back to reach beyond the head to the base of the pectoral fins or even to halfway along the anal fin (*T. setirostris*). The function of this long maxilla is not known. The most highly specialized of the Indo-Pacific forms are the species of *Coilia* the Rat-tailed anchovies, in which the body tapers to a long filament with a very small tail fin on the end, the anal fin running the entire length and containing over a hundred finrays. In addition, the upper rays of the pectoral fins are filamentous. Although members of *Coilia* are found in shallow coastal waters or muddy estuaries, one species has very prominent rows of silvery light organs (photophores) along the lower flanks.

In addition to the anchovy fisheries of

Reconstruction of an anaspid, note the eight gill pores behind the head, and the down-turned tail lobe.

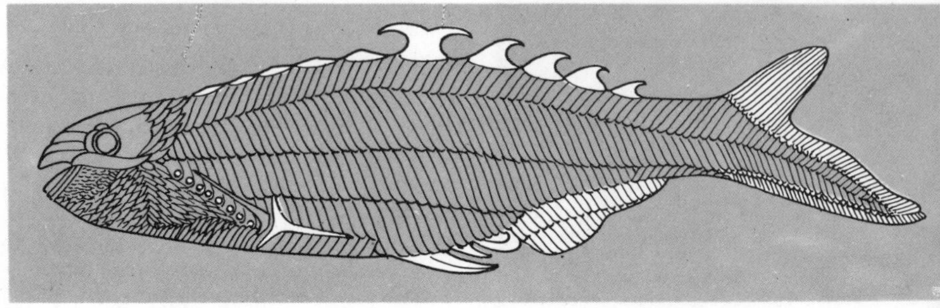

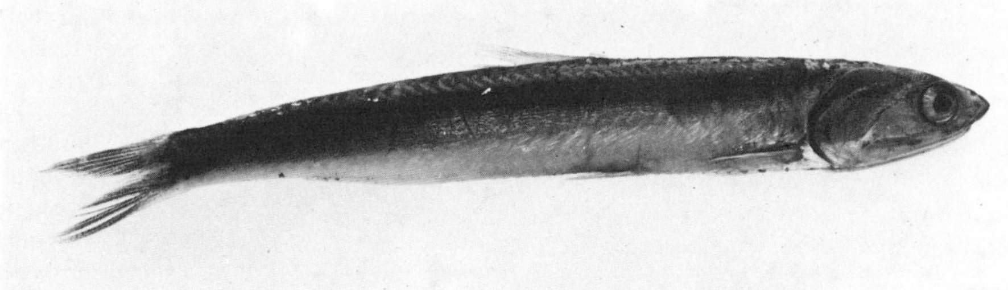

The anchovy, a small, herring-like fish that exists in enormous numbers, especially in tropical seas.

temperate waters, fairly large local fisheries are found in the Indo-Pacific region concentrating on the small, 4–5 in (10–13 cm) species of *Stolephorus*. The anchovies are also an important source of live bait for the tuna fisheries, especially off the Pacific coasts of Central America where the anchoveta *Cetengraulis mysticetus* is commonly used. FAMILY: Engraulidae, ORDER: Clupeiformes, CLASS: Pisces.

ANCHOVETA DILEMMA. Within the last 20–30 years Peru has become one of the major fishing countries of the world. Its fishing industry is based on one species—the anchoveta that swarms in incredible numbers in the cool Humboldt current. It was only in 1950 that the first factory was built to convert the anchovetas into fishmeal fertilizer. In the next few years many more were built and in 1959 300,000 tons of fishmeal were produced, making Peru the fifth most important fishing nation. The bonanza continued and in 1965 the yield was 9 million tons.

Unfortunately the anchoveta industry appears to be clashing with one of Peru's traditional sources of income. For thousands of years anchovetas have been preyed on by cormorants, pelicans and boobies and their droppings accumulated in the nesting colonies to form beds of guano sometimes 100 ft thick. This has been an important source of fertilizer for over 100 years and a valuable export for Peru, but recently the stocks of guano have declined drastically. It seems that the Peruvians' optimism that there were enough anchovetas for both fishmeal factories and seabirds was misplaced and that the seabirds are now suffering from overfishing by man. Unfortunately, with the capital invested in the fishing, it will prove difficult to limit the harvest to prevent overfishing.

ANEMONE, carnivorous, soft-bodied marine animals (Cnidaria, Anthozoa) with a prominent crown of retractile tentacles. Often brightly coloured and commonly found intertidally, they are related to corals and jellyfishes and are named for their resemblance to flowers. They are treated under Sea anemones.

ANEMONEFISH, alternative name for the clownfish.

ANGEL FISHES, name used for three different groups of fish:

a) common name in the United States for members of the Chaetodontidae, a family of coral fishes here termed the butterflyfishes;

b) alternative name for the monkfish;

c) to the aquarist, Angel fishes are members of the freshwater genus *Pterophyllum* of the family Cichlidae. These are highly compressed, deep-bodied fishes with slender, filamentous pelvic rays. When seen head-on through a growth of water plants, the extreme narrowness of the body makes the fish look like just another plant stem. The light brown flanks are marked with four darker vertical bars, so that even from the side the fish blends with its surroundings.

There are still problems concerning the numbers of species in the genus *Pterophyllum*, but three are usually recognized, *P. eimeki*, *P. altum* and *P. scalare*. Identification is difficult for the amateur and will become more so because the hybrids between *P. eimeki* and *P. scalare* are commonly sold. *P. altum* is imported less often than the other two species.

P. scalare is the largest of the three species in the Amazon, grows to a total length of 6 in (15 cm) and has a body height (including fins) of $10\frac{1}{4}$ in (26 cm). However when kept in an aquarium it does not grow so large. Breeding in captivity is not difficult, the main problem being to recognize the sexes and this is best overcome by allowing the fishes to pair off themselves. They spawn on broad-leaved plants which have previously been cleaned by the fishes themselves. After the eggs have been deposited, the parents continually fan them and at 86°F (30°C) the young hatch in about 30 hours. The parents assist the young to hatch by chewing at the eggs and spitting the young onto leaves. There they hang suspended from short threads until the parents remove them to a shallow depression or nest in the sand. After four to five days the young, who may number as many as a

Freshwater Angel fishes, popular with aquarists.

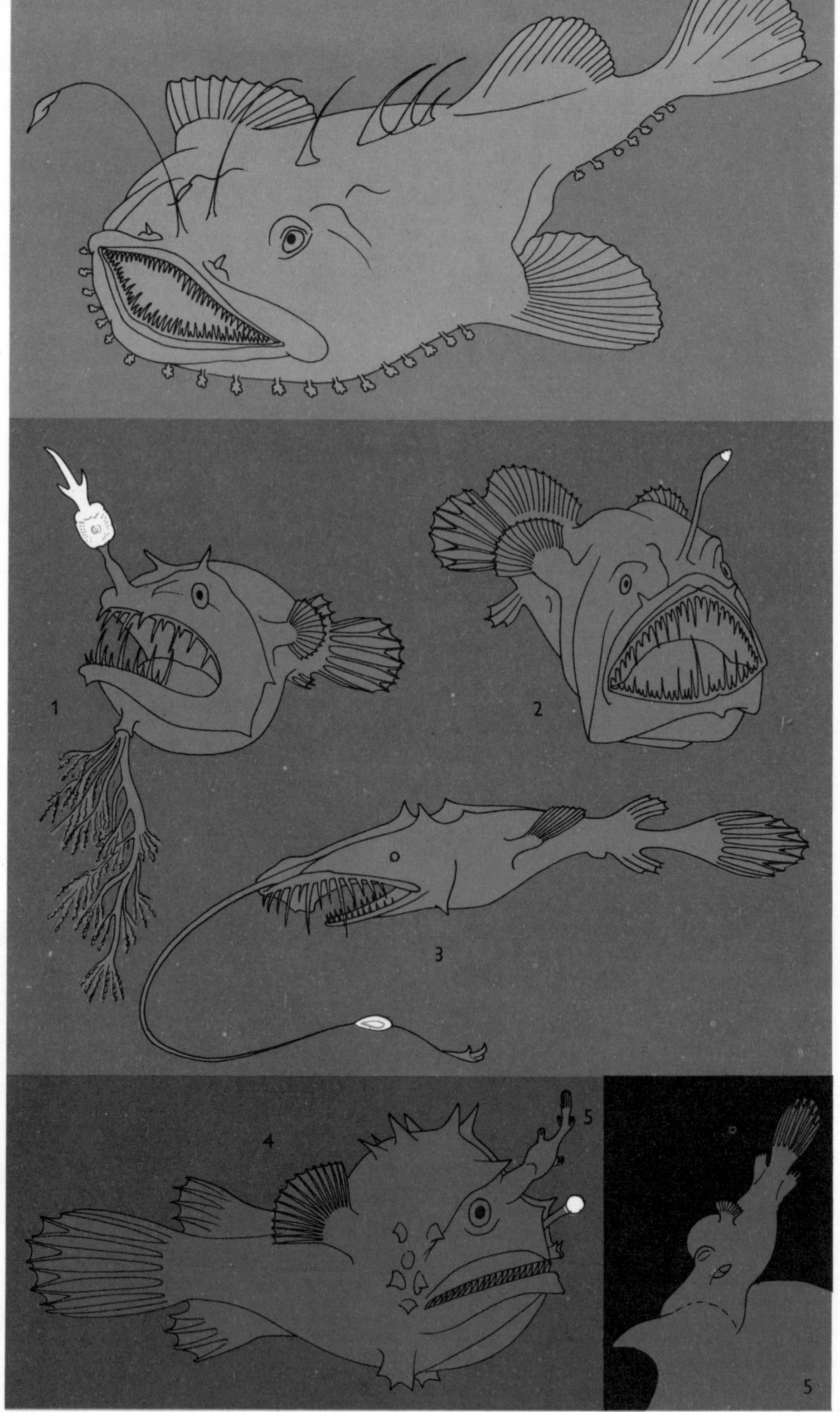

Types of anglerfishes: Common anglerfish (top), deep-sea anglerfishes (centre) including 1) *Linophryne arboriper*, 2) *Melanocetus johnsoni*, 3) *Lasiognathus saccostoma*, with various forms of lure, and (bottom) female ceratioid anglerfish *Photocorynus spiniceps*, bearing a dwarf male (5), shown enlarged to right.

thousand, are able to swim and the parents lead their brood out of the nest. FAMILY: Cichlidae, ORDER: Perciformes, CLASS: Pisces.

ANGEL SHARKS or monkfishes, sharks, the large pectoral fins of which give them a 'hybrid' appearance between a shark and a ray. Unlike the rays, the pectoral fins of Angel sharks are not joined to the head. There are two dorsal fins, no anal fin and the nostrils have two barbels that extend into the mouth. The latter is almost terminal and not underslung as in most sharks. Angel sharks are found principally in temperate waters and they feed mainly on fishes. The monkfish *Squatina squatina* of European waters is the largest, reaching 8 ft (2·4 m) in length and weighing 160 lb (73 kg). It is found in British waters, chiefly off the south coast, and enters shallow waters in summer. Of the several species known, *S. dumeril* occurs off American Atlantic coasts and *S. californica* off American Pacific coasts. FAMILY: Squatinidae, ORDER: Pleurotremata, CLASS: Chondrichthyes.

ANGLERFISHES, a highly specialized group of marine fishes found in all oceans and at all depths, from shallow waters down to the abyssal trenches. The anglerfishes can be divided into three main suborders: the Lophioidea, the Antennarioidea and the Ceratioidea. The three groups share certain anatomical features, the most outstanding and the one that has given them their common name being the tendency for the first ray of the dorsal fin to be long and to develop a lure at its tip with which the anglerfish 'angles' for its prey. In addition, the pectoral fins in many species are borne on a fleshy limb, which adds to the bizarre appearance of the fish and gave rise to a former scientific name for the whole group, the Pediculati.

The first group of anglerfishes, the Lophioidea, are shallow water fishes. The Common anglerfish *Lophius piscatorius,* sometimes known as the Fishing frog, is found around European and American coasts. It is a greatly flattened fish, lying like a huge disc on the sea bottom. The mouth is enormous and the jaws are lined with sharp, needle-like teeth. The eyes are on the top of the head and the brown body is fringed with small flaps of skin so that the outline of the fish is broken and the fish itself rendered inconspicuous. The anterior rays of the dorsal fin are very long and are separated from the rest of the fin. They function as the fishing rod or illicium, the first ray having a small flap of tissue at its tip to act as a lure. This lure is dangled in front of the mouth and when small fishes come to investigate the huge mouth is suddenly opened and then closed over them. The mouth is capacious and food can be stored there until it is swallowed. It is interesting to note that Aristotle, who well merits the title of Father of Zoology, recorded this curious feeding habit over 2,000 years ago. Anglers seem to eat anything that is available. In spite of their rather sluggish appearance, they have been seen at the surface and it is not uncommon to find seagulls in their stomachs. They are large fishes, reaching 4 ft (120 cm) in length. The spawn of the anglerfish is also peculiar. The eggs are contained in a long ribbon of mucus 1–3 ft (30–90 cm) wide and up to 50 ft (16 m) long. These long ribbons are often reported floating at the surface of the sea.

The second group of anglers, the Antennarioidea, includes two important families. The family Antennariidae comprises species

An anglerfish *Antennarius* lies in wait on the sea-bed to catch passing prey.

that are flattened from side to side (not from top to bottom as in the lophioids). One of the best known members is the Sargassum weed fish *Histrio* spp. The second family is the Ogcocephalidae, often called the batfishes (a name also used for the genus *Platax*). The batfishes are flattened like the lophioids and have large heads and fairly small bodies. The most striking feature is the limb-like pectoral fins which are muscular and are used to crawl about the bottom with a slow, deliberate waddle. The lure is hidden in a tube above the mouth and it can be projected out when the fish is hungry; the tube gives the fish a rather sharp-nosed appearance. Batfishes grow to about 15 in (38 cm) and are found in both the Atlantic and Pacific Oceans.

There is no doubt that the third suborder of anglers, the Ceratioidea or Deep-sea anglers, are amongst the most fascinating of all fishes. They are clearly separated from the other anglers by the absence of pelvic fins. Unlike the other two groups, the ceratioids do not stay on the bottom but are essentially midwater fishes of the deep seas. In this group, the body is rounded and not flattened, but the characteristic fishing lure is present. The existence of these fishes was not suspected until the 1830s when a Danish sea captain discovered one washed up on the shores of Greenland. Captain Holboell's discovery has been commemorated in the naming of one of the giants of this group, *Ceratias holboelli,* a species that grows to 36 in (90 cm). Most of the ceratioids, however, are only a few inches long. They are usually dark brown or black, without scales and with a fragile, velvety skin, although some have warty projections on the body.

It is one thing to fish with a lure in clear, shallow water but obviously this would be ineffective in depths where little or no light penetrates. The Deep-sea anglerfishes have overcome this in a remarkable way, the lure being luminescent. In members of the genus *Linophryne* there is also a luminescent, tree-like barbel hanging from the chin, as well as the luminescent lure. In *Ceratias* and *Lasiognathus* there is a further specialization. The illicium can be slowly retracted so that the prey is drawn closer to the jaws before it is finally seized. Considering that the illicium is merely a modified finray, it is remarkable that it can be manoeuvred in this manner. In *Lasiognathus saccostoma* there is a slender line beyond the luminous bait, at the end of which is a series of horny hooks; these are not, however, used like fishing hooks. The ultimate sophistication in lures is found in the bottom-living *Galatheathauma,* a fish that lives at depths of 12,000 ft (about 4,000 m). In this fish the luminescent organ is on the roof of the mouth, thus tempting the prey right inside.

The extraordinary breeding habits of the Deep-sea anglerfishes, in which the male becomes parasitic on the female, have been described in the article on deep-sea fishes. The young, which look fairly 'normal' by comparison with the adults, spend their larval life in tropical and subtropical surface waters. The eyes are normal in size, but as the juveniles metamorphose into the adult they sink slowly into the deeper waters and the eyes cease to grow larger. Thereafter, the eyes become smaller and smaller in comparison with the body, so that they are often hard to find in the adult.

Food is not easy to come by in the ocean depths and the anglerfishes cannot afford to miss any opportunities, even if the prey is larger than the predator. A specimen of *Melanocoetus,* for example, measuring only 3½ in (9 cm) in length, has been found with a 6 in (15 cm) lanternfish coiled up in its elastic stomach. These anglers are for the most part small and are not rapid swimmers, relying on their lures to attract their prey to them. ORDER: Lophiiformes, CLASS: Pisces.

ANGLERFISHES, our knowledge of the deep-sea anglerfishes has come gradually and it is only with the recent introduction of deep-sea craft and under-water television that observations could be made on the living fishes. Prior to this records have been limited to specimens brought up in trawls or found at the surface. It seems that some deep-sea fishes come to the surface at night and this may explain the finding of the first deep-sea angler ever to be seen. It was washed ashore on the west coast of Greenland and named *Ceriatias holboelli* after its discoverer, Lieutenant-Commander Holbøll of the Royal Danish Navy. It is now known to live throughout the oceans.

ANGUID LIZARDS, a family of small to medium-sized lizards usually classified in seven genera with about 75 species. This family comprises standard lizard-like forms and limbless, snake-like ones, presenting a problem in classification. In the skull the temporal arch is complete and the teeth are solid, not hollow, and attached to the inner jaw bone. The tongue is protrusible and can be withdrawn into a case-like sheath. Nearly all anguids have a skin armour of overlapping scales with bony plates beneath them. Many anguids have particularly long tails that can be shed by *autotomy, in moments of danger. The lost tail is regenerated in a few weeks, but it never grows as long as the original tail and is supported by an unjointed cartilage bar so autotomy cannot occur again in the regenerated tail.

The distribution of anguids is discontinuous. A number of species are found in Central America and on the Caribbean islands, but many of these have only a small range, and some are so rare they are known only from the original specimens from which they were named. In America the anguids range from British Columbia in the north to Argentina in the south but they are absent from large areas in between. There are only two genera with very few species in Europe, northwest Africa and western and southeast Asia, but amongst these we find the *Slow worm *Anguis fragilis* the best known of the family. There are no anguids in Africa south of the Sahara or in Australia.

Six species of *Ophisaurus* are found in the Old World and five in America. They are relics of a once abundant genus and fossils can be found in places where *Ophisaurus* no longer occurs. The Scheltopusik *O. apodus* with a length of about 3 ft (90 cm) is the most impressive of the genus and of the family and can be found from the northern part of the Balkan peninsula through Asia Minor and the Caucasus to Turkestan. Like all species of *Ophisaurus,* the Scheltopusik is legless, snake-like and its body well armoured with a great number of bony scales. There is a furrow on each side of the body enabling the lizard to move its otherwise rather rigid body sideways. Insects alone are not enough to feed a strong Scheltopusik; it also eats snails and small rodents, crushing these with its powerful jaws. A lot of people fear the Scheltopusik more than any snake and even believe it, incorrectly, to be poisonous. The other *Ophisaurus* species of the Old World live in comparatively restricted areas. The New World Glass snake lives in the central and southern part of Northern America and in Mexico. As far as is known all *Ophisaurus* species lay eggs.

About 30 species of the Alligator lizard *Gerrhonotus* can be found in North and Central America. Their body structure is more primitive than that of the snake-like anguids. In *Gerrhonotus* the limbs are well developed, the head and body are protected by scales. Alligator lizards are ground dwellers, but some species are able climbers making use of their tails. Their food consists of insects which they stalk and seize, leaping at them from a short distance. Alligator lizards may be viviparous or oviparous.

Less well-known are the galliwasps of the genus *Diploglossus.* They are rather shapeless anguids with small but well developed legs. There are about 30 species in Central America, South America and on a few islands of the West Indies. A number of species have only rarely been found and it is probable that some of the island species have become extinct already, perhaps exterminated through the introduction of predators. The differences in colouration between adult and young is often quite remarkable. The young Brazilian *Diploglossus fasciatus* has striking transverse black and white stripes but in the adult the stripes are lengthwise.

Finally the South American Snake lizard of the genus *Ophiodes* has to be mentioned. There are four species in the open plains south of the Amazon basin. They are very snake-like, the front limbs being absent but one-toed flaps remain of the hind legs. Unlike Glass snakes the Snake lizards have no side furrows. FAMILY: Anguidae, ORDER: Squamata, CLASS: Reptilia. K.K.

ANGWANTIBO *Arctocebus calabarensis,* a small, golden brown mammal related to lorises and monkeys, with forward-directed, large eyes and a pointed snout. Its head and body measure 9 in (22·5 cm) with a 2 in (5 cm) tail almost hidden in the fur. Each hand has a widely opposed thumb, a very small nailless index finger and a short third finger. The big toe is widely opposed to the other toes. These grasping extremities are very powerful, and it is said that the angwantibo spends most of its time hanging upside-down from branches. Like the potto and the loris it is very slow-moving and walks with a deliberate, clasping pace, its hands and feet acting like pincers.

The angwantibo is completely arboreal and lives high up in the trees in the tropical forest belt of West Africa from the Niger to the Congo, where it is rarely seen, which explains why so little is known about it. It seems not to make a nest and probably sleeps clasped to a fork of a tree, like the potto. It is omnivorous but the main item of diet is probably insects, supplemented by soft fruits, this being reflected in its dentition, which has long, pointed canines and well-developed sharp cusps on the cheekteeth (premolars and molars).

As with most of the Primates, there is only one baby at a birth, after a gestation of about 4 months, and it climbs directly onto the mother's fur. Thereafter, it is carried around by the mother until reaching independence. There seems to be no well-defined breeding season, but there may be an annual rise and fall in the number of births. The angwantibo is apparently solitary or pair-living, so the baby probably moves off to establish its own home range or territory as soon as it is independent of the mother.

The angwantibo is one of the distant relatives of man placed in the suborder Prosimii. This basically means that it has retained a number of very primitive characters from the ancestral primate stock. It is placed in the family Lorisidae, along with the lorises and pottos, since it shares with them the slow-moving gait, the reduction of the fingers, the forward-directed eyes and the carriage of young on the fur. In fact, the angwantibo was originally regarded as a potto, and it has often been referred to as the Golden potto and placed in the same genus *Perodicticus.* FAMILY: Lorisidae, ORDER: Primates, CLASS: Mammalia. R.D.M.

Harmless snake-like Scheltopusik lizard.

ANIMALS IN ART, have been an aspect of major significance in relatively few civilizations. When civilizations have assigned particular importance to animal images it has generally been because of their association with religious or magico-religious beliefs.

During the Paleolithic era, the hunting peoples of southwest Europe and Africa depended wholly for subsistence on their ability to kill animals. In an attempt to make their existence less precarious they performed magical rites which they believed would ensure both a plentiful supply of animals, and the success of hunting expeditions. As a part of the rites they produced the first pictorial representations of reality. In Europe they took the form of paintings on the walls of caves depicting mammoths, bison, ibexes, horses and reindeer. In Africa the images of ostriches, elephants, hippopotami, and crocodiles were drawn on exposed slabs of rock. According to prehistoric man's beliefs, if he were to gain power over the will of the animals he hunted it was necessary for him to assume their identity by means of imitation. The naturalistic representations of animals fulfilled this imitative function.

The art of many early hunting cultures, in different areas of the world, was based on similar magical beliefs. In southern Africa the animal art of the Bushmen does not appear to have been so strictly utilitarian as that of the hunters of Europe and North Africa. Although they were bound by the same beliefs there is a decorative element in their paintings which seems to indicate an awareness and enjoyment of the creative process outside of its role in hunting. However, their representations of animals are above all naturalistic, in contrast to the human figures which appear in some of their paintings. The human figure was drawn in a highly stylized manner because the portrayal of a particular person would, they believed, have given the artist power over that person.

Animals, quite naturally, continued to play an important role in African art. An especially fine example of more recent African animal art is provided by the Benin bronzes, sculptures of legendary animals, of the 16th and 17th centuries, used for weighing out gold along the Gold Coast (Ghana).

Representations of animals are a prominent feature of Egyptian art as a result of the totemic animal cult which existed in early Egyptian civilisation. The divine animal gods (e.g. Hathor – cow, Anubis – jackal, Horus – falcon, Sekhmet – lioness) assumed a hybrid form in which human bodies were surmounted by animal heads. The lion, as far as the Egyptians were concerned, was the king of beasts and the priests developed a whole system of theology and cosmology of

Female angwantibo carries her infant on her back.

which it was the subject. It, or part of it, appears in what is probably the most famous piece of Egyptian animal art, the Sphinx, which is composed of the head of a Pharaoh and the body of a lion.

In Egyptian funerary art animals are depicted not as gods but as man's fellow inhabitants of Earth. It was the Egyptian custom to bury, along with the dead man and his possessions, representations of the people and animals that had surrounded him in life, so that they could accompany him in his after-life. Later this custom developed to include paintings on the walls of the tomb illustrating the dead man's life on earth. The scenes in tomb paintings of men hunting, fishing, and playing with the cats, dogs, and tame monkeys that they kept as pets, bear witness to the genuine love that the Egyptians had for animal life. The paintings, sculptures, and relief carvings that this civilization produced display a homogeneity which is the consequence of the artists' adherence to a set of strict stylistic conventions. There is an imposed sense of order and harmony which induces a slight air of austerity and remoteness, but despite this the images retain a high degree of naturalism.

There are marked similarities between the Egyptian civilization and the highly developed civilizations of pre-Columbian America. The Totec, Aztec and Mayan cultures of Central and South America were also based upon a totemic animal cult. The puma is represented as a sacred animal, and the images of eagles, coyotes, jaguars and plumed serpents appear endowed with mythological and cosmological significances.

*Chinese art presents the observer with a profusion of representations of animals, both real and mythical, which functioned as elements in a complex system of symbolism.

Greek art began, more or less, where Egyptian art left off. The earliest examples of Greek animal art were produced by the fishing peoples of Mycenia and Crete when they decorated their pottery with representations of marine life. These images of Water snails, shellfish and octopuses very much accept the stylistic limits of Egyptian art. However, during the great Greek era man stopped accepting and began questioning, and the desire for knowledge and understanding brought science and philosophy into being and affected art in such a way as to change fundamentally the nature of the activity. Art became a means of real investigation and artists began to experiment in an attempt to come to terms with natural form. From this study, a degree of realism was attained which bestowed upon the manifestations of the divine gods in animal form a power and dynamism never before achieved. Because of their passionate and sympathetic concern for nature, the Greeks intuitively introduced a spiritual quality into their animal images. Roman attempts to emulate Greek art were merely superficial representations of reality, conspicuously lacking in the majestic spirituality of Greek works.

This miniature represents the fable of the monkey and the turtle. It was added in 1557 to the manuscript Humayun-name, Turkish translation of an original Sanscrit text from the third century AD.

Christianity was disturbed by the concentration of the Greeks on form and found it difficult to accept the realistic art that was its inheritance. They feared that such naturalistic images could possibly promote idolatory. Animal representations, because of their historical associations with magical beliefs and rites, were considered especially dangerous because they could, it was felt, encourage a return to paganism. Such fears produced a change in both the role and the representation of animals. They were used as symbols, allegorical figures alluding to ideas or concepts; a function which did not require animals to be realistically depicted. Consequently there was a drift away from naturalism into formalism and stylization.

Late in the 14th century there was, in Italy, a resurgence of interest in Antiquity, and by the first decade of the 15th century the classical revival, or Renaissance, was beginning to have its effect. Even though man was the focus of Renaissance attention, the quest for scientific knowledge meant that animal life was closely studied. The scientific attitude was apparent in the art of the Renaissance, and Leonardo, Pisanello, and Dürer, all produced magnificent animal drawings by exact analytical observation.

The occurrence of animal forms in contemporary art does not serve any particular cultural function, it is merely the result of the artists' subjective judgement, and thus animals appear sporadically and with varying purpose. B.E.

ANIMALS IN LITERATURE, probably made their most notable appearance in Aesop's Fables. Aesop lived as a slave in Greece during the 6th century BC, and was regarded as the foremost exponent of the fable, a traditional literary form which is thought to have existed in the wisdom literature of much earlier civilizations. In these simple and amusing animal tales Aesop was not concerned with describing the behaviour of animals, rather he portrayed, by means of animal characters, the motives and actions of human beings. The different animals each represent a particular human characteristic; for example, the fox represents slyness, the lamb timidity, the wolf greed, and the lion courage and dignity. Each story attempts, through the interaction of animal characters, to convey a 'moral', or useful lesson, relevant to human behaviour. It was this didactic element that, in the eyes of the Greeks, raised Aesop's Fables from the status of folk-tales to that of wisdom literature.

Proverbs, as a literary form, have an affinity with fables, and many proverbial phrases such as 'a wolf in sheep's clothing', and 'never count your chickens before they hatch', are derived from fables by Aesop.

Jean De La Fontaine (1621–1695) wrote a collection of animal fables which are numbered among the great works of French literature. He used the fable tradition, and especially the fables of Aesop, as his source material, from which his peculiar talent produced dramas of real subtlety and comedy.

Finally, animal characters have been used by George Orwell in Animal Farm, to act out a satire on Stalinist Russia during the revolution. B.E.

ANIMAL SOCIOLOGY. Many animals live together in permanent or semi-permanent associations consisting of members of one species. Examples are herds of cattle, schools of fish, colonies of honeybees. Often these animals react to each other behaviourally in such a way that signals are exchanged which produce special behaviour patterns. When animals interact in this way they can be said to be social.

Even the simplest associations of animals seem to bring advantages to the individuals which comprise them. In particular an animal isolated from the group survives less well than those which are together. Brittlestars (Ophiuroidea) will clump together in an otherwise bare tank. When provided with glass rods they will cling to these instead of each other, so it appears that the brittlestars seek maximum contact stimulation on their bodies. This may be provided either by glass rods or by other members of the species. Increased survival in these circumstances was described by Allee as the group effect and remains unexplained. However, the advantages of some other associations are more obvious. Protection is one. A flock of starlings closes formation when threatened by a Peregrine falcon, for then the falcon hesitates to dive upon them since in taking one of them it risks injury from colliding with the rest. Anchovies form dense shoals which move round in circles when a Horse mackerel is near. The mackerel will be confused by the number of flashing bodies and is therefore less likely to take any of the anchovies so long as they remain part of the shoal. Another advantage is that when danger threatens warning is more likely to be given in time if

A mixed flock of knot and dunlin.

there are a number of animals together: there are more eyes and ears to pick up signs of danger. Baboons and impala form mixed troops in the East African savannah. Warning cries from either are enough to give the alarm and show the presence of, say, a cheetah. Such advantages offset the conspicuousness of a large animal group.

Additionally, animals in a group mutually stimulate each other. One result is they tend to mature earlier than solitary animals of the same species. Male locusts *(Schistocerca gregaria)* produce a pheromone which causes accelerated maturation in other males of the same species. Social animals also tend to imitate each other. For example, a chick that has just finished feeding will start to eat once more if it is placed with a group of hungry chicks that have just begun to eat. This effect is social facilitation. It is responsible for the biologically advantageous synchronization of reproductive activities. Thus in many species of seabirds reproduction begins earlier and is over more quickly in a large colony than in a small one. In this way the period during which the young of the colony are vulnerable to attack by predators is minimized.

Some animal societies are very highly organized so that the members of each society have special behaviour patterns which combine to the advantage of the whole. This is best demonstrated by the social insects, like honeybees or termites. A honeybee colony consists of a queen with many thousands of workers which are her female offspring. Once a year male insects (drones) make their appearance. The work of the colony is carried out by the workers who are morphologically adapted for collecting and carrying pollen and nectar. Their tasks in the colony, besides foraging, include the building of a honeycomb from plates of wax secreted by glands on their bodies, cleaning and repairing the honeycomb to be used again, tending and feeding the larvae and guarding the hive entrance. The males exist solely to fertilize the young virgin queens on their mating flight. Thus, the members of the colony are all of the same family since they all come from eggs laid by the same parent.

It is characteristic of the majority of social insects that individuals within the colony continually exchange food. This food sharing behaviour is known as trophallaxis. It appears to be the bond which holds the colony together. An insect separated from its colony soon dies and even a small group of them survives only a little longer than a single animal.

Termites have a similarly structured society, though since these are hemimetabolous insects, their larvae are active and play an important part in the colony, forming a large part of the worker force. There are specialized adult individuals whose function is to act as guards, others which act as workers and others which are supplementary reproductives. Unlike a honeybee, a termite does not take part in all the activities of the colony during its life-time. Termites also differ from honeybees in that the male remains with the queen for long periods after the establishment of a new colony. Thus it can be seen that the colonies of social insects are highly organized reproductive systems and carry out the function most efficiently.

Many vertebrate social groups are a mixture of the sexes. Groups of apes and monkeys (see primate societies) often consist of enlarged families that include a number of near relatives. Howler monkeys, for example, travel in bands typically made up of three males, eight females, three dependent infants and four young adults. There is no elaborate group behaviour which results in building anything like the honeybee comb or a termite's nest, nor are individuals specially adapted to carry out one function. Moreover, a single individual is able to survive away from the rest.

The summer herds of Red deer consist of both sexes. In them the males fight for dominance and, so, for mates. These relationships have to be re-established each September and they last only for the short rutting period. Outside this period the hinds form a coherent herd with young animals aged less than three years. In this herd a hind is the leader and, indeed, she will also take over the lead during the rutting season if serious danger threatens. The males form a separate herd, loosely bound. The main factor in keeping a flock of sheep together is the mother-child relationship. Thus a ewe will follow her mother even after she has had a lamb herself.

The structure of the societies of vertebrates which are not nomadic is slightly different. Prairie dogs, which are rodents, make burrows in the great plains of America. These burrows are grouped to form 'townships' of several acres in extent. The mound around a burrow entrance not only protects the tunnels from flooding but also serves as a grandstand from which the owners of the territory signal their ownership or give the alarm in moments of danger. Within the townships the burrows are divided into coteries, or neighbourhood groups, averaging one male, three females and six offspring. Each member burrows and protects the boundaries of its territory with an elaborate ritual of behaviour.

Outside the breeding season, many birds relinquish their territories and form flocks which feed together. Members of these flocks are often related together in a *dominance hierarchy. Because they are banded together, each bird obtains food more easily than others, because they are helping each other to search, and each individual has a remarkably fixed relationship to the others. Such hierarchies exist in most vertebrate societies, during the reproductive period if not outside it.

Typical then of vertebrate societies are these hierarchies, which appear to be absent in other animal societies. In birds, mammals and ants another characteristic is that individuals groom each other. This is not always for a functional purpose; it does not increase when the animals' pelts or feathers are more dirty, but it seems to suppress aggressive responses and acts to keep the peace in the society.

All animal societies depend upon communication between its members. A honeybee successful in foraging performs a dance on her return to the hive which signals the distance and direction of the food source she has visited. Another example of signalling is when a dominant animal behaves in a way which is immediately recognized by the others in the group, so it does not have to be

A family group of baboons and (opposite) the serried ranks of a shoal of marine fishes afford protection, by weight of numbers, for individual members.

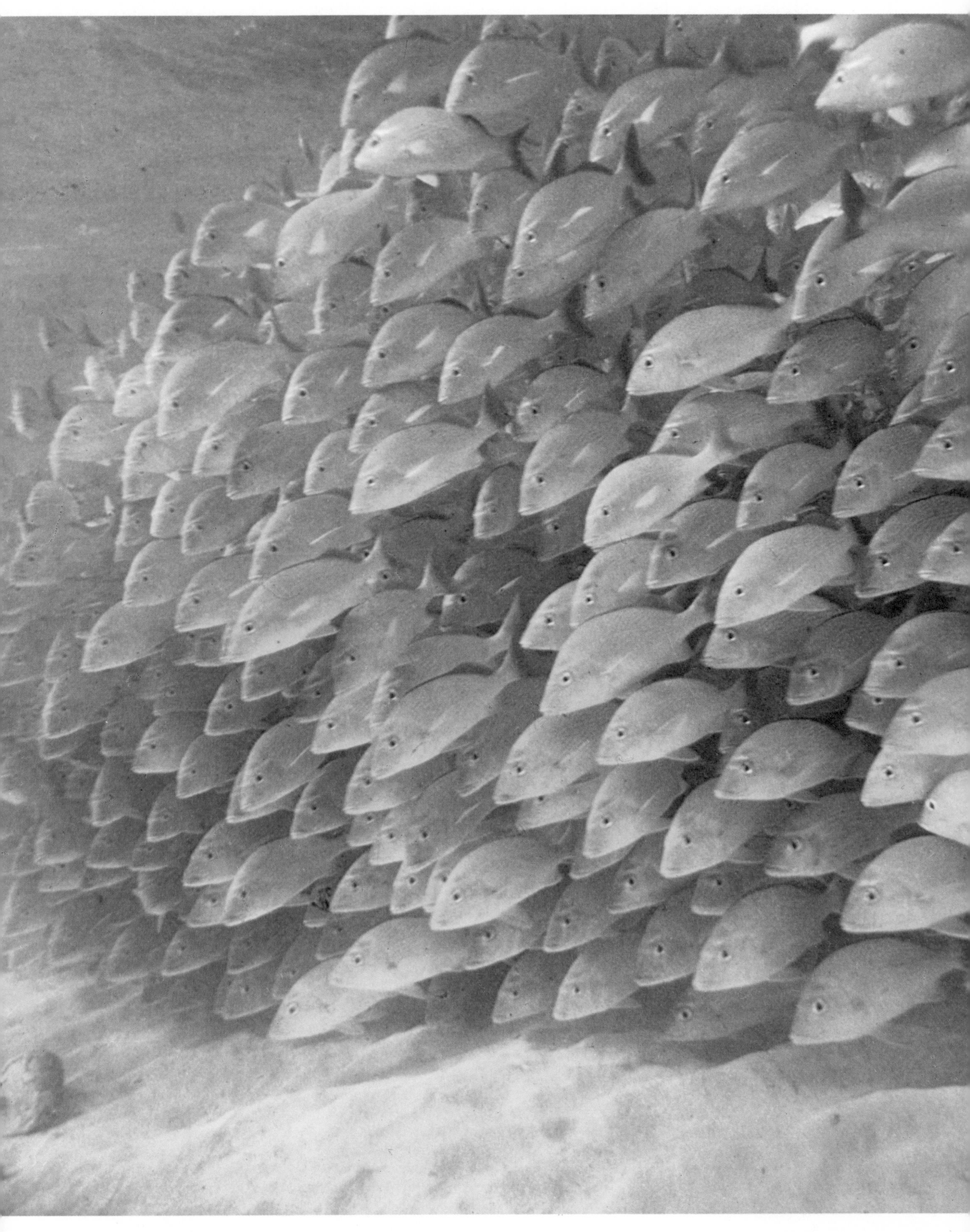

continually fighting to maintain its position. Alarm calls are another form of signalling. They are understandable by all members of the group so have obvious value.

It is plain that few animals live solitary lives entirely without contact with other members of their species. Reproduction would often be impossible if this were so. The need for selection of the right species and sex means that a system of recognition is necessary. This rests on the exchange of a series of signals. Such mutual signalling constitutes a social interchange. Thus social life is possible outside the family group. J.D.C.

ANIS, three species of cuckoos, genus *Crotophaga* of southern USA, Central and South America, inhabiting clearings and open country of the tropical lowlands. Of medium size, they have a mainly black plumage, slightly glossed with bronze, green or blue. Their tails are long and appear to be loosely joined to the body, while the legs and wings are relatively short. The birds often look awkward and ungainly. The most conspicuous feature is the bill which on the Smooth-billed ani *Crotophaga ani* is very deep and laterally flattened, appearing large and arched in outline from the side, narrow and blade-like from in front. In the Groove-billed ani *C. sulcirostris* it is less deep and has several longitudinal grooves on each side, while in the Greater ani *C. major* the narrow flattened ridge is much reduced and confined to the basal part of the bill.

Anis are highly sociable and usually keep together and move about in small groups within a territory. Groups of Smooth-billed anis will defend their territory against intruders of their own species, but the other two species appear to be more tolerant. They feed extensively on the ground, running, hopping and fluttering along. Their food consists of insects, particularly grasshoppers, but they will take small lizards, and also berries of various kinds. In farming regions they accompany grazing cattle to catch the insects they disturb and will also jump up to take the ticks from the legs of cattle.

Their flight appears weak and slow with flapping alternating with level gliding. The smaller species seem rather helpless in a high wind, but the Greater ani flies strongly. Off the ground they perch awkwardly with swinging and oscillating tails, and when resting huddle together in a close group and in such situations will frequently preen each other.

The anis have various unmusical calls; querulous and whining, or rattling and clucking in the Smooth-billed ani, shriller and more chattering in the Groove-billed ani, while the Greater ani makes guttural croaks and bubbling calls.

A group of anis will usually nest communally, although at times a single pair may nest on their own. The nest, built in a tree, is a cup made of sticks, with an inner cup of finer material; the whole structure being very bulky if a number of birds are involved. Green leaves are used for the final lining and both twigs and leaves may be added while incubation is in progress. Several females will lay in one nest. A single bird lays four or five eggs and up to 29 have been found in one nest. In such a pile of eggs those at the bottom are not incubated sufficiently and fail to hatch. The eggs are blue-shelled, but the blue is covered with a white layer, thin enough in places for a blue tint to be apparent and become scratched during incubation. The several females in the group share both incubation and the care of the nestlings. FAMILY: Cuculidae, ORDER: Cuculiformes, CLASS: Aves.

ANIS. The sociable habits of the anis extend to their huddling together on a branch to roost at night and in the early morning. They also perch in the sun with their wings extended and both habits suggest that they get chilled easily. This is supported by temperature measurements made on two captive Smooth-billed anis. Their body temperatures fell from 41°C in the evening to 33–34°C by 4 am the next morning. Their temperatures slowly returned to normal by the late morning.

ANKYLOSAURS, Cretaceous dinosaurs belonging to the Ornithischia. These quadrupedal herbivores demonstrate the greatest degree of armour plating found in dinosaurs. Some reached a length of 20 ft (6 m) and in all the much flattened head and trunk were protected on their upper surface by a mosaic of bony plates. Commonly the tail had a flexible armour of bony rings and in some species long bony spikes for defence projected from the shoulder and tail regions. The teeth were weak or absent. The group had a world-wide distribution. Well known forms are *Polacanthus* from England and *Nodosaurus* from North America.

ANNUAL FISHES, species that, for climatic reasons, complete their life cycle in a single year. In hot countries which have one or two well defined rainy seasons with an intervening rainless period, many of the smaller pools dry up between the rains. Nevertheless, such pools are often colonized by fishes, the so-called annual fishes, which deposit their eggs in the mud before the start of the dry season. As the pools dry out, the parents die but their eggs remain in the hardened mud, protected from desiccation by their tough outer membranes. Months later, with the onset of the rains, the pools refill and the eggs complete their development and hatch. Even when they are kept in an aquarium, the parents still die because their entire metabolic cycle is geared to this short period of life. Further, to raise the eggs in an aquarium it is essential to siphon out the water in order to provide the necessary dry period. There are four New World genera of toothcarps (Cyprinodontidae), comprising about 24 species, which are annual fishes (*Austrofundulus, Cynolebias, Pterolebias* and *Rachovia*), including the beautiful Argentine pearlfishes. African annual fishes include members of the genera *Nothobranchius* and *Aphyosemion*.

ANOA, the name of two small species of buffalo on the island of Celebes differing from the Water buffalo and tamarao in their small size, rounded skulls, slender build and straight horns. They are placed in the subgenus *Anoa* of the genus *Bubalus*. The horns in both species are back-pointing in line with the forehead. The Lowland anoa *Bubalus (Anoa) depressicornis* is 34 in (86 cm) high with horns 12 in (30 cm) long in males, 9 in (21·7 cm) in females. Both sexes are jet black with sparse hair and the legs are white below the knee and hocks. The horns in adults are strong ridged and triangular in section at the base. The Mountain anoa *B. (A.) quarlesi* is only 28 in (69 cm) high with horns $6\frac{1}{2}$ in (16 cm) long in both sexes. The horns are simple, smooth and conical even in adults. Both sexes are usually black with thick woolly hair and the white on the legs is restricted to a pair of spots above the hoofs. Calves of both species are golden brown; adult Mountain anoas are sometimes brown.

Both species are found all over Celebes but there are signs that the lowland species is becoming rare, as cultivation is spreading rapidly on the island. Anoas live in pairs, and wallow like Water buffalo to protect themselves from flies. They are rather dangerous, aggressive animals and cannot be caged with any other species in captivity. Moreover the male must be removed after he has serviced the cows. Both in Melbourne Zoo and in Catskill Game Park, anoa bulls have killed their cows. The Melbourne bull killed the calf as well and tried to kill his keeper. In Woburn Park the Duke of Bedford kept a pair at the beginning of the century. They would graze under the belly of a deer, then raise their heads sharply, stabbing the deer in the belly. After several deer had been killed, the anoas were caught and stabled by themselves. FAMILY: Bovidae, ORDER: Artiodactyla, CLASS: Mammalia. C.G.

ANOLE, American lizard-like reptiles of the family Iguanidae. There are 165 species, of which the best known is the Green anole *Anolis carolinensis*. Anoles, which are also known as American chamaeleons from their ability to change colour rapidly, range from

5–19 in (12·5–47·5 cm) in length. The toes of anoles are armed with small sharp claws and have adhesive pads of minute transverse ridges which enable them to cling to rough and smooth surfaces alike. The Green anole is active in daylight and moves continuously and rapidly searching for insects in bushes and trees. Male anoles have a reddish throat sac which is extended to deter rival males from encroaching on another's territory. FAMILY: Iguanidae, ORDER: Squamata, CLASS: Reptilia.

ANOMOCOELA, amphibians belonging to the suborder Anomocoela with procoelous vertebrae and lacking ribs. The single family Pelobatidae has members in Europe, North America and Asia. They are known as Spadefoot toads because of their ability to burrow using a crescent-shaped horny projection on the side of the foot with which to dig. The Western American form *Scaphiopus couchi* lives in semi-desert regions and may burrow several feet underground to avoid desiccation. The European spadefoot *Pelobates fuscus* lives in sandy areas and on capture emits a secretion which is said to smell of garlic, hence its German name 'Knoblauchskröte', Garlic toad. ORDER: Anura, CLASS: Amphibia.

ANOMURA, the suborder of decapod crustaceans which includes the Hermit crabs, Squat lobsters (at least in one sense of the term) and also several related animals in which the abdomen is much shortened so that they have come to resemble the true crabs. Best known of these perhaps is the Robber crab of the South Pacific Islands renowned for its ability to climb coconut trees and for its alleged ability to open the nuts. It is possible also that the Sponge crab belongs here though it is most usually classified as a true crab. ORDER: Crustacea, PHYLUM: Arthropoda.

ANTARCTIC CODS, fishes belonging to the family Nototheniidae, but in no way related to the true cods. They are placed in a suborder that includes the icefishes. The Antarctic cods are confined to the ocean surrounding Antarctica and live in waters which are permanently only just above freezing. They are generally sluggish bottom-living forms with large heads and jaws and show their relationship to other perch-like fishes in the presence of spines on the first part of the dorsal fin. FAMILY: Nototheniidae, ORDER: Perciformes, CLASS: Pisces.

ANTARCTIC FAUNA, the environmental conditions and fauna of this area are dealt with under Polar faunas.

ANTBIRDS, a large diverse family (Formicariidae) of rather small American perching birds, sometimes called 'antthrushes', though that name is now usually restricted to particular genera (*Formicarius, Chamaeza,* etc). There are 223 species all less than 12 in (30 cm) long. Combinations of the prefix 'ant' with other bird names (shrike, wren, vireo and pitta) or with general terms (catcher and creeper) are used to designate other genera. The plumage is in shades of black, grey, brown, rufous, chestnut, olive and white, and the females often differ from the males in having black replaced by brown, rufous or chestnut. There is often a short crest, and the feathers of the back, rump and flanks are long, loose and silky. The wings are short and rounded, the bill stout and strong with a hooked upper mandible and the feet and legs strong and well developed. The voice is generally harsh and unmusical.

The family is confined to wooded areas, essentially lowland and mountain forest, in Central and South America, from southern Mexico to Argentina, Bolivia and Peru. It reaches Trinidad and Tobago, but not the Antilles, and is absent from Chile and the treeless areas south of La Plata, extending farther south on the eastern side of the Andes than it does on the western side.

Breeding is known for only a few species, and these may not be typical of the family. The nest may be a woven cup suspended by the rim from a forked twig (*Sakesphorus* spp) or may be a normal nest supported in a fork (*Myrmeciza* spp), but some species are said to nest in holes or on the ground. Two white eggs with blotches, spots or scrawls of brown, purple, lavender, or reddish hues, often as a zone at the larger end, seem to be the normal clutch, but one species of antshrike commonly lays three eggs. The interval of laying is about 48 hours in the Black-crested antshrike *Sakesphorus canadensis,* but it is not known if that is representative of the family. The incubation period, determined in few species, is between 14 and 17 days, the nestling period between 9 and 13. The sexes share duties at the nest, and the female broods at night in those few species adequately studied.

These birds live in thickets and forest undergrowth or in areas with good cover, but some genera of antwrens and antvireos hunt through the trees well above the ground. The flight is neither strong nor sustained, and some species are unwilling to cross open areas. A close association with Soldier ants is established in species such as the Spotted antbird *Hylophylax naevioides,* so that the distribution, activity and feeding of the birds is probably dependent on the activities of the ants. The prefix 'ant' has presumably been extended from these species associating with ants to the whole family, but this is misleading since many genera (e.g. *Sake-*

This Hermit crab off the Philippines uses a mollusc shell for protection.

sphorus) apparently never associate with ants. Moreover the resemblance of many species to shrikes, wrens, thrushes, etc is so slight that the popular names are generally unhelpful. FAMILY: Formicariidae, ORDER: Passeriformes, CLASS: Aves. S.M.

ANTEATER, the comprehensive name for several South American mammals including the Giant anteater, the tamandua and the Two-toed anteater. There are several other mammals adapted to feeding on ants or, more especially, termites, the so-called White ants. To avoid confusion it is best to speak of these last as ant-eaters (with a hyphen), since they do not belong to the family Myrmecophagidae or anteaters (without a hyphen). The ant-eaters are the echidna or Spiny ant-eater, the numbat or Banded ant-eater and the pangolin or Scaly ant-eater. The aardvark and aardwolf are also ant-eaters and show the same adaptations as the others, such as weak teeth and long tongues, but they are not usually referred to as ant-eaters (see edentates and tamandua).

ANTELOPES, slenderly built, graceful, swift-moving hollow-horned ruminants. As thus defined, the term covers all members of the Bovidae except for the cattle-buffalo group and the sheep, goats and goat-antelopes, as well as the American pronghorn, the sole living member of the family Antilocapridae. There is therefore no single zoological grouping which can be translated as 'antelopes'.

A general survey of antelopes (except the pronghorn) and their relatives appears under the heading Bovidae: and detailed descriptions of the various kinds of antelopes under their respective names including addax, blaauwbok, blackbuck, bongo, chiru, dibatag, duiker, Dwarf antelope, eland, Four-horned antelope, gazelle, gnu, hartebeest, impala, kudu, nilgai, oryx, reedbuck, rhebok, Roan antelope, Sable antelope, saiga and waterbuck.

ANTHOZOA, name given to a class of the phylum Cnidaria which includes the corals and Sea anemones.

ANTHROPOIDEA, a suborder of Primates: the so-called 'Higher Primates'—monkeys, apes and man. They differ from the Prosimii (Lower Primates) in their reduced olfactory (smelling) system and shorter snout, at least in most forms, bigger brains and greater intelligence, forward-facing orbits giving stereoscopic vision, and greater manual dexterity. Instead of the moist, naked muzzle with the upper lip bound to the gum—an adaptation for the sense of smell found in prosimians as in many other mammals—the Anthropoidea have a hairy nose and free upper lip, so that the olfactory elaboration has been lost and replaced by a much greater facial mobility: facial communication is highly developed among the Anthropoidea. The tarsier is the only prosimian with a similar muzzle, and may be closely related to the stock from which the Anthropoidea evolved.

Baboon and her baby, and (opposite) a female guenon monkey with her growing offspring.

The Anthropoidea are a very diverse group which includes, as well as man and apes, some very different animals all popularly lumped together as 'monkeys'. They are classified as follows:

Infraorder 1 Platyrrhini		
Family Callitrichidae		
Genera:	*Callimico*	Goeldi's marmosets
	Saguinus	Tamarins
	Leontideus	Golden marmosets
	Callithrix	Common marmoset
	Cebuella	Pygmy marmosets
Family Cebidae		
Subfamily Cebinae		
Genera:	*Callicebus*	Titis
	Pithecia	Sakis
	Cacajao	Uakaris
	Cebus	Capuchin monkeys
Subfamily Aotinae		
Genera:	*Aotus*	Douroucouli
	Saimiri	Squirrel monkeys
Subfamily Atelinae		
Genera:	*Alouatta*	Howler monkeys
	Lagothrix	Woolly monkeys
	Ateles	Spider monkeys
Infraorder 2 Catarrhini		
Superfamily A Cercopithecoidea		
Family Cercopithecidae		
Subfamily Cercopithecinae		
Genera:	*Cercopithecus*	Guenons
	Erythrocebus	Patas monkeys
	Macaca	Macaques
	Theropithecus	Geladas
	Cercocebus	Mangabeys
	Papio	Baboons
Subfamily Colobinae		
Genera:	*Colobus*	Colobus
	Presbytis	Langurs
	Pygathrix	Douc and Snub-nos monkeys
	Nasalis	Proboscis monkeys
Superfamily B Hominoidea		
Family Pongidae		
Genera:	*Hylobates*	Gibbons
	Pongo	Orang-utans
	Pan	Gorillas and chimpazees
Family Hominidae		
Genus	*Homo*	Man

The differences between Platyrrhini and Catarrhini seem rather subtle and unimportant, but in fact their fundamental nature is shown by their consistency; no fossil classifiable as one of the Anthropoidea can be demonstrated to be their common ancestor, and the probability is that the two anthropoid infraorders evolved separately from the prosimian family Omomyidae in the Eocene and Oligocene. All the Platyrrhini have three premolars on each side of each jaw, so that the usual dental formula is $\frac{2.1.3.3}{2.1.3.3}$ (some platyrrhines, however, have only two molars instead of three); the catar-

The Anthropoidea, showing their range of form and main lines of evolutionary development, blue to platyrrhine monkeys, red to catarrhine monkeys and to apes and man.

Entelles
angabeys
Gibbons
Gorilles
Colobes
ercopithèques
Homme
Pongidés
Australopithèques
opithèques
Ramapithèques
M. Wilson

rhines have only two, making the dental formula $\frac{2.1.2.3}{2.1.2.3}$. The catarrhines tend to have large curved canines in the males but small ones in the females (man and gibbons being exceptions here); the platyrrhines have rather short canines in both sexes.

In platyrrhines, which means 'flat nosed', the nasal septum is very broad, with the nostrils widely spaced; in catarrhines, meaning 'downward nosed', the septum is narrow and the nostrils look forward and downward. This is one of the few ways in which the two groups can be told at a glance from their external appearance.

The thumb of platyrrhines is not very mobile, and is aligned alongside the other fingers. In picking up an object, it is as likely to be placed between fingers and palm or between digits two and three, as between thumb and forefinger. In the catarrhines the thumb is mobile and at least partly opposable, and objects can often be picked up with considerable delicacy.

In all Anthropoidea there is a menstrual cycle with monthly bleeding, but in catarrhines the bleeding is much more marked, and the female also undergoes cyclic changes in sexual skin—sometimes the skin swells up and is filled with a watery fluid.

The family Omomyidae arose in the Eocene and quickly spread so that its range extended across Eurasia and North America. It survived in North America until the Miocene, when the last known representative, the specialized genus *Ekgmowechashala,* flourished. However, in the Oligocene, there were already very advanced forms, such as *Rooneyia* from Texas. By the upper Oligocene, the Omomyidae had extended their range into South America, which was for a relatively short period joined to North America before finally becoming isolated from it until the Pleistocene. Already an adaptive radiation of forms was taking place. The upper Oligocene genus *Dolichocebus,* the first platyrrhine genus, is recognizably a marmoset; while in the Miocene the ancestors of the three subfamilies of Cebidae were established. The only significant changes needed to turn a North American, early or middle Oligocene omomyid into a South American, upper Oligocene platyrrhine monkey are an enlargement of the braincase and a decrease in the size of the facial skeleton and jaws. The fact that the major groups were established during the Miocene demonstrates how distinct and long-established are the main groups of platyrrhines, and indicates that on entering South America the platyrrhines rapidly branched out to fill vacant niches.

Among living platyrrhines, the family Callitrichidae are in many ways the most primitive, with many tactile hairs (vibrissae), including a tuft on the wrist where no other monkeys have them. Marmosets have claws on all their digits except the great toe where there is a nail as in most other Primates. There is controversy at the present time over whether the claws of marmosets are primitive (inherited from pre-Primate ancestors) or specialized (a fairly recent development of marmosets, from ancestors who had nails). Most marmosets also lack the third molars: but so also do some Cebidae, so this is a less fundamental difference. Marmosets are small squirrel-like short-faced monkeys which tend to live in pairs; they generally bear two young at a time, unlike most other Primates.

The Cebidae are rather larger monkeys, with nails on all digits, but these are often rather convex and almost claw-like. They are very difficult to classify, and are often divided into six or seven subfamilies, almost one to each genus! The classification given here is based on the studies of J. Anthony, R. I. Pocock and P. Hershkovitz.

The subfamily Cebinae are not very unspecialized: they do not have prehensile tails, or enlarged orbits, or any of the advanced characters of their relatives. They all have rather straight, small faces, big rounded braincases, and coarse or silky long hair. The hand always forms a single grasping unit, with the thumb closely aligned with the other fingers. The tail is generally long, thickly-furred, and used as a balancing organ, although some Capuchin monkeys can hang by them. The Capuchin monkey, the most 'advanced' of the subfamily, is highly intelligent, and usually scores in mental tests only a little less than the apes—considerably more than the Old World monkeys.

Female gorilla.

The subfamily Aotinae includes two genera with big eyes and long, low skulls, well-developed sensory pads on the hands and short, close upstanding fur. The Douroucouli or Night monkey is the only Higher Primate that is nocturnal; it consequently has fewer facial gestures than other anthropoids, but a far more complex repertoire of vocalizations.

The subfamily Atelinae are the most highly specialized of the New World monkeys. All members have long tails which are thoroughly prehensile, and modified on the underside towards the tip with hairless skin forming dermatoglyphics ('fingerprints') which aid grasping. The tail is highly sensitive and is used as a fifth limb, both in locomotion and to stabilize the animal while feeding.

Marmosets and some cebids, such as titis and douroucoulis, move by a scurrying type of locomotion, often with a galloping gait; the legs are considerably longer than the arms, and it is worth remembering that their immediate ancestors, the omomyids, were 'vertical clingers and leapers'. Capuchins and sakis have limbs of more nearly equal length and are more truly quadrupedal. Finally the Atelinae, most markedly the Spider monkeys, move at least partially by brachiation (arm-swinging). Spider monkeys have arms longer than their legs; sometimes they walk quadrupedally, and sometimes they swing through the branches with their arms and tail, the legs dangling down.

The earliest Catarrhini are Eocene: that is to say, they arose from their omomyid ancestors earlier than the platyrrhines arose from theirs. The earliest catarrhine genus, *Amphipithecus* from the upper Eocene of Burma, still had three premolars like its omomyid ancestors and like the platyrrhines; so did the Oligocene family Parapithecidae, whose remains are abundant in deposits at the Fayûm in Egypt. Already in the Oligocene, however, some forms with the reduced number of premolars existed: *Propliopithecus* from the middle Oligocene, and its descendant *Aegyptopithecus* of the upper Oligocene, both from the Fayûm. The latter, at least the males, had rather large canines like most catarrhines. A complete skull of *Aegyptopithecus* was recently discovered in Egypt by Elwyn Simons, of Yale, making this the best-known Oligocene Primate. The face was still long and the braincase small, but certain characters definitely foreshadow later catarrhines.

The two superfamilies of catarrhines are each distinguished by strong adaptive characters: the Cercopithecoidea have cheekteeth modified with crests for hard chewing, and the males have a sharp edge defined by a groove on the back of the canines; the Hominoidea have primitive teeth but a limb skeleton very specialized for their type of locomotion; brachiation.

Brachiation (arm-swinging), independently evolved by the Pongidae and the Atelinae of the New World, involves changes

Common marmoset.

of the muscles and skeleton which are thoroughgoing and easily recognizable. The most specialized brachiator is the gibbon, and this is also the only Old World anthropoid which brachiates as a normal mode of progression throughout its life-cycle. (Among the 'great apes', gorillas brachiate only when young, and chimpanzees and orang-utans brachiate only sporadically). The 'brachiation complex' means that the animal's anatomy is modified, so that the chest is very broad, with the shoulder-blades at the back, and a great deal of mobility at the shoulder, so that the animal concerned has a wider reach with its arms. The elbow joint, on the other hand, is very stable, but the wrist is loose and flexible. Since the posture of the creature is vertical most of the time, this requires certain changes in the skull (which must be balanced at the top of the spine) and the pelvis. The lumbar vertebrae are very large and are few in number, making the small of the back rather solid, and the sacrum (the fused bone where the spine and pelvis meet) is large and incorporates a number of vertebrae. Finally, the internal organs are suspended in a different direction from quadrupeds, and have to be supported; so the tail is dispensed with and its remnants are fused and inturned, to form a bony shelf, the coccyx.

The gibbon brachiates as a normal mode of locomotion, and its agility and rhythm are very pleasing to watch. The orang-utan is arboreal, like the gibbon, but it is too heavy to do much brachiating. The chimpanzee and gorilla are specialized for life on the ground, on top of their brachiating specializations: they walk quadrupedally on the middle joints of their fingers, a type of locomotion known as 'knuckle-walking'. Man is placed in a separate family, Hominidae, because—although he still has much of the brachiation complex inherited from his more apelike ancestors—he is intensely specialized for bipedal walking.

Since most fossils are known by their teeth, and the teeth of Old World monkeys are more specialized than those of apes, it is easier to say whether a given fossil form is a specialized monkey than if it is a specialized ape. Consequently, most fossil catarrhines are classified as apes 'by default': the Miocene genus *Dryopithecus*, very common in deposits in Africa, India and Europe, has primitive ape-like teeth, but as its limbs become better known it is becoming clearer and clearer that, to start off with, it was a quadruped like monkeys, and its brachiating characters developed during the course of the Miocene. It is not until the middle Miocene that we find traces of cercopithecoid teeth, so that it seems that the apes came first, and Old World monkeys evolved from them.

The primitive teeth of pongids are suitable for the ancestral primate diet of fruit. The specialized teeth of cercopithecoids are good for feeding on much coarser, harsher vegetation, such as leaves, and it seems that when these monkeys evolved they were more efficient at leaf-eating than apes, and so displaced them. Apes then specialized in fruit-eating, which they did by developing the ability to hang by the arms, at the ends of branches where the fruit grows. The degree to which the cercopithecoids displaced them is reflected in their relative abundance today, monkeys being far more numerous and successful than apes, and in the fact that after the Miocene only monkeys have been found as fossils—apes, in other words, became so rare that they appear not to be present in Pliocene and Pleistocene deposits.

It is noticeable that the ape/monkey split was taking place in the Old World at a time—middle Miocene—when the main groups of New World monkeys (platyrrhines) had already arisen and become established. The Old World monkeys are a rather close-knit group, with only the two subfamilies marking a divergence of any importance. The three genera of apes are rather more distinct, and the gibbons in particular may have become distinct before all the anatomical characters of the 'great apes' were established.

Man's ancestors first became distinct from those of apes at the very end of the Miocene: the genus *Ramapithecus,* now recognized as the earliest hominid, has been found in Kenya, India and China. It is thought probable that the orang-utan's ancestors had already become distinct by this time, since the gorilla, chimpanzee and man share some anatomical specializations, also some reactions of the blood and shape of the chromosomes, which are lacking in orang-utan and gibbon. Consequently, some specialists now prefer to classify the Hominoidea as follows:

Family Hylobatidae		
Genus:	*Hylobates*	Gibbons (sometimes divided into 2–3 genera)
Family Pongidae		
Genus:	*Pongo*	Orang-utans
Family Hominidae		
Genera:	*Pan*	Gorillas and chimpanzees
	Homo	Man

ANTHROPOMORPHISM, the attribution of human qualities to animals. Usually this consists of seeing human motives and emotions in the behaviour of animals. This can be used as a means of explaining the behaviour. But this explanation is by the transference of introspection into one's own behaviour–probably a uniquely human ability–to the working of an animal's nervous system. It also carries the implication that animals possess something akin to the human mind.

Psychology as a science depends upon the possibility of analysis of behaviour by introspection; by extension, since it is accepted that human beings all have minds of a similar kind, the analysis can be made into a generalization applicable to all men. It is impossible, however, for an animal to convey what is going on in its mind (if it has one).

Psychology is therefore a subjective science while ethology, the study of animal behaviour, strives to be an objective one. Tinbergen in 1942 called for such objective descriptions of animal behaviour using words which as far as possible do not carry an emotive content. Ideally, therefore, one should avoid such words as 'alarm' and 'fear', for they carry the implication of something akin to human emotion. In practice it is difficult to avoid the use of such words and they are frequently employed to avoid the lengthy and verbose phrases that would be necessary in their place. But it is easier to avoid the imputation of human motives and purpose to an animal. By adhering to Tinbergen's ideals as rigorously as is practicable, it is possible to make a description of behaviour which is comparable with those of other workers on the same species in different circumstances, or on different species. Since ethology depends very much on such comparisons this is plainly a valuable discipline.

The idea that an animal behaves purposefully in a way which leads to a biologically useful goal is natural, but unscientific. It is not necessary to suppose that an action pattern triggered by some environmental stimulus is being carried on with an end in view. This is most particularly true when the behaviour is one which seems to be largely innate. When an animal has learned that a certain action brings a reward of food one can more reasonably postulate that the action is carried out for the purpose of obtaining food. Notwithstanding this, and provided that the dangers are understood, anthropomorphism is a useful tool in designing experiments to be more appropriate for the animal's abilities and can provide useful clues for further objective work. J.D.C.

ANTING. An unusual piece of bird behaviour has attracted special attention since 1934. Before then it had been talked about but it had been regarded as an old wive's tale. In this, a bird takes an ant in its beak, raises one wing (both in some species) and appears to rub the ant on the underside of the long flight feathers. It then either swallows the ant or throws it aside, picks up another and repeats the action perhaps with the other wing. The action is performed with the bird giving every appearance of excitement. The tail is usually turned to one side or under the body, and the anting bird will often tumble as a result of the contortions into which it throws itself and it may even tread on its own tail and trip itself up. Some 250 species of birds all belonging to the order Passeriformes are known to ant. Anting may also be carried out with a variety of aromatic or pungent substances such as lemon juice, vinegar, certain berries, beetles, moths, hot ashes, smoke and fire. It is unpredictable in the sense that some birds seem to be confirmed anters, others indulge only occasionally and there are some individuals that seem never to ant. There are also

European jay in anting contortions.

those that ant a few times at a very early age and never again and those that fail to ant throughout a lifetime and then do so a few times before they die. On the face of it it would seem that the birds are using the formic acid given out by ants and the other substances, as a means of ridding themselves of skin parasites. This is a view usually taken only by those who have not studied the subject sufficiently, as the evidence is against this explanation. For example, in the only careful test made the only mites killed by the formic acid were those that benefit the bird by feeding on dead scales of its skin. The harmful mites went unscathed. So far as aviary birds are concerned the more infected by skin parasites they are the less they are disposed to ant. Another suggestion is that the formic acid acts as a tonic to the feathers. One paradoxical aspect of anting is that all birds so far observed critically begin anting with the left wing and they anoint their feathers with the formic acid or other substances, on average, three times on the left wing to every once on the right wing. This suggests the behaviour is to some extent ritualized.

One remarkable feature is the anting with fire, which causes birds to carry glowing embers or lighted cigarettes onto thatched roofs or into their nests so setting them on fire, and there is reason to believe that of a surprising high percentage of buildings set on fire this has been the cause. A bird anting with fire on a burning nest would look like the conventional picture of the *phoenix, and it may be that it was such a bird that Pliny referred to as a false phoenix seen in Rome. M.B.

ANT LIONS, name given to the larvae of a group of insects belonging to the Neuroptera and related to the Lacewing flies. The larval Ant lion digs itself a small conical pit in sand or soft soil and buries itself at the bottom of

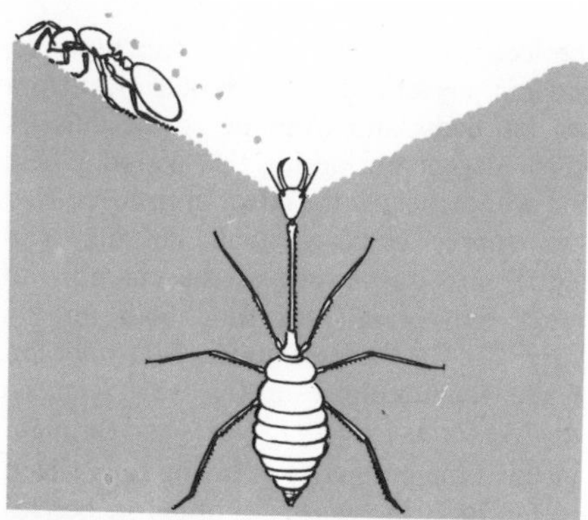

Southeast Asian Ant lion, with very long 'neck' waits for small insects to slide into its pit.

it. Ants and other small insects wandering across the ground fall into the pit and are seized by the Ant lion before they are able to escape up the loose soil of the pit walls. Ant lions, *Myrmeleon* spp, are common in southern Europe and the family is very widely distributed in tropical and subtropical regions.

The adult Ant lion fly bears a superficial resemblance to the thin-bodied dragonflies, from which it is easily distinguished, however, by its long clubbed antennae and two prominent parallel veins in the wings which have no cross veinlets between them. Some of the tropical species may have a wing-span of up to 4 or 5 in (10–12½ cm). Their wings are usually of equal size, translucent with mottled patches. Some tropical species have enormously elongated hindwings drawn out at the ends so that they are shaped roughly like a squash racquet. Ant lions are nocturnal and their weak flight, achieved with their seemingly oversized wings, makes them conspicuous as they fly around lights.

The larvae generally have pear-shaped bodies with enormous curved mandibles. Some species in Southeast Asia have a greatly elongated prothorax which gives the impression of a very long neck and therefore a rather bizarre appearance. FAMILY: Mymeleontidae, SUBORDER: Planipennia, ORDER: Neuroptera, CLASS: Insecta, PHYLUM: Arthropoda. R.C.F.

Larva of Ant lion *Myrmeleon alternatus*.

ANTPIPITS is or rather was, the name given to the family of insectivorous birds, Conopophagidae, sometimes also known as 'gnat-eaters', which inhabit the forests of tropical South America. The group was split

Adult Ant lions are seldom on the wing by day.

into two genera. The first, *Conopophaga* spp, are large robin-sized ball-like birds with long thin legs and short wings and tails, which live among the lower branches of trees. The other, *Corythopis,* has two species of smaller, more elongated, pipit-like and pipit-sized, birds inhabiting the forest floor. Recent studies on the internal structure of these birds suggest that the genus *Conopophaga* should be placed with the antbirds and *Corythopis* with the Tyrant flycatchers. FAMILY: Conopophagidae, ORDER: Passeriformes, CLASS: Aves.

ANTS, small insects of which 3,500 species have been described from the tropics and the temperate zones. All are social living in colonies, which may consist of a few individuals, as in the Ponerinae, or as many as 100,000 individuals in, for example, the Wood ant *Formica rufa*. An ant is recognizable by its 'waist' or petiole formed by a narrow segment or segments between abdomen and thorax. Females and males are winged when they leave the nest but are wingless at other times. Winged ants, which fly slowly in great clouds at certain times of the year, are not a separate species but the reproductive members of colonies which have left to swarm.

Ants are very clearly polymorphic with worker, male and female castes. Males of all species are rather alike being winged and having well developed eyes and long antennae. They are usually to be found only at certain times of the year, for they do not survive mating for long and are not readmitted to the nest after the nuptial flight.

With very few exceptions, all species of ants have a clearly recognizable worker caste consisting of sterile females whose function is to forage, build the nest and care for the young. They are wingless and often their eyes are small. In many species the workers do not produce eggs but in some they lay eggs which are used to feed young larvae. These eggs, as they are not fertilized, could only give rise to males. Workers vary in size and typically those hatched from the first eggs laid by a queen establishing a new nest are smaller than those forming the bulk of the population. However, there may be a spread of size at all times in the colony, the smaller ones then seem to pass most of their time within the nest while the larger ones protect the nest and forage. But there may be two very clearly defined kinds of workers and in this case the larger ones, known as the soldiers, have very large, strongly chitinized heads and strong mandibles. As their name implies one of their functions is to fight to protect the nest, but in addition they may help the smaller workers when they have found a large piece of food that needs to be broken up before it is transported to the nest.

As in honeybees, but unlike termites, the ant queen is solitary and not accompanied by a male when she establishes a nest. She is usually larger than males or workers but has fully functional mouthparts. After fertilization, which generally takes place in the air, the queen lands and pulls off her wings with her jaws or rubs them off against a solid object. She then begins to excavate a small chamber within which she remains until the following year. Very soon she lays a few eggs which will develop into workers. She tends these eggs and when the larvae hatch she feeds them upon salivary secretions depending, herself, solely upon nutriment from her fat body and from her flight muscles which degenerate during this period. These first workers show the effect of their reduced food supply in being small, but they can nevertheless break out of the chamber to forage and bring back food both for the queen and for the later young. Many species of ants found colonies in this way. A queen may live for as long as 15 years and throughout this time is capable of laying eggs which are fertilized by sperm deposited in her receptaculum seminis during the mating flight.

The eggs of ants are white and not more than $\frac{1}{50}$ in (0·5 mm) long. The 'ants eggs' sold as fish food are the cocoons of ants and not the true eggs. Workers carry the eggs about as conditions within the nest change, always maintaining them in that part of the nest where the conditions are optimum. They are licked by the workers and this keeps them free of fungal infection. The larvae are grub-like with a head and about 13 segments. They are legless but seem, in some species, to solicit food from workers by side-to-side movements of the front end of their bodies. They are kept in piles of equal size and of roughly equal age. Should there be a larger individual in the pile more attention will be paid by the 'nurses' to that one. Therefore sorting the larvae so that all are of the same size ensures that each gets a fair share of attention.

On the whole the larvae are fed upon regurgitated liquid material. The foragers transfer food to other workers and the same kinds of trophallactic relationships exist amongst ants as amongst honeybees. In some primitive ants (Ponerinae) insect prey is given to the larvae, which are active enough to tear it apart, and de-husked seeds are given to the larvae of Harvest ants. In due course the larvae pupate, often first spinning a cocoon around themselves. Workers aid them in breaking out of this covering when they have changed to the adult form. The caste of an ant is determined by the amount of food which is fed to it as a larva. Those destined to be reproductives are given a high protein diet while the future workers receive a largely carbohydrate diet. Whether the ant is male or female is genetically determined and as in all Hymenoptera the female ants, i.e. queens and workers, have XX chromosomes and the males have XY.

Colonies of ants live in a great variety of structures, usually made by themselves. Many make galleries in the soil with chambers scattered through the depth of the nest. In these chambers broods are kept, or seeds stored as food, or fungus grown upon beds of macerated leaves. These fungus gardens are typical of the Leaf-cutter ants of the tropics (Attinae) which strip nearby trees

Wood ant nests may be more than 3 ft (1 m) high.

to obtain the material upon which to grow their fungus. Their young are fed upon the bromatia, bodies produced by the fungus only in this underground situation. The nests of Leaf-cutter ants, which are a serious agricultural pest, go very deep, making them difficult to destroy.

Other species make mound nests. The Wood ant of Europe digs down a short distance and makes part of its nest below ground but above it piles pine needles, small twigs and the like between which the galleries of the nest penetrate. The entrances to the passages are closed when it is necessary to conserve heat within the mound and are re-opened if the internal temperature rises too high. Some of the smaller ants, like *Leptothorax,* which have colonies of relatively few individuals, may live under the bark of sticks lying on the ground. 'Paper' made from wood chewed by the insects themselves is another building material, while some tropical species occupy chambers within plants. The plants response to this is often to produce gall-like formations which become riddled with the ants' galleries. One unusual type of nest is built by the Tailor ant *Oecophylla smaragdina*. Workers hold two leaves together, grasping one with their mandibles while gripping the other with their hindlegs. Other workers, holding larvae in their jaws, 'sew' the leaves together by moving the heads of the larvae to touch first one leaf and then the other. The larvae produce silk which holds the leaves firmly together. This ant is a serious pest of coffee plantations, for it keeps various plant-pest insects within its leaf-house where they are protected against insecticidal sprays.

Army ant soldier with workers.

The Army ants (Dorylinae) cannot be said to have any permanent dwelling place and they do not construct a nest. They move in long columns over the countryside clearing it of other insects and even small birds and

Wood ant guard on the alert (top left) and (below) Wood ant worker carrying a cocoon to safety.

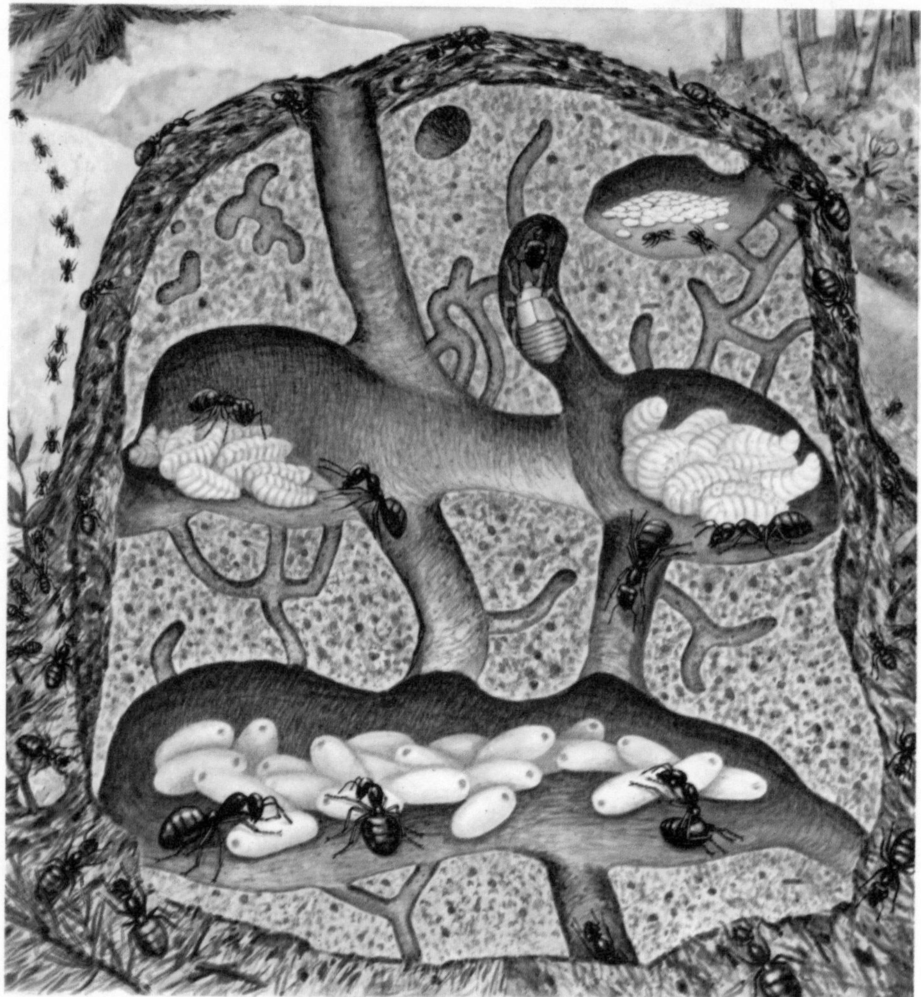

Cross-section of the nest of Wood ants with (top right) eggs, (underneath) a guest, (middle left) small larvae, (middle right) big larvae, (bottom) pupae.

Busy scene at entrance to an ant's nest.

mammals as they go. Each night they bivouac below a log or in a similar situation and march on the next morning. Periodically they settle for a longer period in a hole or within a hollow log. These phases occur just after the queen has laid her eggs and when there are no larvae in the colony.

Such Army ants are, together with the ponerine ants, the most primitive ants and are entirely carnivorous. More highly evolved ants have a vegetarian diet. Some collect seeds and use them for food. They bite off the radicles of the seeds and thus prevent them from germinating. In warm weather these Harvester ants can be seen to bring the seeds to the surface and lay them out to dry. The most highly evolved ants have taken to a purely liquid diet, obtaining nectar from flowers or secretions from certain plant-eating insects. The habit of looking after aphids to obtain food from them is widespread. Sometimes ants will protect such greenfly by building shelters over them or, in the case of *Lasius flavus,* excavating 'stables' around the rootlets upon which the aphids feed. The honeydew collected by the ants is a food surplus to the greenfly's requirements which is exuded from its anus. *Lasius niger's* habit of keeping blackfly colonies clean by removal of the honeydew has been demonstrated to increase the reproductive rate of the aphids. When not attended by the ants the honeydew gathers around the aphids, becomes infected by fungi and other microorganisms and reduces the aphids' reproductive potential.

Other insects are also symbiotic, living within the ants' nests. Some (synechthrans) scavenge in the nest and are treated with hostility by the ants; others (synoekets) are tolerated and are mostly small and inconspicuous. But a further group, the symphiles are true guests and are welcomed by the ants as they supply them with attractive secretions. *Lomechusa,* a beetle like the majority of these guests, has tufts of secretory hairs on its body from which the ants lick what are, apparently, much appreciated substances. The young of the symphiles may even be reared by the ants themselves, even though occasionally these young eat the ant larvae.

Various kinds of relationships between one ant species and another have arisen. It may be that two species will occupy the same nest. Some ants make slaves, thus *Formica sanguinea* will remove the cocoons from *F. fusca* nests and rear the *fusca* workers in their own colonies. These add to the labour force of the *sanguinea* and are completely accepted by the workers of this species. Other ants are social parasites. *Anergates atratulus* has no workers. Queens of this species invade nests of *Tetramorium caespitum* so that their eggs may be tended by the *Tetramorium* workers. The relationship may end by the *Anergates* killing the host queen and the take-over is complete. SUPERFAMILY: Formicoidea, ORDER: Hymenoptera, CLASS: Insecta, PHYLUM: Arthropoda. J.D.C.

ANTS IN COLUMNS, stories of the Army ants of the tropics, also known as Soldier, Driver or Legionary ants, are often exaggerated. Yet there is no doubt that a column of Army ants is an impressive sight. The individual ants may be over 1 in (2·5 cm) long and a column may be many yards long. Their usual prey is small arthropods and when Army ants invade a house they perform a useful service in clearing it of insect pests. Vertebrates are usually able to escape because the column only travels at about 50 ft (15 m) per hour although tethered horses and cattle may be eaten alive.

In South America Army ants attract a crowd of 'camp followers' who feed on the small animals flushed by the ants. The first indication of an approaching column may be the flocks of small birds flying and hopping through the undergrowth over the ants. Some, such as the antbirds, motmots, tanagers and woodcreepers, make a regular habit of following Army ants and they are joined by migrants from North America. Parasitic flies also follow the swarms of ants to lay their eggs in the ants' prey.

ANURA, tailless amphibians, including frogs and toads, which are the most successful of living amphibians, with some 250 genera and around 2,600 species. They are widely distributed throughout temperate and tropical regions except for a number of small islands in the Pacific. Some species live in the inclement conditions of Patagonia and others within the Arctic Circle in Europe.

Living frogs and toads have short squat bodies, large eyes and long hindlimbs. The length of the hindlimb is partially due to the presence of an 'extra joint' formed by the elongation of certain ankle bones. The presence of large hindlimbs is a major difference between the anurans and the tailed amphibians or Caudata, the salamanders and newts, in which the limbs are small and of roughly equal size. The other group of living amphibians, the caecilians or Apoda, are limbless. The distances covered by leaping frogs has been of considerable interest, as in the 'frog-jumping' contests in North America. Tests have shown that smaller frogs can generally jump greater distances relative to their size than the larger frogs. For example the large bullfrog *Rana catesbeiana* can leap a distance equal to nine times its own length, whereas the smaller Sharp-nosed frog *Rana oxyrhyncha* can cover a distance equal to 40 times its own body length.

The anuran vertebral column has usually only nine vertebrae and the first of these has two small areas (facets) which articulate with the hind end of the skull. The last vertebra, termed the sacral, usually bears lateral extensions which articulate with the pelvic girdle. Behind the sacral vertebra is a rod-shaped bone, the urostyle, which is thought to be derived from a number of fused, post-sacral, vertebrae. Ribs are usually absent.

The term 'toad' tends to be used in an ambiguous way; it should be restricted to the family Bufonidae, the true toads. Toads are usually more plump and less graceful than frogs and have relatively shorter hindlimbs. They have a large parotid gland just behind the head on either side and the skin frequently has a granular or warty appearance. Frogs lack parotid glands and their skin is fairly smooth.

Anurans are largely dependent on water for reproduction. Fertilization is usually external and the eggs are laid in a gelatinous mass as spawn. The life history usually involves a free-swimming stage, or tadpole, which swims by means of a tail that is lost during metamorphosis. Some anurans have departed from the usual type of life history. For example, Archey's frog *Leiopelma archeyi* (family Ascaphidae) lays its eggs under stones, the larvae developing within the egg capsule, omitting the free-swimming stage and hatching as miniature frogs.

Mating in frogs and toads involves *amplexus, or gripping of the female by the male, so that the sperm may be shed onto the eggs as they leave the female. Frogs may remain in amplexus for a number of days and a single male may undergo amplexus with a number of females at different times. Anurans often lay large numbers of eggs and a single female Marine toad *Bufo marinus* (family Bufonidae) may produce as many as 35,000 eggs. In unmated females the eggs are usually resorbed. Anurans often develop secondary sexual characteristics, that is, features which apart from the structure of the male and female reproductive system serve to distinguish the sexes. Generally the females are larger than the males. The males usually have stouter forelimbs than the females and the male forelimb is often specially modified to grasp the female during amplexus.

A characteristic of frogs and toads is the presence of a tympanic membrane on either side of the head, behind the eye. This is sensitive to air-borne vibrations and performs much the same function as the ear-drum in mammals and is correlated with the ability of frogs and toads to produce sounds. The Caudates and apodans are generally voiceless and lack a tympanic membrane, but are thought to perceive vibrations in the sub-stratum either through the lower jaw or the forelimbs. The voice in anurans also tends to be a secondary sexual characteristic since it is usually more fully developed in the male than in the female. The sounds are produced by a well developed vocal apparatus and are often amplified by the resonance of large vocal sacs. The calls of anurans differ in pitch, duration, frequency and harmonics and each species has its own particular call, although the sounds produced by closely related species are often very similar. The call of the male is largely used to attract the female at breeding time but may also be used to establish a territory. The male bullfrog takes up a 'calling station' each night at a particular spot. His call serves to warn others of his territory. Occasionally frogs which breed in spring also call at other times of the year. The Squirrel frog *Hyla squirella* (family Hylidae) has a distinctive call when the rains come in autumn, so is often termed the Rain frog. Not all frogs and toads have a voice and the Striped mountain toad *Bufo rosei,* of South Africa, has neither voice nor tympanic membrane. The Tailed frog *Ascaphus truei* (family Ascaphidae) which inhabits swift-moving mountain streams is also silent.

One of the largest anurans is the Roccoco toad *Bufo paracnemis* of Brazil which is 10 in (25 cm) long, whereas the tiny Grass frog *Hyla ocularis* is about $\frac{3}{4}$ in (1·8 cm) in length.

The anurans have a long geological history. They were probably in existence in the Carboniferous period 340 million years ago and can be traced back with certainty 230 million years to the Triassic form *Triadobatrachus* (=*Protobatrachus*). This had a skull similar to that of modern frogs but the trunk was longer and ribs were present. *Vieraella* from the early Jurassic, 180 million years ago, had a skeleton remarkably similar to that of the modern forms and most modern anuran families seem to have been in existence since the Cretaceous, 130 million years ago. This suggests that modern anurans have evolved from long-bodied forms but unfortunately we can say little of the very early ancestry of the anurans, which is true also of the caudates and apodans. This makes it extremely difficult to decide whether the anurans, caudates and apodans are closely related to each other or whether any two are closer to each other than to a third. Current opinion favours the view that the three modern amphibian groups have probably evolved from a common ancestor and should be considered as a natural group, the Lissamphibia.

The classification of frogs and toads has always presented problems. The feature which seems to be most useful is the structure of the vertebrae. On this basis it is generally agreed there are five anuran suborders with 12 families.

It is generally supposed that the families Ascaphidae, Discoglossidae and Pipidae are the most primitive. ORDER: Anura, CLASS: Amphibia. R.L.

Classification of the Anura.
Suborder Amphicoela: Family Ascaphidae
Suborder Opisthocoela: Families Discoglossidae, Pipidae
Suborder Procoela: Families Atelopodidae, Bufonidae, Hylidae, Leptodactylidae, Rhynophrynidae
Suborder Anomocoela: Family Pelobatidae
Suborder Diplasocoela: Families Microhylidae, Ranidae, Rhacophoridae

ANUS, the posterior opening of the alimentary canal. It is controlled by a circular muscle (or sphincter).

APE, a term loosely used to mean any species of Higher Primate except man, especially one without a tail (such as Barbary 'ape', Celebes 'ape', both of which are species of macaques); but more strictly, one of the 'anthropoid apes', the family Pongidae. Thus narrowed down, the term 'ape' denotes any one of the four types closest to man among the Primates: the gorilla, chimpanzee, orang-utan and gibbon.

Apes share a morphology that was evolved basically as an adaptation to brachiation, that is swinging by the arms through the trees. Today, only the gibbon is a habitual brachiator, although both the orang-utan and the chimpanzee will sometimes brachiate. The gorilla is largely terrestrial. The fundamental morphology that aligns the apes with man, and separates them from the Old World monkeys is present in all: an upright trunk, broad chest and shoulders, well-developed muscles of the back and upper arm, great mobility at the shoulder and wrist joints, stability at the elbow joint, powerful hands with short thumbs, no tail, broad pelvis, and a widely separated great toe. Man corresponds with the apes in all except the short thumb and separated great toe. These adaptations to the great toe and thumb allow apes to reach out in many directions, remain suspended by their hands for long periods, and use their feet as additional grasping organs. Living apes have long arms and short legs, and their hands are habitually held in a hook, with the fingers bent and it is not surprising that the two which spend most of their time on the ground—the gorilla and chimpanzee—have developed a specialized way of walking, on the knuckles.

Apes are like man in a number of other ways also. The tail is not only lost, its remnants are turned inwards and fused into a small shelf-like bone, the coccyx, which helps to support the viscera in the upright position. They have a vermiform appendix to the caecum. They have more complex brains than do Old World monkeys, and are more intelligent. All the apes show a good deal of manipulative skill in captivity.

An ancestral ape, *Dryopithecus,* flourished in the Miocene of East Africa, Europe and southern Asia; the earliest species were quadrupedal, and these did not develop their locomotor specializations until late in the Miocene. A second genus, the more lightly built *Pliopithecus,* existed alongside *Dryopithecus* throughout the Miocene and members of this genus have often been considered ancestral to gibbons, but the evidence for this is very dubious. At the end of the Miocene,

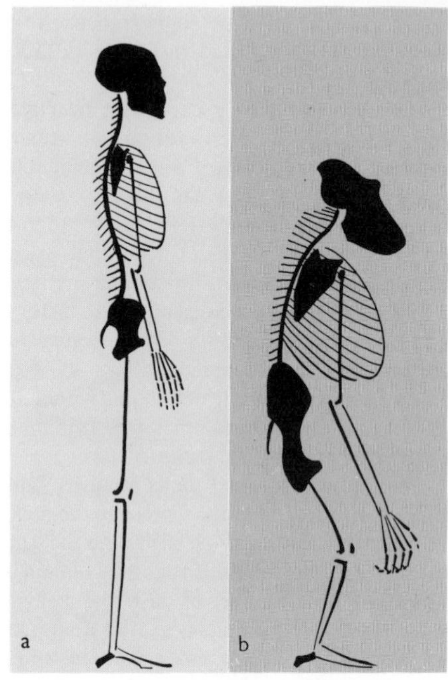

Skeletons of a) man and b) a man-like ape, showing modifications of bones linked with man's upright stance.

apes became scarce and it is evident that the rapidly evolving Old World monkeys had taken over most of the ecological niches. Even today, with the exception of gibbons, apes are becoming rare. FAMILY: Pongidae, ORDER: Primates, CLASS: Mammalia. C.P.G.

APHIDS, greenflies or plant-lice, sap-feeding insects of the superfamily Aphidoidea, order Homoptera. This order also contains cicadas, Scale insects, Spittle bugs and whiteflies.

There are about 4,000 known species of aphids—about 540 in Britain. Some are restricted to specific climatic or vegetational zones, while others, such as the Peach-potato aphid *Myzus persicae* and the Cabbage aphid *Brevicoryne brassicae,* are cosmopolitan. They are grouped into nine families, of which the family Aphididae is the largest with about 60% of the recorded species.

Aphids are small soft-bodied insects with piercing mouthparts and the tubular proboscis or rostrum usually has four evident segments. They feed by piercing the tissues of plants with their proboscis to take up the sap. The legs, usually long and slender, end in a bi-segmented tarsus and a pair of claws. The four wings, when present, are transparent and the hindwings are narrower and smaller than the forewings. The antennae have three to six segments, the last usually having a narrowed prolongation, the flagellum or unguis. Most species have paired cylindrical tubes or cones, the cornicles or siphunculi, projecting from the upper surface of the fifth or sixth abdominal segment. The last abdominal tergite is usually prolonged over the anus into a cauda.

Aphids are among the most important insect pests of plants, not only causing direct damage by feeding but indirect damage by transmitting viruses. Some, such as the Peach-potato aphid, are polyphagous, that is they feed on a number of different plants, but other species, such as the Sycamore aphid *Drepanosiphum platanoidis,* are monophagous, feeding only on one kind of plant. Many species feed exclusively on leaves and young shoots, others on the branches of woody trees and shrubs, others below ground on roots, and some live in galls.

Aphids are remarkable for their mode of development and reproduction, individuals of the same species often having a wide range of forms. Adult males and females may be winged (alate) or wingless (apterous) and the females may produce eggs (oviparity) or living young (viviparity). Females may be sexual, requiring fertilization, or they may reproduce parthenogenetically. In most families only the sexual females lay eggs, the parthenogenetic females being viviparous, but in two of the smaller families, the Adelgidae and Phylloxeridae, both the sexual and parthenogenetic females lay eggs.

Life cycles. Many species have a complex life-cycle, the sexual generation living on one kind of plant, the primary host, and the parthenogenetic generations living on others, the secondary hosts. In some species, however, the sexual and parthenogenetic generations occur on the same host. By contrast, some species have no sexual phase and reproduce only by parthenogenesis.

Species that alternate between hosts usually spend the winter as eggs laid on the primary host, often a woody plant. An example is the Black bean aphid *Aphis fabae.* Its eggs are laid on the Spindle tree and on the sterile Guelder rose. They hatch in spring to produce wingless females, the fundatrices, which reproduce parthenogenetically and viviparously. Their progeny, the fundatrigeniae, reproduce in the same way, but in the third or later generations winged parthenogenetic viviparous females, the migrantes, are produced. These migrate to her-

baceous secondary hosts, such as beans, sugarbeet and poppies, during May and June and establish colonies. Throughout the summer new generations of winged or wingless parthenogenetic viviparous females, the alienicolae, are produced on these plants and the winged forms fly to establish colonies on other plants. Towards the end of summer or during early autumn, winged males and winged viviparous females, the gynoparae, are produced, which return to the winter hosts. The gynoparae reproduce parthenogenetically to produce wingless sexual females, the oviparae. The males and oviparae mate and eggs are laid.

This kind of life-cycle is typical of many aphids in temperate climates, but other species that alternate between woody winter and herbaceous summer hosts may also overwinter as adult and nymphal viviparous females. Thus the Peach-potato aphid overwinters in egg form on peach and on other *Prunus* species, from which it migrates to many species of secondary hosts including potatoes, sugarbeet and turnips. However, in average winters in Britain more individuals may overwinter viviparously on secondary hosts than as eggs on primary hosts and in many hot countries the aphid reproduces only by parthenogenesis.

In contrast to host-alternating species, others live continuously on one kind of plant, such as trees or grasses. For example, the Sycamore aphid lays eggs on the sycamore tree, *Acer pseudoplatanus,* and on related species. The fundatrices are winged and all the subsequent generations, produced parthenogenetically and viviparously, are also winged. These may disperse from the tree on which they were born, but only to hosts of the same or related species. Similarly the Grain aphid *Sitobion avenae* which lives only on grasses and cereals, reproduces parthenogenetically throughout spring and summer and lays eggs during autumn.

Aphids are remarkable not only because of their differing life-cycle and ways of reproducing, but also for their fecundity. Many parthenogenetic viviparous females can produce 50 or more young, and these are so well developed that at birth they contain embryos. Under favourable conditions the nymphs become adult and start to reproduce in about ten days. This process may continue for many generations while host and environment remain suitable. However, their reproduction usually falls short of its potential, for host plants and weather become unsuitable, many are killed by predators, parasites and disease and many die during migration.

Migration. Aphid species that alternate seasonally between primary and secondary

Wood ants 'milking' black aphids.

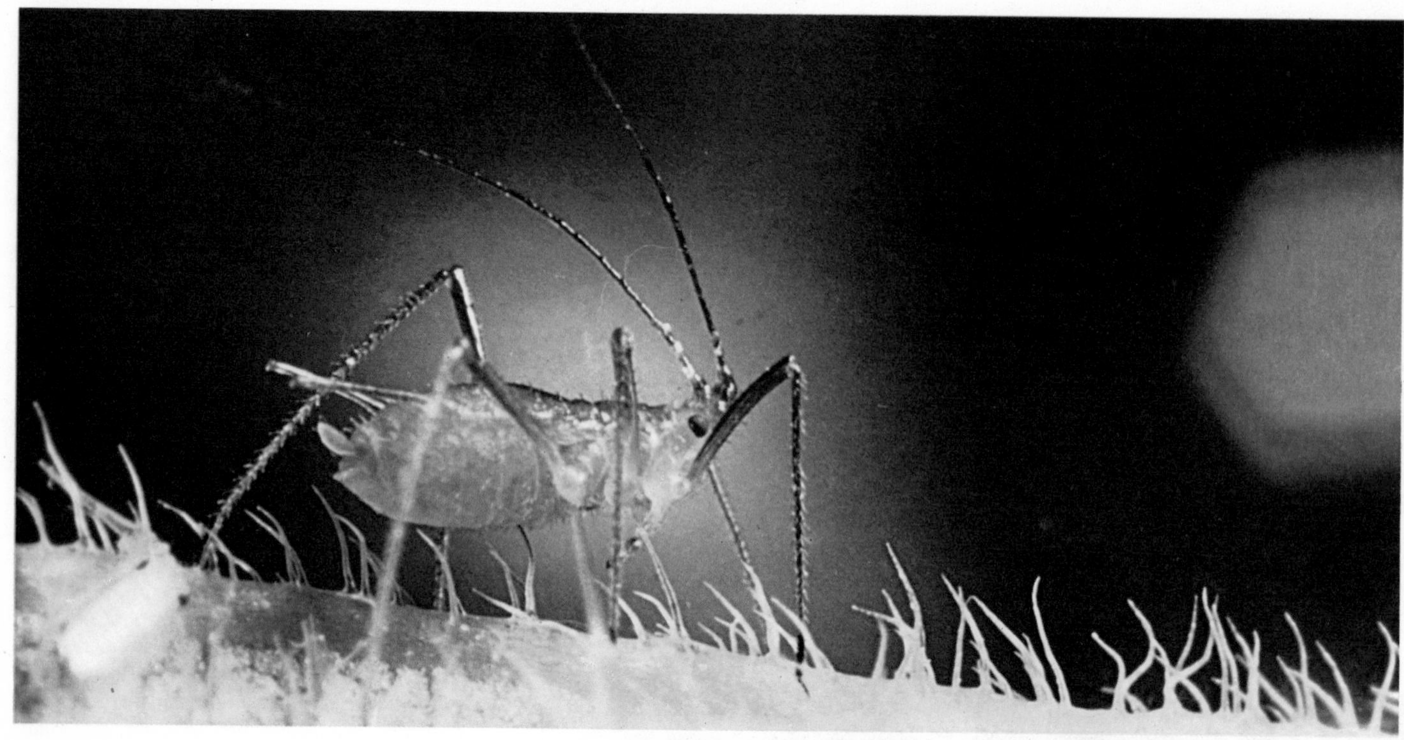

Wingless female aphid giving birth parthenogenetically.

hosts are sometimes termed migratory, and those living throughout the year on one kind of host, non-migratory. However, many so-called non-migrant species fly long distances between hosts. Thus in the United States the Spotted alfalfa aphid *Therioaphis trifolii* and the greenbug *Schizaphis* often migrate many hundreds of miles. By contrast, not all alatae even of a typical migrant species, such as the Black bean aphid, migrate and a small proportion never fly at all, but remain permanently on the plants on which they were born.

Migration may be induced by many factors, including overcrowding on the host, changes in the food supply, temperature or length of day. These factors affect development and behaviour and lead to the production of winged migrants.

Migration occurs in early adult life. Typical migrants have an almost irrepressible urge to fly as soon as they are flight mature. Reproduction is usually inhibited and usually only cold or darkness delays flight. They take off upward towards light and soon reach air currents that may carry them long distances. After a time they descend and settle on plants, and then, depending on the suitability of the plant as a host and on the length of time they have flown, they either remain and reproduce or take off again. After a few days, the flight muscles of those that remain on suitable hosts may degenerate, so that the ability to fly is lost.

Autolysis—the breakdown and absorption—of the flight muscles occurs in many, but not all, species and exceptions include the Sycamore aphid and some other tree species. These aphids can fly for most of their adult lives that most flights are local.

Aphids are very weak fliers and the distances they migrate depend on the strength and direction of the air currents they enter. The average duration of single flights seems to be between one and three hours; some single flights are much shorter, others much longer, and distances travelled may range from a few yards to hundreds of miles. Records of long distance migration are circumstantial, but there is much evidence to indicate that the greenbug and other cereal aphids often migrate hundreds of miles from south to north in the United States and that the Cowpea aphid *Aphis craccivora* migrates 200–300 miles (320–480 km) into the coastal regions near Sydney, Australia. These are two examples of the many long-distance migrations that occur.

Migrating aphids probably find hosts by chance, for they seem unable to discriminate between host and non-host until they have alighted. Attraction to hosts from a distance has never been proved and the visual powers of flying aphids probably only allows discrimination between plants and background, or between plants of very different colour, rather than between hosts and non-hosts. Thus finding a host is hazardous and undoubtedly most migrants die in the process. Success in colonizing new areas depends largely on the production of enormous numbers of migrants.

Feeding. Aphids feed by inserting their needle-like mouthparts, the stylets, into a plant. The pressure of sap within the tissues forces it into the stylets and gut, but on occasions aphids may also suck.

The stylets are long and flexible, an outer pair, the mandibular stylets, closely sheathing an inner pair, the maxillary stylets. The maxillary stylets fit together lengthways and where their innermost surfaces come together two longitudinal canals are formed, an anterior food canal and a posterior salivary canal. The stylets are ensheathed in the rostrum, from which they protrude when inserted into plants.

The stylets are pushed into plants partly by the action of muscles attached to the bases of the stylets in the head, and partly by a clamping action of the rostrum on the stylets. Penetration may be aided by the secretion of saliva, for in many species this contains the enzyme pectinase which dissolves the middle lamellae of plant cells. Many species feed on the sap of cells in or near the phloem, but some, notably the adelgids, seem to feed mainly on parenchyma, while others live on mosses which have only rudimentary vascular tissues.

The turgor pressure within the cells forces sap into the stylets, for when the embedded stylets of aphids are severed from the head, sap continues to exude from the cut end for a time. However, aphids can control their rate of feeding and this rate may be increased by sucking, for they can imbibe through a membrane liquids that are not under pressure and some increase their feeding rate when attended by ants.

The sap ingested is usually rich in carbohydrates, most of which is excreted either in the ingested or a converted form. By contrast, much of the nitrogen in the sap, in the form of amino-acids or amides, is assimilated, at least 55% by the Large willow aphid *Tuberolachnus saligna* feeding on willow stems.

Excretion. Aphids and related insects, such as scale insects and cicadas, excrete a clear fluid called honeydew. From very early times deposits of honeydew on or near plants have attracted interest, especially because of their large sugar content. The 'mannas' collected and consumed by peasants in the Middle East are mainly the accumulated excreta of aphids and scale insects, the deposits hardening and crystallizing in the sun.

The composition of aphid honeydew depends on the host plant and on the species of aphid. Fresh droplets are usually complex mixtures and contain sugars, amino-acids, amides, organic acids, alcohols, auxins and salts; carbohydrates comprising most of the dry matter. Thus fresh honeydew of the Cabbage aphid, feeding on swedes, contains about 11% dry matter, of which 88% is carbohydrate and 7% nitrogenous compounds.

Different species expel honeydew in different ways. In many the tip of the abdomen is raised and the droplet is then either flicked from the anus by one of the hindlegs or by the cauda, or is expelled by contraction of the abdomen or rectum. Some species, the bodies of which are heavily coated with wax, such as the Woolly aphid *Eriosoma lanigerum,* do not dislodge the droplets from the anus; droplets solidify, or become covered with wax, and then fall off.

The honeydew of some aphids is much sought after as a source of food by ants and some other insects.

Ant attendance. Many aphid species are attended by ants which collect and feed on their honeydew, the aphids often being referred to as 'ant-cows'. Some species are more or less adapted to live with ants and do not thrive without them. This association is termed myrmecophily. Other species are merely visited by ants on their host plants, the aphids benefit by the removal of the sticky honeydew and some by the protection afforded by the ants against parasites and predators. Thus the Common black ant *Lasius niger* attacks ladybirds, anthocorid bugs and syrphid larvae feeding on colonies of the Black bean aphid.

Many of the subterranean aphids feed on the roots of plants penetrating ant nests and it is in this situation that aphids receive the best care and protection. The Artichoke tuber aphid *Trama troglodytes* and other species of *Trama, Anoecia* and *Tetraneura,* to mention a few, often occur in nests of the Mound ant *Lasius flavus* and at least 17 species of aphids have been found in nests of the Common black ant in Europe.

The care and protection afforded by ants sometimes extends to aphid eggs, which are collected during autumn and stored within the nests until spring. The nymphs emerging during spring may be carried by the ants to the roots or shoots of suitable host plants. This occurs with the Corn root aphid *Aphis maidiradicis,* which overwinter as eggs in the nests of *Lasius niger americanus* in North America.

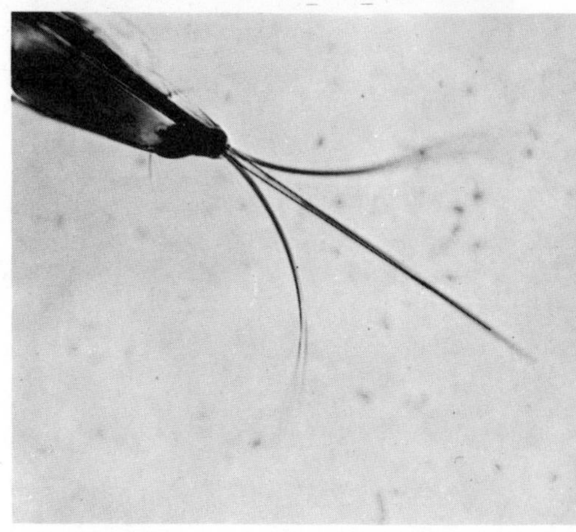

Mouthparts of the black Bean aphid showing rostrum and stylets which pierce food plants.

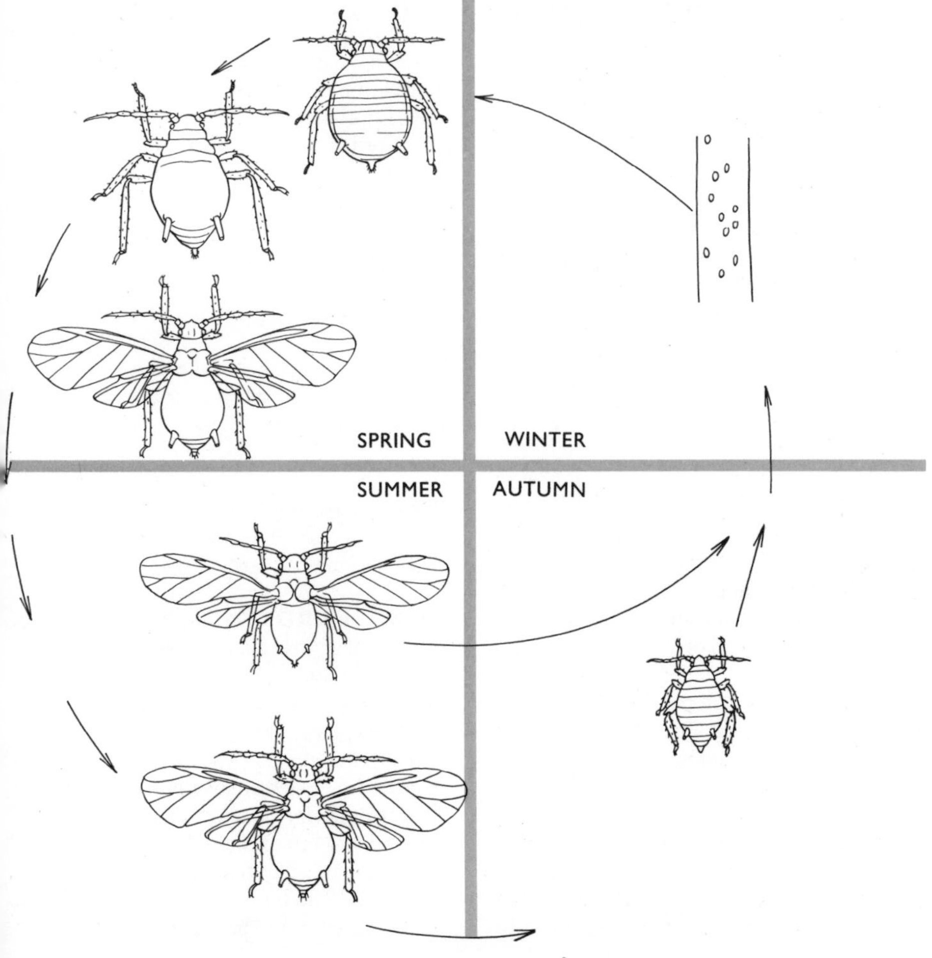

Life-history of aphids. Eggs (top right) hatch to give wingless females which reproduce parthenogenetically (top left). After several generations, wingless females (bottom right) are produced in autumn which mate with winged males (upper figure bottom left) and lay winterresistant eggs.

Natural enemies. Many insects and fungi attack aphids and can exact a heavy toll of populations, even preventing outbreaks on certain crops, but generally their effect is to lessen rather than control populations.

The main insect predators are ladybirds, hoverflies, lacewings and anthocorid bugs. Only the larvae of hoverflies and lacewings, but both larval and adult ladybirds and anthocorids, feed on aphids. The larva of the Two spot ladybird *Adalia bipunctata* eats about 15–20 aphids daily and can consume 200–500 during its development.

The main parasites are small wasps of the hymenopterous families Aphidiidae and Aphelinidae. These wasps lay their eggs in the bodies of aphids and the larvae feed on the internal tissues, eventually killing their hosts. One such wasp, *Aphelinus mali,* has been used successfully to control the Woolly aphid on apple trees in many countries.

The most important disease organisms of aphids are fungi, mainly of the genus *Entomophthora.* They are sometimes the most important natural factor limiting populations. Thus *Entomophthora aphidis* has almost obliterated populations of the Woolly pine needle aphid *Schizolachnus piniradiatae* in certain areas of Canada.

Black Bean aphids, showing winged and wingless forms.

Damage. Aphids cause direct damage to plants by feeding and indirect damage by transmitting viruses or by fouling with honeydew. Direct damage may result in wilting, distortion, stunting and defoliation. Thus heavy infestations of the Black bean aphid and the Cabbage aphid cause wilting and stunting, with consequent loss of yield, of beans and brassicas respectively; early attack may check growth beyond recovery. Sometimes leaves are so distorted that they cannot function properly. Thus the Peach-potato aphid and the Leaf-curling plum aphid *Brachycaudus helichrysi*, commonly cause the leaves of peach and plum to curl. Severe defoliation sometimes occurs, as with spruce infested with the Spruce aphid *Elatobium abietinum*.

Some aphids cause abnormal growth of tissue on the plants on which they feed. The Woolly aphid produces swellings or pseudogalls on the wood of apple trees, the bark rupturing and woody tissue growing out to form large roughened and creviced masses. Other species induce the formation of true galls. Thus the purse galls on the leaf petioles of poplars are caused by the Lettuce root aphid *Pemphigus bursarius* and the pine-apple galls, or pseudocones, of spruce are caused by the Spruce gall *Adelges abietis*.

The honeydew excreted by aphids damages some plants. The honeydew may cover the leaves and impair photosynthesis, or it may act as a substrate for the development of fungi, especially sooty moulds. Sometimes, as with the Leaf-curling plum aphid infesting the flowers of red clover, the seeds are fouled and may stick together in masses.

Often direct feeding damage or fouling with honeydew becomes apparent only when aphids are numerous, but a single aphid can transmit a virus to a susceptible plant on which it feeds.

Of the 250 known plant viruses, about 65% are transmitted by aphids. Many are acquired from infected plants during a brief feed of only a few seconds, and are transmitted to other plants within minutes. With such viruses aphids remain infective for only a short time, less than an hour when feeding and a few hours when fasting; hence these viruses are termed non-persistent. Examples are Potato virus Y and Cucumber mosaic.

Other aphid-transmitted viruses require hours or days of feeding by the aphid before the latter can acquire and transmit them, but, once infective, the aphid will remain so for many days, sometimes for life. These viruses, such as Potato leaf roll and Barley yellow dwarf, are termed persistent and may be carried considerable distances by flying aphids.

The non-persistent viruses and certain others are thought to be carried on or within the stylets and are termed stylet-borne. These comprise at least 60% of known aphid-transmitted viruses. By contrast, many of the persistent viruses are ingested and pass through the haemolymph to the salivary glands, with or without multiplication. They pass into plants again with the saliva during feeding. These viruses are called circulative.

Aphids differ in their importance as vectors. The Peach-potato aphid transmits more than 100 different viruses, of which at least 70 are stylet-borne and ten circulative. By contrast, the Sycamore aphid and the Lettuce root aphid are not known to transmit any viruses. SUPERFAMILY: Aphidoidea, ORDER: Homoptera, CLASS: Insecta, PHYLUM: Arthropoda. A.J.C.

APHIDS, the close relationship between aphids and ants appears to be based on a case of mistaken identity. According to a German zoologist, W. Kloft, the ants mistake the hind end of an aphid for the front end of an ant. When two ants meet they 'palpate', caressing each other with their antennae, and one may regurgitate liquid food for the other to eat. Aphids unwittingly mimic this behaviour. When an aphid is palpated by an ant it waves its hind legs in a disturbance response, so imitating the waving of an ant's antennae. Furthermore, the drop of honeydew at the anus is like the drop of food at an ant's mouth. Kloft tested this idea with models. A simple rounded model was ignored by ants but they were attracted by models with two bristles resembling antennae. He also found that well-fed ants tried to feed the rear ends of aphids which seems to clinch the idea that they are mistaking them for other ants.

If, however, the ant-aphid relationship started as a mistake on the part of the ants, they have capitalized on their mistake to their considerable profit.

APODA, or caecilians, limbless worm-like amphibians which burrow in the ground in tropical countries. See caecilians.

APOSTLEBIRD *Struthidea cinerea,* a babbler-like Australian species, one of three in the family of *mudnest-builders. These fluffy, grey birds, with short thick bills, are highly sociable, living in groups, and are named after the 12 Apostles. When resting they huddle together and preen each other. They live in dry areas of eastern Australia, feeding on a mixed diet of insects and seeds. They run clumsily, climb with short leaps and fly weakly. The sexes are alike. The nest is a basin-shaped mud structure reinforced with grass, built on a horizontal limb, in which the group nests communally. Another name for these birds is Happy families, from the way they keep together. The name 'apostlebirds' seems to be from the way they travel about in flocks of a dozen. FAMILY: Grallinidae, ORDER: Passeriformes, CLASS: Aves.

APPEASEMENT BEHAVIOUR. Aggression between two animals of the same species may often be prevented from becoming actual fighting by appeasement or submissive behaviour on the part of one of them. An advantage of possessing a behavioural mechanism which reduces combat and aggressive display is that the animals can live more closely together and yet be peaceable.

The probability of aggression is much increased by certain stimuli, the most potent of which is aggressive behaviour by the opponent. Hence it is not surprising to find that much appeasement behaviour is the antithesis of aggressive behaviour. It is particularly important for a female approaching a male in courtship to reduce his initially aggressive response to her. Zebra finch males have sleeked feathers when aggressive and take up a horizontal (the most intensively aggressive) or a vertical stance. A submissive female puffs out her feathers and holds her body in a more normal oblique position. The females of other birds can be seen to perform activities typical of young birds, such as food begging. This reversion to youth is effective for young birds are rarely attacked by their elders, nor do the young attack the old.

The appeasement postures of a Blackheaded gull consists of head flagging. In this movement the beak is turned away from the opponent by rapid sideways turn of the head, so that all the rival sees is the back of the other gull's head. This has been said to be like a man sheathing his sword to demonstrate his peaceful intentions. A dog shows appeasement behaviour which is the very opposite of attack, by lying on its back and permitting its opponent to sniff its body. This has the effect of exposing its vulnerable underside, but the origin of the behaviour seems to lie in demonstrating a lack of aggressive intent rather than to be like a man baring his chest and daring his opponent to shoot.

Flight is a strong stimulus for an opponent to attack. Therefore reduction of any indication of flight is also the source of many appeasement signals. Thus, immobility is characteristic of many of them. The submissive dog, for example, remains quite still during the inspection.

Evocation of other behaviour in the attacker is another method of appeasement. The shrieks and squeals of defeated mammals and birds may have a scaring effect and cause the attacker to turn tail. The offer to groom is important in a social species for not only does it reduce aggression but it also permits the two animals to remain in close contact. Likewise, in some primates, sexual presentation is effective in reducing aggression by eliciting mounting behaviour from the attacker, the animals therefore remaining together while at the same time the behavioural stimulus is radically changed.

Appeasement behaviour has the biologically important effect of reducing maladaptive aggression. This is particularly important for maintaining peaceful relations in animal societies. J.D.C.

APPENDICULARIA, the best-known, though not the most abundant genus of Larvacea. This tadpole-like creature is widely distributed from the poles to the tropics in the upper sunlit layers of the oceans, where it feeds on the minute plant life of the plankton. ORDER: Copelata, CLASS: Larvacea, SUBPHYLUM: Urochordata, PHYLUM: Chordata.

APPETITIVE BEHAVIOUR is when a hungry or thirsty animal seeks food or water; it may do so in ways which are different each time it does this. This phase of the animal's activities is brought to an end by one or several consummatory acts which in themselves bring to an end the internal state which motivated the appetitive behaviour. Thus a hungry animal finding food eats until it is satiated, removing in this way the state of hunger which induced its search.

Appeasement is shown by animals adopting an attitude of submission. In the Blackheaded gull it consists of head-flagging preceded, according to some ornithologists, by the lowered posture shown here.

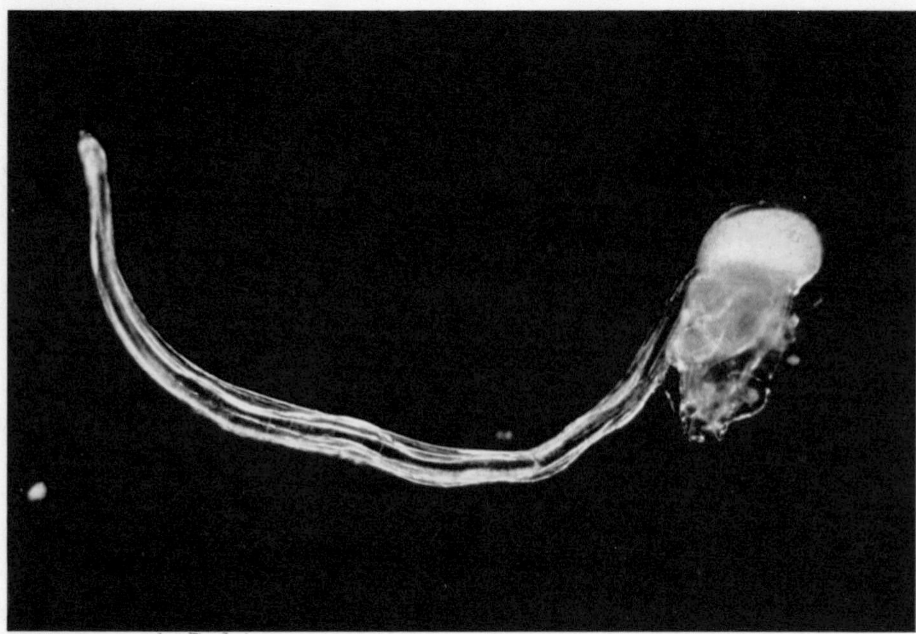

Larva of *Oikopleura*, the long tail is used for locomotion and to produce a feeding current which carries food to the mouth situated on the right of the body.

This phase of searching is of importance in many patterns of behaviour, but it is easiest to give examples from feeding behaviour. Few hungry animals find themselves in places where they are simply confronted by food waiting to be eaten. They need to seek their food. The behaviour during the search is appetitive, that of actually feeding and swallowing is consumptive. Some animals carry out a random search: wireworms, the larvae of Laterid beetles, for example, feed on the succulent young rootlets of plants, destroying acres of crops if they are in the soil in any great number. Their search is a *kinesis, the larvae reacting to gradients of the sugar which emanates from the roots. A similar random search describes the appetitive behaviour of the larvae of Ladybird beetles. These feed on greenfly *Aphis fabae*. But they do not perceive them even at a distance of 3–5 mm. They crawl mainly at random over a flat surface, although on a plant the edges and veins of leaves to some extent canalize their movements. The colonies of aphis often occur close to the veins so that the chance of encountering them is enhanced. At intervals, a larva stops and moves the front part of its body from side to side with its abdomen fixed temporarily to the leaf surface. In this way an area larger than the actual track is searched. After feeding it moves with many small turns which has the effect of keeping it in the area where it has been successful and where it is likely to encounter yet another aphid. This is known as klinokinesis. The searching behaviour may, however, be orientated, as when a blood sucking tick moves towards any object the temperature of which is above that of the surroundings. As this ectoparasite feeds on warm-blooded animals, this behaviour leads it to a potential host where it will be able to find food.

The forms of appetitive behaviour mentioned thus far have been examples of inborn behaviour. Sometimes the behaviour is acquired. A dog will learn where its food bowl is and look for food there at the time of day when it is usually fed. A foraging honeybee is guided to the flowers which are producing abundant nectar by the dances of successful foragers. Its appetitive behaviour is therefore determined by the activities of another animal. On the other hand, once found the food is recognized again by the appearance of conspicuous objects close to it and the way to the food is found by landmarks along the ground and light patterns from the sky.

Appetitive behaviour is not, however, restricted to feeding. To give another example, a newt which rises to the surface to fill its lungs with air is showing appetitive behaviour which leads it to oxygen-containing air.

A characteristic of appetitive behaviour is that it is brought to an end by a consummatory act. A hungry animal which takes in food becomes satiated, though not necessarily after one meal only. When the newt has filled its lungs, the appetitive behaviour ceases. Sometimes one can see that a complex pattern of behaviour can be broken down into constituent parts, each with a consummatory act preceded by appetitive behaviour. Thus a bird building a nest may begin by searching for large twigs to make the base of it. When that part of the nest is completed, the sides are constructed with smaller materials. Collecting mud and shaping it into a cup follows. Finally, the cup is lined with grass and hair. Each part of this pattern ends only when one kind of activity, say, the building of the sides, has been completed.

Lorenz considered that much of what had in the past been called instinctive behaviour is made up of two sequences, appetitive behaviour and the consummatory act both forming a fixed action pattern. Appetitive behaviour is variable; one individual may find its food in different ways on consecutive occasions. It is also often adaptive, most particularly when the animal uses learning in its appetitive behaviour. This gives the air of variability to what is, by definition, inborn behaviour. But Lorenz sees the fixed action patterns as the truly rigid inborn core of the instinct.

Part of the essence of appetitive behaviour is that is is motivated by a *drive; the different drives produce characteristic kinds of action. But when the consummatory act is performed the motivation is switched off, as it were. At the same time that this gives appetitive behaviour a purposive look, as it leads to a biologically useful end, it also serves to distinguish it from exploration. Exploration is an end in itself activated, it appears, by a drive for exploration. The consummatory act is a period spent in such exploration. J.D.C.

APUS, the old name for a genus of *Tadpole shrimps, now referred to as *Triops*. ORDER: Notostraca, SUBCLASS: Branchiopoda, CLASS: Crustacea, PHYLUM: Arthropoda.

AQUARIUM, alternatively aquavivarium, was the name originally given to a tank of water kept in a hot-house for cultivating aquatic plants. It is now generally used for any vessel containing live marine or freshwater plants and animals or the building housing the tanks. In 1790, Sir John Graham Dalzell, had constructed a number of tanks in which to keep aquatic animals for study. The real history of the modern aquarium started, however, about 1841, when N. B. Ward succeeded in growing seaweeds in artificial seawater and also constructed an aquarium to show how aquatic plants could be grown for purifying tank water. Other investigators discovered how a balance could be kept between the aquatic plants and animals. In 1856, H. P. Gosse, who did so much to popularize the study of marine animals on the shore, published his book, *The Aquarium*. This gave a tremendous fillip not only to the study of marine zoology but to the keeping of private aquaria. The first public aquarium to exhibit aquatic plants and animals had been opened in the London Zoological Gardens in 1853. This proved a great success and many other public aquaria were subsequently opened. The Westminster Aquarium was opened in 1876, with an aeration circuit nearly three miles long.